# LECTURES

ON

# HOMILETICS AND PREACHING;

## BY EBENEZER PORTER, D.D.

PRESIDENT OF THE THEOLOGICAL SEMINARY, ANDOVER.

WITH A PREFACE, AN APPENDIX, AND COPIOUS NOTES,

## BY THE REV. J. JONES, M.A.

INCUMBENT MINISTER OF ST. ANDREW'S CHURCH, LIVERPOOL.

PUBLISHED BY R. B. SEELEY AND W. BURNSIDE:
AND SOLD BY L. AND J. SEELEY,
FLEET STREET, LONDON,
MDCCCXXXV.

TO

THE RIGHT REVEREND

JOHN BIRD SUMNER, D. D.

LORD BISHOP OF CHESTER,

THIS ENGLISH EDITION

OF A VALUABLE TRANSATLANTIC PUBLICATION,

REVISED AND RE-PUBLISHED AT HIS SUGGESTION,

IS RESPECTFULLY DEDICATED,

BY HIS HUMBLE AND OBLIGED SERVANT,

THE EDITOR.

# PREFACE BY THE EDITOR.

ONE of the most important considerations connected
with the Christian Ministry, and too frequently lost
sight of in the present day, is its divine institution.
When our Saviour quitted this lower world, he left the
government of his church expressly in the hands of his
Apostles, whom he promised to endow with every
necessary gift, and whose decrees he declared should be
binding upon his disciples to the end of time. Their
official acts were virtually the acts of Christ himself,
for they acted not only by his delegated authority, but
under the immediate influence of his Holy Spirit. Now
we know from their own writings, as well as from the
testimony of ecclesiastical history, that they not only
ordained men to the ministry themselves, but gave
authority to others to do the same. Thus were Timothy
and Titus empowered and enjoined to "set in order
things that were wanting" in the several churches which
they visited, "and to ordain elders in every city." From
that day to this, elders have been ordained by men who
were severally authorized by their immediate predecessors; and of every one who has been thus ordained, it
may be said, in the language of St. Paul, that "a dispensation of the gospel has been given to him, and that
woe will be unto him if he preach not the gospel."

That the ministers of God's word and sacraments are
to be considered as divinely appointed to their respective
offices, may be deduced also from the general tenor of the
writings of the New Testament.  The apostle Paul, in
adverting to the various agencies which were then employed for the benefit of the church, and the spread of
Christianity, traces them all up to the great Head of the
church, as their origin and source.  " When he ascended
up on high, he led captivity captive, and gave gifts unto
men. . . . And he gave some apostles, and some prophets, and some evangelists, and some pastors and teachers; for the perfecting of the saints, for the work of the
ministry, for the edifying of the body of Christ."[1]  In a
similar manner he speaks of himself and his fellow-
labourers, in his Second Epistle to the Corinthians,[2]
where he traces up all to the same divine source:  " All
things are of God . . . . who *hath given* to us the ministry of reconciliation."  And in the same chapter he
adds, " Now then we are ambassadors for Christ, as
though God did beseech you by us."  And is there not
an important sense in which every Christian minister,
inwardly moved by the Holy Ghost to ' desire the office
of a presbyter,' as a thing preeminently ' good,' and
regularly set apart to the same, by the imposition of
authorized hands, may now be regarded as an " Ambassador for Christ ? "  And is he not justified in claiming
from professed Christians such a recognition of his divine
appointment, as is implied in the words of the apostle;
" Let a man so account of us as of the ministers of
Christ, and stewards of the mysteries of God ? "

[1] Eph. iv. 8, 11, 12.                    [2] Chap. v. 18.

But how much soever the ministerial office may be contemned by others; how low soever their conceptions of its authority or its source; the minister himself must " magnify his office." It is of the utmost importance, that he entertain elevated notions both of its *sanctity* and its *dignity*. The welfare of the people committed to his charge, no less than the formation and maintenance of his own character requires him to be well persuaded " of what dignity, and of how great importance the office is, whereunto he has been called." Hence the stress which is laid upon it in the Ordination Service of our church. ' And now again,' (observes the Bishop, whilst addressing those about to be admitted into the priestly office,) we exhort you, in the name of our Lord Jesus Christ, that you have in remembrance into how high a dignity, and to how weighty an office and charge ye are called, that is to say, to be messengers, watchmen, and stewards of the Lord, to teach and to premonish, to feed and provide for the Lord's family : to seek for Christ's sheep that are dispersed abroad, and for his children who are in the midst of this naughty world, that they may be saved through Christ for ever.'

There is a sense, doubtless, in which a Christian presbyter may be justly styled the minister or pastor of his *flock—their* watchmen, *their* messenger, *their* steward : but in a still higher and far more appropriate sense he is the minister of CHRIST, the watchman of the LORD OF HOSTS, the messenger of JEHOVAH, the steward of GOD. As far as it respects the objects of his care, and watchfulness, and ministration, he is *theirs*, but when his original appointment, the source of his authority, his ulti-

mate responsibility are referred to, he is wholly and
entirely the LORD'S.

Such is the scriptural view which he should take of
the transcendant dignity of his sacred office. If he
regard it with less respect and veneration, he will not
fail to act in many respects in a manner at variance with
its true character—a more secular spirit, and meaner
motives and designs than become the sacred office, will
be sure to mar his ministrations. "The moment we permit ourselves to think lightly of the Christian ministry,
our right arm is withered, nothing but imbecility and
relaxation remains. For no man ever excelled in a
profession to which he did not feel an attachment bor-
dering on enthusiasm; though in other professions what
is enthusiasm, is in ours the dictate of sobriety and
truth." [1]

The reluctance which some persons feel to admit this
view of the subject, may have arisen in part from a just
indignation at the claims which have been set up by an
arrogant priesthood to the almost idolatrous homage of a
superstitious and ignorant people. But it should be
remembered that the abuse of a doctrine or a truth is no
just argument against the legitimate use. What, though
proud and ambitious men arrogate *to themselves* that
which is due only to their *office*, do they thereby make
void the declarations and appointments of the unchange-
able and faithful God? No: "let God be true, though
every man be found a liar,"—let his own divine institution
be had in honour, though all who are invested with it be

[1] Hall's Sermon on the Discouragements and Supports of the
Christian Ministry.

deserving only of his displeasure. There is no necessary connexion between the dignity of the office, and that of the person who sustains it. The Christian minister who has felt the power of the gospel on his own heart, instead of priding himself upon his supposed personal dignity, will be filled with self-abasement at the thought of his unworthiness to be entrusted with so weighty a charge. His feelings will be those of the Apostle when he exclaimed " who is sufficient for these things?" Whilst he magnifies his office he will debase himself. In this, as well as in every thing else connected with the ministerial profession, St. Paul is indeed an illustrious example. He entertained at once the most exalted idea of his office, and the most humble opinion respecting himself. " Unto me," he observes, " who am less than the least of all saints, is this grace given, that I should preach among the Gentiles the unsearchable riches of Christ." [1] What more lowly expression could he use, than that which he here employs or rather invents, [2] to designate his personal unworthiness? It did not satisfy him to say that he was "inferior" to other saints, or even the " least" of all saints : such was his humility that he could scarcely deem himself worthy to be numbered amongst them at all; and he could only say that, if it were possible, he was " less than the least."

And yet we know, as well from his own testimony as from the history of his life, that he was not a whit behind the chiefest of the Apostles. If there be a cha-

---

[1] Ephesians iii. 8.

[2] ἐλαχιστοτερος a comparative, formed from the superlative ἐλαχιστος.

racter unfolded to us in the pages of sacred history,
whether of the Old Testament or the New, more strikingly noble, disinterested, and benevolent than another,
it is that of the Apostle Paul. From the moment he
was arrested by the voice of his Redeemer, and entrusted
with the Gospel, he acted as a magnanimous champion
in his cause, and was successful beyond all example as a
Preacher of " the faith which once he destroyed." He
was a burning and a shining light ; "in all things approving himself as the minister of God, in much patience, in
afflictions, in necessities, in distresses, in stripes, in im-
prisonments, in tumults, in labours, in watchings, in
fastings, by pureness, by knowledge, by long-suffering,
by kindness, by the Holy Ghost, by love unfeigned, by
the word of truth, by the power of God, by the armour
of righteousness on the right hand and on the left, by
honour and dishonour, by evil report and good report."
How greatly are we of this day indebted to him for his
invaluable and edifying writings ! How large a portion
of the New Testament itself is the composition of his
pen ! To how many millions have his words given light
and wisdom, consolation and joy ! It is impossible to
peruse those writings without forming the highest idea
of their author—of the sublimity of his conceptions, the
strength of his faith, the expansion of his heart, the confidence of his hope, the warmth of his affections, the
ardour of his zeal, and the disinterestedness of his purpose. Yet, such was the depth of his humility, and the
penitential regret with which he retraced his steps as a
" persecutor and injurious," that in sincerity of soul he
described himself as " less than the least of all saints !"

And as the Christian Minister is thus taught to humble himself, whilst he magnifies his office, so is he instructed also to regard his appointment as a special *privilege*, which should awaken his gratitude to " the Father of lights, from whom proceedeth every good and perfect gift." " Unto me," says the Apostle, " who am less than the least of all saints, is *this grace* given, that I should preach among the Gentiles the unsearchable riches of Christ." But why, it may be asked, did he esteem such an appointment to be a " grace" or a " favour ? " It was not in those days an office of credit in the world : on the contrary, it was universally branded with infamy. St. Paul, we know, was regarded as a factious dema- gogue—a leader of the sect of the Nazarenes every where spoken against—one who " turned the world upside down." Was it a " favour " to be thus exposed to the world's scorn and persecution ? Was that office to be accounted honourable which insured universal con- tempt, or that appointment valuable which stripped its possessor of every earthly good ? Yet, St. Paul accounted it such ; and, next to his conversion, he thanked God for " putting him into the ministry." He accounted it a favour because it gave him an opportunity of gratifying the benevolent affections of his heart. He longed for the salvation of mankind ; for this he accounted not his life dear unto him. The office was one whose duties he delighted to perform, notwithstanding all the privations and sufferings it imposed. He preached the Gospel " not by constraint, but willingly ; " " not for filthy lucre, but of a ready mind."

He esteemed it a favour also, because it gave him

many opportunities of testifying his gratitude to Christ. So great was his sense of obligation to the Redeemer, that he rejoiced to suffer in his cause, and after his example. Multiplied and grievous as were the tribulations he endured, they depressed not his spirits; nay, rather he learned to glory in them as evidences of his fidelity and love to him "who died for him, and rose again." Nor was he ignorant that his "light afflictions which were but for a moment, would work out for him a more exceeding and eternal weight of glory," whilst he looked steadfastly at things unseen and eternal. He knew that the day of requital would ere long arrive, when the Saviour's smile, and the Saviour's presence would make amends for all; when they who had turned many to righteousness would "shine as the sun in the firmament, and as the stars, for ever and ever."

But there was one other consideration which served to enhance the value of his appointment; namely, the unspeakable excellency of those tidings which he was commissioned to bear. It was given him to preach, what he terms, "the unsearchable riches of Christ." And who amongst the most profound of theologians, that has studied the most deeply, and the most successfully the treasures of wisdom, and knowledge, and love, which are exhibited to us in the cross of the Redeemer, will not freely admit that they pass man's understanding? Behold! what wisdom is displayed in the *contrivance* of our redemption. Careless and carnal minds are disposed to overlook every difficulty which presents itself in the inquiry, How can man be just with God? They regard the all holy One as a Being like unto themselves, whose only impediment to the pardon of sin is the indignation which he feels against the sinner. " But God's ways are not as our ways, nor are our thoughts like his thoughts." Before sin can be pardoned, it must be seen that no injury will accrue to the attributes of the Most High, or to the well-being of the universe. The claims of justice, holiness, and truth, must be severally satisfied, ere mercy can dictate terms of forgiveness. Now the plan devised in the counsels of eternity was one at the same time honourable to God, and benevolent to man ; one whereby mercy and truth met together, righteousness and peace embraced each other ; one by which God remained just, though the justifier of those that believe in Jesus. The perfect life, and the atoning death, the glorious resurrection and triumphant ascension of Jesus of Nazareth, achieved this plan, " brought life and immortality to light, and opened the kingdom of heaven to all believers." Can we contemplate the *plan* or its *execution* without exclaiming in the language of the Apostle, " O the depth of the wisdom and knowledge of God ; how unsearchable are his thoughts, and his ways past finding out."

And what riches of liberality ; what treasures of compassion and love are exhibited in the gospel of Christ. " God spared not his own Son, but delivered him up for us all." " God so loved the world, that he gave his only begotten Son, that whosoever believeth in him should not perish, but have everlasting life." What the Father refused not, the Son delighted to give : he gave himself a ransom for all, first stripping himself of his glory, the glory which he had before the world was, assuming our nature in its lowest form, and voluntarily

subjecting himself to hardship, suffering, and contempt.
" Being in the form of God, he thought it not robbery
to be equal with God, but made himself of no reputation,
and took upon him the form of a servant, and was made
in the likeness of men ; and being found in fashion as a
man, he humbled himself, and became obedient unto
death, even the death of the cross." " Greater love,'
says our Saviour, " hath no man than this, that a man
lay down his life for his friends."   " Scarcely," says the
Apostle, " for a righteous man will one die ; yet, perad-
venture for a *good* (or *benevolent*) man, some would
even dare to die; but God commendeth his love towards
us, in that while we were yet sinners, Christ died for
us."   O unsearchable riches of the love of Christ!   The
more we try to estimate its value, the more it appears
to pass man's wisdom.   It is indeed our duty and our
privilege to study to comprehend with all saints what is
" the breadth and length, and depth and height, and to
know the love of Christ ; " but we shall find, after all, that
" it passeth knowledge."   May our contemplations of it
be more and more profitable to our souls, and be rendered
subservient to the increase of our love to him, who thus
loved us even unto death !

The unsearchable riches of Christ may be considered
also with reference to the efficacy of his atonement, and
the invaluable blessings which he hath purchased, and
now confers upon his people.   He became a propitiation for the sins, not of a few, but of a multitude whom
no man can number; not for a separate people, but for
every nation under heaven; not for a limited period, but
for every age, past, present, and to come.   He is the

propitiation for the sins of the *whole world.*  His blood cleanseth from all sin ; and "whosoever cometh unto him he will in no wise cast out."    What he purchased by his death, he is now ever living to bestow upon the contrite supplicant.    He is exalted at the right hand of God, to be "a Prince and a Saviour, to give repentance unto Israel, and the forgiveness of sins."  He "ascended up on high and received gifts for men, yea, even for the rebellious, that the Lord God might dwell among us." And what are those gifts ?   Are they not *unsearchable ?* Who can tell, for instance, the value of *pardon?*  Surely no one, till he first compute the value of a soul, and the duration of eternity.   Or who can estimate aright the blessedness of heaven ?   " Eye hath not seen, nor ear heard, nor hath it entered into the heart of man to con-/ceive, the things which God hath prepared for them that love him."

Such are the unsearchable riches of Christ, which St. Paul in common with his Apostolic brethren, thought it so great a favour to be allowed to promulgate.   And such assuredly are the doctrines which every enlightened minister will study to adopt for himself, and rejoice to preach unto others.   For, as it has been well expressed by an enlightened and distinguished prelate, 'If the Christian minister boasts of deriving his commission to preach the Gospel by an uninterrupted succession from the hands of the Apostles, consistency requires that he should apply to the same Apostles for the doctrine which he is to deliver. ' [1]

[1] Bishop Sumner's Apostolic Preaching.

But supposing that a correct and comprehensive view of the doctrines of Christianity has been attained, and that their momentous importance is justly felt and appreciated, the Christian minister may still feel considerable perplexity as to the best mode of communicating them from the pulpit. The young and inexperienced minister, who is anxious to approve himself unto God as "a workman that needeth not to be ashamed, rightly dividing the word of truth," cannot fail to feel his want of much instruction on this point, and will turn with the deepest interest to every source of information within his reach. ' It is impossible indeed to contemplate calmly the situation of a young man, who is first called to appear in this most important, most responsible post, and who ascends the pulpit with little advantage from previous instruction, and with none from previous exercise. " It is impossible indeed to see him, preparing to teach others, and to see hundreds hanging on his lips, for that word which is to feed their souls; without mourning over the circumstances under which this part of the ministry is generally commenced. He may have knowledge, he may have zeal, he may have affection, he may have qualities which hereafter may render him eminently useful; but his first efforts in preaching are generally nothing better than experiments which only lead to conviction of error. He naturally begins by imitating the manner of some one whom he has been accustomed to admire, or by attempting some mode which he has been imagining to himself; but his first efforts are attempts in an art which he has never studied, and where he has no adviser to direct him. Even the theory of the system is unknown, and it is probable that years must elapse, before experience and reflection will lead him to discover that mode of preaching which is suited to his powers, and best calculated to edify his hearers." [1]

Hence the importance of furnishing the youthful minister with specific instruction on the subject of preaching. It is to be regretted however that whilst there is no lack of valuable treatises on the pastoral duties generally, the want of a separate, complete and satisfactory work on this particular department of them has long been felt. How far the following attempt of Dr. Porter, in his character of Professor of Sacred Rhetoric, may be justly regarded as supplying this want, the Editor will not presume to determine. He feels assured however that it will be found, to say the least, to contain much valuable instruction, and to suggest many useful hints. The object which the Author had in view, and the reasons which induced him to compose the work are thus briefly explained by himself. 'In entering on my labours as Bartlet Professor of Sacred Rhetoric in this Seminary, I found the office to be in some respects a new one in the business of theological instruction. After an examination of the many books which have been written on Sacred Rhetoric, it became manifest, that I must be called to traverse a field, to a considerable extent untrodden by any of my predecessors. One of the first difficulties which met me as an Instructor of our Senior Class, was the want of any single work that I was satisfied to put into their hands, as a text-book on Homiletics. The

---

[1] Mr. Raikes' Remarks on Clerical Education.

best thing of the kind, as far as it went, was Fenelon's
Dialogues : but this little work is too limited in its range
of subjects, and too desultory as to classification of the
matter which it does contain, to occupy any considerable
time of students so advanced in knowledge as our Senior
Class are expected to be. This deficiency is not supplied, in any adequate manner, by Claude's Essay; nor
by the few judicious Lectures of Blair on preaching ; nor
by those of Campbell on Pulpit Eloquence.

‘ This state of the case left me no option as to the
course to be pursued. It was plainly necessary for me
to adapt my instructions to the immediate necessities of
my pupils, and to give them aid on those principles
which they were at once to apply in practice. Hence
my precepts took a systematic form as designed to
exhibit a connected view of the points which are
requisite to a theological student, just beginning to
compose sermons.

‘ Next to a warm and sanctified heart, and a sound
understanding, knowledge respecting his own sacred
employment is necessary to make the preacher a workman that needeth not to be ashamed. No man can learn
to preach by study merely. He must be taught of God,
or he will never understand the Gospel. He must love
Christ, or he will never feel the motives of the Gospel,
nor exhibit its truths in demonstration of the Spirit and
with power. But neither will piety alone render him
skilful and powerful in the pulpit. Besides respectable
native endowments, he must have others that can result
only from study. The preaching of the gospel is a
science, which has elementary principles. Other things

being equal, he will best succeed in this sacred work who best understands and applies these principles.'

Having thus introduced the Author to the English reader, and given him due precedence in the statement of his own reasons for composing the following work, it now becomes the Editor to state the circumstances under which he has undertaken the task of revising it, and what additions and alterations he has presumed to make.

Soon after the publication of the original work in America last year, a copy found its way into the hands of his respected Diocesan, by whose kind recommendation and encouragement he was led to peruse, and subsequently to prepare it for the London press. In its original character and shape how valuable soever the greater part of its contents, it could never have made its way among the English clergy. To say nothing of occasional peculiarities in style and phraseology, there was much irrelevant matter, and some few objectionable passages which required emendation or elision. Certain additions also appeared to be necessary in order to render the work more complete. To each of these departments of his labours, the Editor has given as much time and attention as his numerous pastoral engagements would permit. In the use of the pruning-knife he has studied moderation, never altering a single sentence without an apparent necessity; and yet he has not scrupled to lop off occasionally with a more formidable weapon, large portions of wild and overgrown branches, together with a few unsightly excrescences which seemed at once to deform and injure the goodly tree.

In attempting to supply a few of the more obvious deficiencies in the original work, the Editor has thrown together some remarks on the delivery of Sermons from the Pulpit—on the synopsis of a discourse—and on other subjects of importance to the novitiate, in the form of Appendices and Notes.

The extent of the alterations which he has made, and the measure of success with which he has attempted to improve the work can be determined only by those who have the opportunity to compare the two editions together. Whilst, however, he is convinced that there are other hands by which the Editorial task would have been accomplished in a far superior manner, yet he feels equally assured that the work as it is now presented, cannot fail, with God's blessing, to prove a useful and interesting publication to the younger clergy.

Many of the writings to which reference is made in the notes, are familiar, it is probable, to the majority of his readers : to all others the Editor would venture to recommend them as fraught with wisdom, and calculated to be highly useful to Christian ministers of every standing and grade. He would particularly refer to Remarks on Clerical Education, by the Rev. H. Raikes, M. A. Chancellor of the Diocese of Chester ; The Christian Preacher, by Dr. Williams, containing treatises by Bishop Wilkins, Dr. Watts, Dr. Doddridge, and others; Cecil's Remains ; Budd on Infant Baptism, in which many valuable observations will be found ; Herbert's Country Parson ; Burnet's Pastoral Care ; Baxter's Reformed Pastor ; and, above all, the comprehensive and valuable work of Mr. Bridges on the Christian

Ministry. The most elaborate work on preaching is undoubtedly that of Claude. It is however, far too stiff and formal ever to become popular, or to be studied with an adequate degree of interest. Mr. Simeon has done more perhaps than any one else could have done to make the work read by young divines; but whilst the " Skeletons " to which he has attached his favourite Preceptor, continue to be held in esteem, the Essay itself is too generally neglected, if not despised. It is not the only instance in which the scholar has been seen to excel his master, and the example to surpass the precept.

It only now remains that the Editor should, as a Christian minister addressing his younger brethren in the Lord, remind them of the sacredness of this, as well as of every other part of their appropriate study.

If the chief end of man be to glorify God—if, " whether we eat or drink, or whatsoever we do, we should do all to his glory "—how obviously are we bound in a matter so nearly allied to his honour as that of promulgating the gospel of his Son, to keep that end intently in view. In all things we should study to approve ourselves unto God—to preach not ourselves, but Jesus Christ; and to strive to gain the approbation of our hearers no further than is consistent with their real and eternal well-being. If popularity be regarded by us as an *end* to be pursued for its own sake, rather than as a *means* to promote the honour of Christ in the salvation of men, we betray a spirit inconsistent with that of a true and faithful pastor, and must be classed with those of whom St. Paul speaks when he says, " All seek their own; not the things which are Jesus Christ's."

And though we may have our reward in the plaudits of admiring friends, we can never entertain a well-grounded hope of receiving at last, the approving testimony of Him who shall say to every trustworthy and disinterested herald of salvation, " Well done, good and faithful servant, enter thou into the joy of thy Lord."

# CONTENTS.

## LECT. XV.

## LECT. XVI.

## LECT. XVII.

## LECT. XVIII.

## LECT. XIX.

## LECT. XX.

## LECT. XXI.

## LECT. XXII.

## LECT. XXIII.

---

# APPENDIX.

## I.

## II.

## III.

## IV.

# SYLLABUS

## OF THE FOLLOWING LECTURES.

---

## LECTURE I.

### INTRODUCTORY REMARKS.

THE preaching of the gospel is a work, in preparing for which every attainable degree of perfection should be sought.

No one should think himself already so perfect as to be above improvement.

The requisite improvement is not to be made without one's *own* efforts.

Opinion of Johnson on this point; his example, as a critic on himself. This process of correction requires more caution and judgment in regard to a *sermon*, than to an *essay ;* but the danger lies more in wrong habits of writing, than in subsequent correction.

Yet no man can be so perfect a critic on *himself*, as not to need some aid from the judgment of others; for two reasons; the imperceptible influence of *habit*. Partiality to faults which are his *own*.

These principles somewhat modified by age. Other things being equal, the youngest men are generally least patient of criticism.

## LECTURE II.

### HISTORY OF PREACHING.

What do you know of Enoch as a religious Teacher?— and what of Noah?

General form of religious instruction and worship in the patriarchal ages,—what was it?—Tabernacle.

Schools of the Prophets,—what were they?

What change took place after the Captivity, in the quali-

b 2

fications and duties of religious Teachers?—and for what reasons?—Reading of the Scriptures in synagogue worship;—what parts?—in what method?

Priests in Egypt and Persia; their public rank,—privileges,—services.

State of assemblies to whom Christ and the Apostles preached.

*Names* of the preacher and of his discourse, among the Fathers.

*Place* of public worship, among the early Christians. Erection of churches in time of Constantine;—Pulpit,—its name and form;—place of Presbyters and Deacons.

*Time* of preaching;—viz. frequency of on week days; number of services on the same Lord's day; usage of the Romish and the Greek church in this respect.

*Posture* of the preacher,—what?—also of the hearers,—Classification of hearers,—Why their faces to the east?

*Prayer,* before sermon and after.

*Reading the Scriptures.* Connexion between the passage read, and the subject of the sermon;—Consequence, as to unity of sermons.

## LECTURE III.

### HISTORY OF PREACHING.

*Subject of Sermons.* In ancient assemblies, hearers distinguished into two general classes;—Adaptation of subjects to these. Most general character of subjects in the second century;—state of the church as to controversy. Influence of Platonic philosophy, in the third century, on the pulpit. From Chrysostom onward to the 15th century, state of preaching, as to subjects.

*Interpretation of the Scriptures* in sermons among the Fathers. Influence of Origen; to what extent his system prevailed. Influence of mystical interpretation, in substituting human authority for that of the Bible.

*Reasoning in Sermons.* Character of, among the Fathers.

*Preparation of Sermons.* Extemporary method,—by whom introduced;—evidence that St. Augustine and Chrysostom sometimes preached in this manner;—but that general usage was in favor of written sermons.

*Eloquence of Sermons.* The two most distinguished ancient treatises on this subject. Eloquent Latin Fathers;—also Greek Fathers, besides Chrysostom;—extract from the latter.

*Length of Sermons.* Mode of measuring. Customary length, why difficult to be determined from printed sermons of the day.

*Effect of sermons;* as to silence and order in assemblies: —applauses of hearers,—what, and how far encouraged by preachers. -

## LECTURE IV.

### CHOICE OF TEXTS.

From what principle this practice is derived. Why it is no objection to this practice that there is nothing analogous to it in secular oratory.

#### RULES.

1. *A Text should not be chosen as the mere motto of a sermon.* General reason ;—not respectful to the Bible. Which should be chosen first,—the *subject* or the *text.* Campbell's reasons for preferring the former course.[1] Cases in which this must be adopted. Danger to be guarded against. General character of Motto Sermons.

2. *There should be no affectation of peculiarity in the choice of a text.* Professed motive in such cases.—Examples.

3. *A text should contain a complete sense of itself.* Explanation of this rule. When it is violated, what is generally the motive ;—examples of its violation. Omission of words and phrases in the middle of a text, though the sense is not destroyed. What advantages in a concise text. The proper course for the preacher when his text contains more matter than he wishes to discuss.

4. *It should express a complete sense of the inspired writer.* The taking from a compound sentence, a single clause, expressing grammatical sense, may or may not be a violation of this rule.

5. *It should fairly contain or suggest the subject of discourse.* Violations,—where there is a fanciful connexion of *sound* and *sense ;*—examples. Where there is *no* connexion of any sort;—examples. Where the *apparent* sense is not the *true* sense; examples. *Accommodation* of a text; —improper and proper kind of ;—examples.

6. *A text should have simplicity.* Should not demand a nice, philological exposition. Nor a theological discussion to show that the apparent sense is consistent with the preacher's subject. Should not promise great efforts in the preacher.

[1] Lectures on Pulpit Eloquence, p. 267.

## LECTURE V.

### SUBJECTS OF SERMONS.

State of the Church in any period, how to be known from the prevalent strain of preaching. This principle applied to four different periods of the church. Choice of subjects will be according to the principal end of the preacher. Circumstances which have given character to the pulpit at different times;—viz. celebrated models,—great emergencies in the church. Circumstances which at all times will influence a judicious preacher in choosing his subjects:—capacity and cultivation of his hearers;—time and occasion;—his own talents and age;—his relation to the hearers.

*Four general classes of subjects.*

I. *Doctrinal.* Object of a doctrinal sermon. What is meant by *essential* doctrines. From what motives a man who believes these, may yet forbear to preach them. Reasons for preaching them.

II. *Ethical.* Why this term is here preferred to *practical* and *moral;* doctrines are practical. Character of sermons commonly called moral; and influence on hearers. What sort of subjects belong to ethical discourses. Three cautions in public treatment of these.

III. *Historical.* Including *facts* which respect an individual, a period, a community. Eulogies on the dead inexpedient,—why? Maxim ' De mortuis, nil nisi bonum.' Nor may we describe all the *bad* qualities of the dead; the true course. Two *difficulties* in preaching on historical subjects. Several *advantages;* evidence of facts surpasses other kinds,—(*first*) In *familiarity* and *precision: (secondly)* In *vivacity* of *impression. Examples* from the Bible of the difference between abstract teaching, and illustration of facts.

IV. *Hortatory.* The most common *fault* in this sort of discourse; remarks on language of terror and denunciation. Three general remarks as to choice of subjects. The preacher should, Aim at *variety;* Avoid a vain *love of novelty.* Never be perplexed for want of subjects.

## LECTURE VI.

### GENERAL PRINCIPLES.—EXORDIUM.

*Preliminary remarks.* **Necessity of a sound** *judgment* in a preacher; to preserve him from a *mechanical uniformity* in his sermons; and from disregard, on the other hand, of all settled principles, through a *studied peculiarity.* Necessity of *pious feeling;* what character will be imparted to his sermons by the want of this; and by the possession of it. Principal parts of a sermon,—what. This classification only *general,* to be more or less used, according to the subject.

*Exordium.* Its chief object,—what. Chief *obstacles* to the preacher's success, stated. *Prejudice* against his *talents, character,* or *opinions;* how to be treated. *Ignorance* and *indifference* of hearers; the regard which these require, as to the mode of presenting a subject.

An exordium should possess, 1. *Simplicity;* this forbids, Pomp and studied ornament. Warm appeals to passions. Ostentation of learning. Abstruse thought and language. Abruptness. Examples of proper and improper abruptness.

2. *Pertinence;* it should not be foreign from the subject or occasion. Nor general and trite. Influence of pertinence on variety. Introduction from the context,—advantages of.

3. *Delicacy;* This should arise from Reverence towards God, &c.; respect to hearers. It does not require *timidity;* nor formal *apologies* for defects of the preacher; objection to these. It forbids an *angry, austere* manner.

4. *Judicious length;* Practice of old divines; of some modern ones. The kind of matter common in long exordium. Two brief reasons why inexperienced preachers are apt to dilate the first thoughts of a sermon.

## LECTURE VII.

### EXPOSITION.—PROPOSITION.

*Exposition of the Text.* When, after due examination, we suppose ourselves still not to understand a text, what course is proper. Explanatory remarks, may be useful where no *difficulty* is to be removed; and may fall in with the exordium. Where a regular exposition of the text is called for, there is a difference between the office of the *critic* and of the *preacher*.

Practical principles to be observed by the latter.

1. *He may err by supposing too many difficulties in his way.* Tendency of this state of mind in a preacher. To what extent the Bible is a *plain* book; how the supposition, that, on essential points, it is necessarily unintelligible to plain, pious men, is inconsistent with the grand principle of Protestantism. Why reasonable to expect that it would be intelligible to such men, if we consider *by* whom, *for* whom, and for *what purpose*, it was written. Evidence that it *has been* correctly understood by such men. Yet,

2. *He may err by taking it for granted, that the obvious is always the true sense.* Reasons why this ought not to be expected; great diversity of matter and phraseology in the Bible; local customs, figures. Examples of allusions to oriental customs, in which the terms do not obviously convey the true meaning, viz. from language of Moses, and of Christ.

3. *He may err by aiming to find a new sense to his text.* Motives that may lead to this course. Random censures, in sermons, of the received translation; why improper. Excess of criticism in the pulpit,—condemned by Campbell; his reasons. What was the example of Christ and the Apostles in relation to this subject? How a man's critical knowledge, without any ostentation of it, may benefit his hearers.

When the sense of the text is ascertained, and exhibited, it is announced in the

*Proposition.* Difference in the signification of this term as used in *logic*, and as used in *oratory*. Examples of each —Either is proper in a sermon; which most favourable to unity. Manner of announcing propositions. Two suggestions of cautions.

## LECTURE VIII.

### UNITY.

*Unity.* Why is it that some do, and others do not consider *divisions* as inconsistent with unity? Unity different from *sameness*. Unity with and without *variety*. Illustrations. Applied to a dull *uniformity* in the matter and method of sermons.

Unity in a sermon requires that it be,

1. One in *subject*. *Violated*, by too many *preparatory*

topics, diverting hearers from the *main point*, when there is one. Violated by introducing a *system of religion* into each sermon.

2. One in *design*. *Design* a distinct thing from *subject*. Example;—It is this which should leave on the hearers some one distinct and predominant impression.

3. One in adjustment of its parts to the principal end, and to each other. Grand principle in preaching, viz.—a sermon should produce an effect as *a whole*. How accomplished. Its materials should be chosen and arranged with a view to this. Illustration from works of art;—from architecture;—from landscape gardening;—from historic and portrait painting;—from epic and dramatic poetry. Character of a sermon made up of a succession of good remarks, unconnected :—or of striking sentences,—or brilliant passages,—independent of a main object.

4. One in mode of Illustration. Every topic, figure, &c. should serve to fix the main subject more deeply in mind. Does unity forbid divisions?

# LECTURE IX.

### DIVISIONS.

1. *Objections* to divisions. They give an air of stiffness, and take away the interest which an intelligent hearer has in discovering the method for himself. *Ans.* To *intelligent* hearers, divisions are not useless ;—and to *plain* hearers they are indispensable ;—especially in a *spoken* discourse. *Obj.* Divisions are a scholastic device,—unknown in ancient oratory. *Ans.* Ancient orators, though not formal, had method. Examples from Cicero, in which his method was distinctly announced.

2. *Utility* of divisions. By these is meant, not *occult* but *obvious* divisions. Not essential that heads be always marked *numerically;* several ways of marking them to hearers. Doddridge's advice and example. Method promotes *Perspicuity ; Beauty; Brevity ;* how promoted ; *Energy ;*—order strengthens impression by combining the power of separate arguments ; by relieving attention ; and promoting vivacity. *Memory,* is aided ; viz. of the preacher,—and hearers. Illustrated. Kind of sermons that are in fact most easily remembered by common people. Test from the practice of note-taking—and of repeating sermons in families.

# LECTURE X.

### DIVISIONS.

3. *Kinds* of divisions. The *verbal* or *textual;* The *topical.* The principle of each stated. Example of the kind of division required *by each.* The *scholastic;* principle of: Example. Example of a deliberate oration on the same plan.

4. *Rules* by which divisions should be conducted. They should be *Necessary.* When they are so. *Well arranged.* Chief principles of arrangement in different cases, according to order of *cause* and *effect;*—order of *time;* of *genus* and *species.* In some cases, the order of heads is nearly indifferent,—in others it is essential. Examples of both kinds. *Complete.* What is meant. Illustration from light and colours; from a geographical description of a whole by its parts. *Few;* Illustrated by a *map.* Multiplication of divisions in the seventeenth century. *Concise in terms.* Reason of this rule. How brevity of terms is promoted by aid of grammatical *ellipsis.* Examples of brevity in the form of heads, by such an arrangement as to suspend them all on some one connecting term, or clause.

# LECTURE XI.

### ARGUMENT.

Some who allow reasoning to be proper in *secular* oratory, object to it in the *pulpit;* Why? The objection not well grounded. Influence of such an opinion;—on the preacher,—on the hearers. *Moral evidence,* and not *demonstration,* is appropriate to the reasoning of pulpit. Still it does not follow that a knowledge of intellectual philosophy, and of geometry, are useless to the preacher;—nor that religion does not admit of *certainty.*

### *Sources of argument.*

1. The *Bible is the chief source of argument in the pulpit.* On some subjects the *only* source. In regard to subjects and evidence of this sort, what is the proper province of *reason.* How may we fail in giving prominence to the divine testimony. Examples of this defect. On some sub-

jects proofs are mixed, partly from the Bible, partly from other sources.

2. *Consciousness.* Distinction between this and *conscience.* Strength of this evidence. To what purposes this kind of evidence is most applicable.

3. *Common sense.* Why propositions of this class are called self-evident. Example from Tillotson, to show how this sort of evidence may be employed in sermons.

## LECTURE XII.

### ARGUMENT.

4. *Evidence of facts ;*—including experience, testimony and authority. A general law of the material and intellectual worlds stated, according to which facts become the basis of argument. To what extent this sort of evidence may be used in sermons. Cases in which *testimony,* as proof in sermons is liable to abuse. *Authority,*—its abuse, —its true weight. Practical bearing of this last topic on the evidence of what doctrines are taught in the Bible.

*Rules of Argument.*

I. *In reasoning from the Bible, its unperverted meaning must clearly support the point to be proved.*

1. In adducing proofs from the Bible, the grand principle of Protestantism must be adhered to, that our faith must conform to the Bible, and not the Bible to our faith. Violations of this principle ;—Their tendency ;—

2. But though there be no *perversion,* the proof may be obscured, by quoting—too many texts ;—or too *few ;*—or by *bare quotation* of the text, where *comment* also is necessary to show its bearing. Examples on the last point. Cases in which scriptural proof is made out by comparison and induction.

II. *In reasoning, from whatever source, we should consider the influence of passion and prejudice on belief.*

This influence illustrated. Advantage of *Analytic* method in such cases.

## LECTURE XIII.

### ARGUMENT.

III. *Arguments should be simple,—that is, not complicated, nor abstract ;* Grounds of this rule. .Prejudices against

metaphysics often extreme.  A truth may be mysterious,
while the proof that it is a truth is plain.  Use of metaphysics ;—and abuse.  *Rhetorical* reasoning better than
*abstract,* for sermons.  Language of metaphor and imagination not inconsistent with the dignity of religion ;—
example of the Bible.

IV. *Arguments should not be too many.*  Disadvantages
of accumulation.

V. *Should be well arranged.  Remarks* on the best *order*
in introducing proofs from the Bible, when these are connected with a series of proofs from other sources.  Illustrations.   On alternative of *two* places for a topic.   On
relation of *time, cause,* and *effect,* &c.  On *negative* heads.
On the *antithetic* form of reasoning.  On reasoning from
*Authority.*

VI. *Avoid a controversial strain of reasoning.  Three* ways
of refuting objections.  When we must meet them in *form*
—*six* cautions suggested.


# LECTURE XIV.

### CONCLUSION.

*Recapitulation,*—in what cases useful.  Example of Cicero.
*Continued* or *running* application,—when allowable.

Faulty conclusions of sermons.

1. The formal conclusion.  What it is ;—exemplified in
sermons of the Puritans.  Change after the restoration of
Charles II.

2. The *desultory ;*—what leads to this.

3. The *dry;—*what it is.

To make a good conclusion, the preacher must—1. *Aim
at practical effect,*—aim to impress the hearers as individuals.
How far this effect depends on the *design* of the preacher.

2. *Understand the principles of the human mind.*  Aid of
this knowledge in applying truth.  Rule illustrated.  In
applications, difference between *personality* and *individuality ;*—the former, why improper in an uninspired preacher ;
—often alleged, however, when there is no fault in the
preacher.  Application by the agency of conscience.

3. *Arrange the parts of a sermon so, if practicable, that they
may tend to a single effect in the close.  Convergent* method,
and *divergent.*  In adjusting the plan of a sermon, how far
should the topics of conclusion be previously settled ?
*Inferences,*—cautions respecting ;—advantages of.

4. *Make an appeal to the heart.*
*The pathetic,*—Five remarks on; viz.
1. Demands *simplicity* in execution.
2. Not to be confounded with *emotion* generally.
3. Not to be *protracted.*
4. Requires *moral painting.*
5. Though high powers in the pathetic are wanting to a preacher, this is no reason why he should be dull and cold.

## LECTURE XV.

### STYLE OF THE PULPIT.

I. How far it may be *professional* and *peculiar?* Religion must have its own *technical terms.* In other respects, should conform to general laws of style.
II. *Peculiarities,* amounting to faults, arise from—designed *imitation of scriptural language.* Using *familiar* terms *abstractly* or *mystically.* Reading old authors, and catching their diction. Influence of *conversation-dialect.*
III. Properties of a good style for a preacher. 1. *Simplicity.* This requires him,—Never to use a *hard* word, when a plain one will express his meaning. Never to use a *common* word in an *uncommon* sense. To avoid *display of reading.* Metaphysical obscurity;—Classical quotations and allusions. To guard against taking it for granted that words familiar to himself, as a scholar, will be so to plain hearers.
2. *Seriousness.* This is opposed—To ridicule—To levity and witticism in any form—To affected smartness and sparkling ornament.
3. *Earnestness.* What is requisite in the man, to give this quality to his style.

## LECTURE XVI.

### DIRECTIONS IN FORMING A STYLE, GENERALLY.

1. *Remember that thought is the basis of style.*
Writing with no object, except to form a style; its tendency.
2. *Study your own genius.*—Mistake of Plato, writing poetry.
3. Study the best models. In point of style, what benefit may a student for the ministry derive from reading the

*Classics?* What, from reading *poets,* to one who writes only *prose?* Will one acquire the style of popular address by reading *essays?* What period of English literature furnishes the best models? Comparative value of Scotch models. In reading authors as models generally, what cautions requisite?

4. *Maintain the habit of writing.* Perseverance and resolution in this case, important in early life, as connected with subsequent usefulness. Despatch in writing, on what things it depends; habits of Johnson, as to despatch. Change in the characteristics of English style, since the time of Addison; reasons of this change. Over-exactness in writing, and hurry, both to be avoided.

5. Take it for granted that your best performance is capable of subsequent amendment. Different methods adopted by respectable men, in the act of composing, to diminish the labor of correction. Very strong and sacred obligations rest on young ministers of the present day to cultivate skill in writing.


## LECTURE XVII.

### EVANGELICAL PREACHING.

1. *Sermons should be evangelical.*
1. *What is evangelical preaching.*
Different kinds of phraseology to express this, used in the New Testament. Why Christianity, like every other science or system, must be taught by the exhibition of its elementary principles? Difference between a discourse of Socrates, and a Christian sermon, on the same subject, e. g. the being of a God, or the doctrine of immortality—a caution suggested.

II. *All preaching should be evangelical.*
1. Such preaching might *reasonably be expected* to answer better than any other the great ends of preaching. Brief mention of chief points in the evangelical system. Why these are adapted to give special interest to preaching.
2. *Evidence of facts* shows it to be so.

# LECTURE XVIII.

### INSTRUCTIVE PREACHING.

II. *Sermons should be instructive.*
1. *What things are requisite to make a sermon instructive?*
(1) It must have an *important subject.*
(2) Should be *perspicuous*, in *method and language.*
(3) Should be *rich in matter.* To render sermons so, the preacher should have—respectable capacity. Fixed habits of reading and thinking. Should read and think *as a preacher*, and with systematic *classification* of acquired knowledge. In aiming to enrich sermons with matter, should avoid two mistakes—a sweeping generality—and an effort at perpetual novelty.
(4) Should have the form of *discussion*, rather than of the *desultory manner.*
(5) Should exhibit truth in its *connexions.*

# LECTURE XIX.

### INSTRUCTIVE PREACHING.

2. *The preacher should aim to instruct his hearers.*
This appears—(1) From the *constitution of the human mind*, as influenced by *motives.*
(2) From the nature of the gospel—as a system of *truths*, on which is predicated a system of *duties.*
(3) From the best *examples* of preaching.
(4) From the best *effects* of preaching. Ignorance of the gospel in a Christian country, why criminal, and fatal to the souls of men.

# LECTURE XX.

### DIRECTNESS IN PREACHING.

III. *Sermons should have directness ;*—that is, the preacher should so conduct his address, as to make each hearer feel, " He preaches to me."
1. *What constitutes directness in preaching?*—It implies such an exhibition of a subject that the hearers shall— *Understand* it ;—i. e. not in an unknown tongue ; nor on a subject too recondite for their comprehension. Perceive its *pertinence* and *importance to themselves.*

II. Causes which produce *indefinite* and *indirect* preaching.

1. *Want of intellectual precision* in the preacher. Defect in his mind as to—*Native structure*, or, intellectual *habits*. Hence want of discrimination, and adaptation to different classes and characters, among hearers.


## LECTURE XXI.

### DIRECTNESS IN PREACHING.

2. Indefinite preaching may arise from *false taste* in the preacher; that is, want of rhetorical skill in expression. *Generality* in terms, and formation of sentences. The periphrastic drapery of diction illustrated by farther examples. The same principle applied to *figure* in style.

3. Indefinite preaching may arise from *constitutional delicacy of temperament in the preacher*.

4.—From absolute want of piety, or a low state of piety in the preacher. How a man's manner, as to explicit declaration of the truth, will be modified by supreme regard to *himself*, and to God. Use of evangelical terms, while no one doctrine of the gospel is preached. Indefinite language never resorted to in any serious business of this world.


## LECTURE XXII.

### DIRECTNESS IN PREACHING.

5. Indefinite preaching may arise from *wrong theory in the preacher*, as to the best mode of exhibiting divine truth. The principle assumed is, that men are predisposed to love the truth, if skilfully exhibited; and that feelings of opposition must result from some fault in the preacher. Inconsistency of this theory with the Bible and facts.

1. The Bible represents unsanctified men as predisposed, not to love the truth, but to oppose it.

2. The theory in question has no countenance from the ministry of Christ.

3. Nor from the general evidence of facts. Recapitulation. Concluding reflections on the influence of indefinite preaching upon our churches; and on the obligations of ministers to give an explicit and undisguised exhibition of the whole gospel in their sermons.

# LECTURES.

## LECTURE I.

### INTRODUCTORY.

1. THE preaching of the gospel, however contemned and undervalued by philosophers, ' falsely so called,' is a work of *immense importance*. In the magnitude of its objects it surpasses, beyond all comparison, every other employment in which men can engage. This might be illustrated, did my limits allow the detail, by an ample exhibition of facts, showing that the highest degrees of intellectual cultivation, of civil liberty, and of social order, which are found in the most favoured communities, result not so much from all other causes combined, as from the sanctifying influence produced by the faithful preaching of the gospel.

But the consideration which attaches preeminent importance to this work is, that God has appointed it as the grand instrument of *salvation* to men. The scheme of redemption is an object to which all other objects and events, in our world, are subordinate. This is the radiant point, where all the attributes and works of God converge into a blaze of glory. In contemplating the

B

' great mystery of godliness, into which angels desire to look,' we see how infinite wisdom, love, justice, and grace unite in the forgiveness of sin, and in suspending the immortal hopes of sinners on the cross of Christ. Now the principal means which God has instituted to make *known* this scheme of mercy to a lost world, is the preaching of the gospel. This consideration invests the preacher's work with a character of exalted and awful dignity, which very far transcends the most elevated employments of this world. Well did St. Paul say, and had he been an *angel*, well might he have said, " Who is sufficient for these things ?" Surely then, a pious, uninspired man should aim at the highest attainable degree of perfection, in his preparation for this work.

2. No man who has any just conceptions of this work, and of his own acquisitions, will think himself already so perfect as to be above improvement.

He who has made any real progress in wisdom, will see at every step of his researches, a field opening before him, that is absolutely boundless. His sermons cannot be rich in thought, unless his materials are drawn from inexhaustible resources: and to these he cannot have access, without patient, assiduous, well-directed, and long-continued application. But supposing him to be a " scribe well instructed," and furnished with ample stores of biblical and theological learning, he may be very unskilful in " bringing forth " these treasures, for the instruction of others. His style may be vulgar, or inaccurate, or unintelligible, or dry, or feeble.

In one or more of the qualifications requisite to form an able preacher, very few, at any age, or in any circumstances, are free from considerable imperfection. To any *young* man, then, it can be no reproach, to acknowledge himself imperfect.

3. To correct our own defects, and to increase our qualifications for usefulness, is a work which requires our *own* efforts. No process in which a man is merely passive, can transform him into an able preacher, or a useful man in any respect. Important acquisitions, of every kind, must be the result of care and labour. 'There is no royal road' to knowledge in our profession, more than in others. It would indeed be unwise, at this day, for a Christian student to adopt a course like that of the Athenian orator, who transcribed the history of Thucydides eight times with his own hand, that he might learn to imitate the conciseness, strength, and fire of the historian. But the same *industry*, though it may be better applied in this age of books, is as necessary as it was in the age of Demosthenes. [1]

'Men,' says Johnson, 'have sometimes appeared, of such transcendent abilities, that their slightest and most cursory performances excel all that labour and study can enable meaner intellects to compose; as there are regions of which the spontaneous products cannot be equalled in other soils by care and culture. But it is no less dangerous for any man to place *himself* in this rank of understanding, and fancy that *he* is born to be illustrious without labour, than to omit the cares of husbandry, and expect from his ground the blossoms of Arabia.' Johnson was practically acquainted with the principle of Quinctilian, 'that it is the work of correction to add, to retrench, and to change. That it is comparatively easy to determine what parts require amplification or abridgment; but to repress the tumid, to raise the low, to prune the luxuriant, to restrain the extravagant, to condense the diffuse, is a labour of double difficulty.'

It deserves to be remembered that Johnson was neither

[1] See note (1) by the Editor, at the end of the volume.

too indolent nor too fastidious to become a critic on himself. His Rambler, which, as it was first published, competent judges had classed among the finest specimens of English composition, he almost rewrote for subsequent editions. Chalmers, in his biographical preface to the Rambler, has preserved one of its original papers, as a literary curiosity. Any student who will carefully compare this with the corrected copy, and see with what punctilious inspection, this great man revised his own composition, will find himself amply repaid for his trouble.[1]

I am aware that this critical process, when employed in the correction of a *sermon*, needs to be conducted with more caution and judgment, than in the case of an *essay*, where the heart may slumber, while the intellect is engaged in adjusting the parts of sentences. But the fervor of feeling which is indispensable in the compositions of the preacher, is injured, not so much by subsequent correction, as by the refrigerant proceeding too often adopted in the original discussion of a subject, in which the writer forgets his main business, in searching for favorite forms of expression. 1 cannot too often repeat the remark, that the only adequate remedy for this difficulty, is to acquire such *habits* of correctness, that propriety of language shall be spontaneous, and cost no labor of reflection ; while the *thoughts* to be communicated should thus be allowed to engross the attention.

But to form these habits in a young writer, it is necessary that he should be accustomed carefully to revise, after a proper interval, every production of his own pen. That this labour does not necessarily tend to destroy the spirit of a sermon, is evident from the fact, that to·this very process we are indebted for the most animated,

[1] Note (2.)

energetic, and eloquent discourses, that have ever issued from the press. And to the want of this, in a great measure, we may ascribe the superabundant supply of those which deserve a different character.

But patience in revising our own compositions, is not all that is requisite on this subject—because,

4. No man, however accurate, or however desirous of improvement, can be so perfect a critic on *himself*, as not to need at least occasional aid from the judgment of others.

The reasons of this remark, as applicable to the writer of mature and well-disciplined mind, are chiefly two. One is, the imperceptible influence of *habit*. It is not my purpose here, to analyze those laws of mind on which the power of habit depends. The fact is too obvious to require to be proved, that this power does exist, and exert an important influence upon our whole course of thinking and acting. The constant recurrence of any object or event diminishes the interest which it excites in the mind. On this principle, we gradually become familiar with the attitudes, features, voice, and language of one with whom we daily associate, so as not to observe even those peculiarities which would be instantly noticed by a stranger. For a still stronger reason, we become insensible to whatever is peculiar in *ourselves*. Faults that are quite obvious to others, in our use of favourite words and phrases, or in the general method of expressing our thoughts, may excite as little notice in our own minds, as the action of our limbs in walking, or of our lungs in respiration.

The other, and the more important reason, why a man cannot be a perfect critic on himself, is, that he is liable to feel a *partiality* to the faults which need correction, because they are his *own*. This difficulty exists in all its force respecting a composition that is *recent*, and towards which the writer cherishes a fond regard, as possessing a sort of identity with himself. It was the tendency of both the above causes, especially the latter, to pervert a man's judgment of his own performance, that occasioned the precept of the Latin critic, ' nonum in annum prematur.' And with reference to the same tendency, a modern writer, of good sense, remarked; ' The attachment felt to the defects of our style, at the moment of their production, is to be ranked with the sort of oblique taste manifested by idolaters; who usually most reverence those idols, which are most deformed.' This, I apprehend, is peculiarly true of those faults which spring from the heedless darings of affectation, or the sallies of wayward fancy. Pride is always at hand to volunteer its approbation, or at least apology, for our own defects. After the assassination of Cæsar, when Brutus was about to make a speech in the Roman Senate, some of his friends urged Cicero to prepare that speech for him. Cicero replied—' No orator ever believed that another man could write better than himself.'

These principles, especially the latter, which sober experience, and even piety, do not exterminate from any human bosom, may be expected to operate, with peculiar strength, when combined with the ardent temperament of youth. Accordingly, I have always observed in circles of ministers, that, other things being equal, the *youngest* men are least patient of criticism. In any one of ingenuous and intelligent mind, the desire of improvement is in proportion to his intercourse with men and books; his knowledge of himself; in a word, his attainments in real wisdom. In such a man, of course, a partial attachment to his own productions, and his own errors, always abates with the progress of years: but there is danger of its continuing, to an unhappy extent, till the best period of improvement is past. Instead of shrinking from the scrutiny of judicious criticism, therefore, he who understands his own interest will invite it; he will *prize* it, as the invaluable, indispensable auxiliary of his own efforts. He will seek this aid *seasonably,* before his defects acquire insuperable strength by indulgence. And he will desire that such criticism should be impartial and thorough; that it should not spare real blemishes, though he himself might regard them as minor defects, or even as beauties. No one, in the 'plastic' age, ought to be indifferent to *small* faults; because the carelessness that overlooks these, at twenty, if unchecked, will grow into intolerable blundering by *forty.* [1] In a *sermon, peculiarly,* no error of *sentiment* should be deemed too small for animadversion. Let the empiric tamper with his patient's life by random prescriptions, and be comparatively blameless; but let not the preacher tamper with the *Bible*, and the *souls* of *men*. The faults of one sentence from the pulpit, may produce mischief through a *century*, nay through *eternity*.

Let me add, however, one caution to these remarks. See that the habit of criticism does not withdraw your attention from the great end of preaching. There is no necessity, I must say again, that this consequence should follow from attention even to minute accuracy. And yet there is a tendency to this result, which, in minds of a certain cast, ought to be guarded against with unceasing vigilance. Gross blunders in language are inexcusable in a scholar: but it is a thousand times better to violate grammar and rhetoric, and preach the gospel clearly and powerfully, than to be an accurate, dry, uninstructive, phlegmatic preacher. [2]

[1] Hæ nugæ seria ducent. Hor. Ars. Poet.    [2] Note (3)

# LECTURE II.

## HISTORY OF THE PULPIT.

IN discussing the large class of topics which come under the head of Homiletic Theology, frequent allusion to facts will be necessary: and to avoid repetition, it seems proper here to exhibit a brief sketch of the preacher's work, as it has been conducted in different ages. A complete account of the pulpit belongs indeed to the department of ecclesiastical history, in which it deserves a much more prominent and ample consideration than it has hitherto received. But as I cannot devote ten or fifteen lectures to this subject, I must be content to give a mere outline of facts, imperfect as this of necessity must be.

In the early history of the world, we find no evidence that the business of public religious teaching was reduced to method. "Enoch, the seventh from Adam," we are told in the epistle of Jude, "prophesied." The brief history of this patriarch as given by Moses, makes no mention of him as a prophet. But the language ascribed to him by St. Jude, renders it plain that he spoke under a divine commission; and that as a public instructor of his cotemporaries, he taught the unity and moral perfections of God, and the difference, as to present character and final retribution, between saints and sinners.

St. Peter calls Noah " *a preacher of righteousness ;—* the *eighth person who was saved in the ark,*" as our translators understood the place; or as others, with less reason, render it, " *the eighth preacher of right-eousness.*"[1]

In the patriarchal ages, the worship of God was con-fined chiefly to *families*, the head of each family acting as its priest. Moses, Aaron, and Joshua, in their day, often collected the people in solemn assembly, especially in the Tabernacle, and addressed them with powerful effect, in the name of the Lord.[2]

At a still later period, *schools of the prophets* were established at Bethel, Naioth, and Jericho, which seem at first to have been places of worship, where the people assembled, especially on the sabbaths and new moons, for purposes of religious devotion and instruction; and which afterwards became places of education for young men designated to the sacred office. In the reign of Asa, it is said, that Israel had long been " without the true God, and without a teaching priest." In the next reign, Jehoshaphat sent out a great number of itinerant preach-ers, who " taught in Judah, and had the book of the law with them, and went about throughout all the cities of Judah, and taught the people." The peculiarity of garb, the sanctity of manners, the bold and often splendid imagery, and the violent action of these ancient preachers,

---

[1] The same apostle says that to those who in his day were " spirits in prison," Christ preached the gospel by Noah, before the flood. And St. Paul, in the eleventh chapter of Hebrews, alludes to the warning of the approaching deluge, which Noah gave his cotem-poraries, in which he acted under the spirit of prophecy.

[2] The tabernacle was a tent about fifty feet in length and seventeen in breadth. It was divided by a rich curtain into two parts, the *sanctum*, and *sanctum sanctorum*; the latter containing the Ark of the covenant, &c. In this tent, which was so constructed as to be taken down and moved, the Congregation of Israel offered sacrifices, and performed other religious services.

need not here be described, being only circumstantial appendages of their sacred work.

After the captivity, when the inspired code assumed a more regular form, exhibiting the genealogies, the system of jurisprudence, and the sacred ritual of this peculiar people ; and when their language was corrupted by a barbarous mixture of foreign dialects; religious teachers were obliged to become *students*, for the purposes of exposition and interpretation; and their employment, to some extent, became, of course, a learned profession. In the eighth chapter of Nehemiah, one very interesting example of *Ezra's preaching* is recorded. About fifty thousand people were assembled in an open street. The learned scribe, with a large number of preachers on his right and left, stood on an elevated pulpit of wood. When he opened the book of the law, " all the people stood up," and continued standing, during the remainder of the service, which lasted from morning to midday. The preachers alternately " read in the book of the law of God, distinctly, and gave the sense, and caused them to understand the reading ; and all the people wept, when they heard the words of the law."

It is foreign from my purpose here to enter into the controverted question about the origin of *synagogues;* except to say that I am satisfied with the arguments which assign *their origin* to the period after the captivity. The exercises of the Jewish public worship, were prayers, reading the Scriptures, exposition, and miscellaneous exhortation. The prayers, which at first were few and brief, had become in the time of our Saviour so tedious as to be censured by him for their length. The reading of the Pentateuch, in such portions as to finish the whole every year, was a long established custom, which Antiochus Epiphanes having forbidden by a

sanguinary edict, equal portions of the prophets were
substituted; and after the above prohibition was removed, the " law and the prophets " continued to be
read in alternate lessons. The passage which was read
was interpreted in Chaldee, after that became the current
language of the Jews; and then the ruler of the synagogue invited persons of distinction, giving the preference
to strangers, to address the people.

It would be rather amusing than useful to describe the
sacred rites of Pagan nations. Egypt, Carthage, and
Persia, had priests, who were second in rank and wealth
only to their kings. It was doubtless on account of the
veneration in which they were held, as possessing superior learning, and as understanding the mysteries of the
sacred books, and of divine worship, that Joseph
exempted their lands from the assessment laid upon all
the other subjects of Pharaoh. Among the sacred orders
of those nations, the Magi of Persia were most distinguished; and the second Zoroaster might perhaps with
propriety be called the first Mahomet. By his intercourse with the Jews in their captivity, he became
acquainted with their Scriptures, by the help of which
he compiled his *Zendavesta*. In this he inserted many
Psalms of David,—the history of Adam and Eve, of
the creation and deluge, of Moses, Abraham, and the
patriarchs.

The official services of the priests among the Persians,
consisted in giving instructions to the people, as to their
duties to the gods, and in conducting their superstitious
and sanguinary rites of sacrifice. These rites were performed in the open air : and Varro thinks that perform-
ing them in temples, as was afterwards done by the
Greeks and Romans, had a great tendency to corrupt
religion.

The public ministry of John the Baptist, and of Christ and the apostles, is so minutely described in the New Testament as to require no distinct notice in this sketch. The grand characteristics of their preaching, as to doctrine and manner,.will be considered in another place. I will only say here, that our Saviour, as did his apostles after him, and as all *missionaries* must do, in spreading a new religion, taught his hearers wherever they happened to assemble; sometimes from the deck of a ship; at others, from the summit of a mountain; in a private house; in the synagogue; in the temple; just as the circumstances of the time made it convenient. The sermons delivered on these occasions exhibit a combination of simplicity and majesty, of superiority to the applause, and of fervent zeal for the salvation of men, which render them the best models of public instruction.

When they who planted the primitive churches ceased from their labours, the noble simplicity which distinguished their preaching, began to decline. Many of the early Christian Fathers, however, were burning and shining lights, who, by the purity of their doctrines, the fervour of their piety, the fidelity and efficacy of their ministrations, were great blessings to the world. As the state of the pulpit during the first few centuries of the Christian church is to be collected chiefly from sources difficult of access to most persons, it may be proper to class the remainder of my remarks, under distinct heads, with some enlargement on each.

I begin with the *names* by which the preacher and his office were anciently designated. One of these titles was κήρυξ, a crier; borrowed from the business of one, who, as orator of heathen gods or princes, made proclamation in public places with a loud voice. Under this allusion, St. Paul calls himself κήρυξ καὶ ἀπόστολος, and St. Peter calls Noah δικαιοσύνης κήρυξ. This title indeed, was often applied, in early times, to the *deacon*, who called to order at the commencement of public worship. The preacher was besides often called διδάσκαλος, *tractator, concionator,* &c.

The address which he delivered was called by the Greeks ὁμιλία, that is, a familiar discourse, adapted to common people, from ὅμιλος, an assembly, a multitude. The Latins called it *tractatus, disputatio, locutio, sermo,* and *concio,* according to the subject and strain of the discourse.

When the stated preacher was sick, it was customary for the deacons to read the homilies of the Fathers. Indeed it is evident that Stephen and Philip, two of the seven deacons in the apostolic church, were preachers ; [1] and from several passages in St. Paul's epistles, [2] as well as in the primitive fathers, it seems probable that the office of *deacon* was, in many cases, regarded as preparatory to the ministry ; though it did not of itself imply authority to preach.

The duties of deaconesses in the early Christian church, like those of prophetesses in the Jewish, were limited to offices of piety and charity, and to the private instruction of their own sex. The public preaching of women, which was so strictly prohibited by St. Paul, was disallowed in all the orthodox churches of antiquity. Accordingly the Council of Carthage adopted this as one of its canons; " Mulier, quamvis docta et sancta, viros in conventu, docere non praesumat."

---

[1] Acts vii. and viii. 5, 26.     [2] 1 Tim. iii. 13.

GENERAL ORDER OF PUBLIC WORSHIP.

*Place.*—To the Jews, Christ often preached in the
synagogue, and so did the apostles. Among the *early
Christians* religious assemblies often convened in the
streets or fields; but more commonly in the houses of
private persons, especially during seasons of persecution.
In process of time, places of meeting were provided,
which became common property, and took the name of
*churches*,[1] by a figure derived from the assemblies which
were convened in them. What sort of buildings these
were, in the time of Diocletian, Eusebius informs us, in
describing the wonderful prosperity of the church, which
was suddenly darkened by the-strife for preeminence
among its ministers. ' But now,' says he, ' how should
any one be able to describe those multitudes, who,
throughout every city, flocked to embrace the faith of
Christ; and those famous assemblies in the churches?
For which reason, they were no longer contented with
the old edifices, but erected spacious churches from the
very foundations, throughout all the cities.'[2]  And the
churches erected by Constantine, ' were richly adorned
with pictures and images, and bore a striking resemblance
to the pagan temples, both in their outward and inward
form.'

*Pulpit.*—The preacher addressed the people, in these
ancient assemblies, sometimes from the episcopal seat,
and sometimes, especially when baptism was to be
administered, from the steps of the altar.  The common
place of the preacher, however, to give him a full view
of his auditors, and to denote the dignity and authority

---

[1] Εκκλησία.      [2] Euseb. Lib. 8. Cap. 1.—and Mosheim, 1, 383.

of his office, was a sort of rostrum, called *tribunal, sug-
gestum, ambo,* and other names corresponding with the
different purposes for which it was designed.   A very
usual appellation of this  pulpit among the fathers was
' the preacher's throne.'   Thus Gregory Nazianzen says,
' I seemed to myself to be placed on an elevated throne ;
upon lower seats on each side, sat presbyters ; but the
deacons in white vestments, stood, spreading around them
an angelic splendor.'   And Chrysostom calls the pulpit
θρόνος διδασκαλικὸς.   The form of these pulpits was that
of a rostrum, elevated, and somewhat extended ; but they
seem not to have been on the same model as those of
many churches of modern Italy, where the whole person
of the preacher is exposed to the view of his audience.

## TIME OF PREACHING.

In populous cities, where assemblies could easily con-
vene for devotional purposes, it was often customary to
mingle preaching *daily* with public prayers.   Origen and
Augustine preached in this manner ; and hence the frequent allusions of the latter to sermons, which he delivered ' *heri,*' and ' *hesterno die.*'   These things were
differently determined, according to circumstances in
different places.   But the celebration of public worship
on the *first day of the week,* was, in the primitive
churches, an universal custom, founded on the example
and express appointment of the Apostles.

The number of services on the Lord's day was one,
two, or three, according to the disposition of the preacher,
or the zeal or convenience of the hearers.   Basil commonly preached twice   on  the  Christian  Sabbath.
Augustine in the afternoon, often alludes to his morning

discourse.   Chrysostom styles one of his homilies, ' an
exhortation to those who were ashamed to come to sermon after dinner.'   In his tenth homily to the people of
Antioch, he commends them for the full assemblies
which convened for public worship in the afternoon.   It
is probable that he did, at least occasionally, preach a
*third* time, on the same Sabbath; for he certainly did
sometimes preach in the *evening;* it appears from his
fourth homily on Genesis, in which by an eloquent digression, he reproved his hearers for turning their eyes away
from himself to the man that was lighting the lamps.
The Apostolical Constitutions, speaking of the Christian
Sabbath, say,—' On which day, we deliver three sermons in commemoration of him who rose again after
three days.'   The custom of modern Protestant churches,
throughout Christendom, except in very high latitudes,
or very scattered population, requires two services on
each Sabbath.   The ecclesiastical canons of Scotland
require three in the summer and two in the winter;
though general usage dispenses with one of these, in each
division of the year.

It need only be mentioned on this particular, that, in
the Romish church, at different periods, preaching,
except on occasion of some public festival, was entirely
suspended for ages together;—as it has also been in
some branches of the Greek church.


CIRCUMSTANCES CONNECTED WITH PREACHING.


*Posture of the preacher.*—Ancient authorities are
divided on the question, whether the common posture of
the preacher was sitting or standing.   ' The Scribes and
Pharisees *sat* in Moses' seat.'   Our Saviour, having

read a passage from the prophet Isaiah,—" *sat down,*
to teach the people." " He *sat down* and taught the
people out of the ship "—" He *sat* and taught his disciples in the mountain; "—and to his enemies he said,
" I *sat* daily with you, teaching in the temple."

It is certain that sitting to preach was the attitude
adopted frequently by Augustine, and commonly by
Justin, Origen, Athanasius, and Chrysostom. It was
probably the prevailing usage of ancient preachers,
though often departed from by Christ, and by the early
fathers.

*Posture of hearers.*—Justin Martyr says in his second
Apology, that when the sermon was finished in the
church of Rome, the people all *rose up* to pray;—implying that they heard the sermon sitting, and united in
the prayer standing. This was the general custom in the
churches of Italy at that period; and in many churches
of the east. But in the African churches, the indulgence of sitting to hear sermons, was strictly prohibited,
except to the aged and infirm; and standing was the
more prevailing custom of Christian assemblies for a
long period.

Eusebius says that when he preached, in the palace
of Constantine the great, the *Emperor stood,* with the
other auditors, during the whole discourse. And when
he entreated him to sit down on his throne, which was
near, he refused, saying that ease and remissness was
unbecoming in hearers of the divine word; and that
standing in such a case, was only a decent respect to
religion.

*Classification of hearers.*—In ancient Christian assemblies, distinct portions of the church were allotted to
different classes of persons, designated by railings of
wood; so that males were separated from females, and
married from the unmarried.

*Prayers.*—The regular prayers of the ancient churches were offered after the sermon was closed. Ferrarius, however, informs us, that, before the preacher began his discourse, he always invoked divine aid in a short prayer, similar in kind and length, to those occasional supplications, which he offered in the current of his sermon, when any point of unusual difficulty came to be discussed. In the more set prayers at the conclusion of public worship, the people, having been silent to the close, united in the audible response,—Amen.

*Reading the Scriptures.*—The *reading of the scriptures,* either by the preacher, or some one in his stead, always was the first exercise of public worship. The subject of the sermon was usually taken from the passage read, and where the reader was a different person from the preacher, it often happened that a fortuitous selection of the passage at the time, required from the preacher an extempore effort in the exposition. This passage, however, was commonly determined by previous arrangement.

*The Salutation, Pax vobis.*—To secure the attention of the people at the commencement of worship, the deacons commanded silence; the preachers addressed them with an affectionate salutation and benediction; 'peace be with you,'—(the people answering, 'and with thy spirit;') and at the moment of commencing his sermon, he signified by his look, and the movement of his right hand, that he expected them to give audience to what he was about to deliver. This signal of his right hand, Lucan says, Julius Cæsar employed, when about to address the multitude. It was common with ancient orators, heathen and Christian. On such occasions St. Peter "beckoned with his hand;"—and so did .St. Paul, repeatedly.

*Text.*—Ancient preachers did not select a text,

exactly in the modern manner. Sometimes the theme
of discourse was deduced from a short clause of the
lesson read, which was announced at or near the commencement of the sermon. At other times, this theme
was taken from a *whole* lesson; at others, from *several*
lessons. Basil, in one of his homilies, alludes to *three*,
and in another to *four* distinct passages that had been
read that day, from different parts of the Bible. This
accounts in some measure for the fact, that the preaching
of the Fathers had so much of the hortatory and dis-
cussive character, and so little unity of subject and
effect.

# LECTURE III.

*Subjects of sermons.*—Under this head, I might greatly extend my remarks; as a proper survey of the subjects discussed by preachers of different ages, would form a history of the pulpit, far more accurate and complete than any which has been given to the world.

Among the early fathers, sermons were adapted to two general classes of hearers, the *catechumens* and the *faithful,* or, (as they were sometimes called,) *imperiti* and *initiati.* In addressing the latter, abstruse doctrines, and the sacred mysteries of religion were often discussed; while the preacher, in instructing the catechumens, passed over these entirely, or touched them very lightly, dwelling on those simple truths and duties, which were adapted to their circumstances. Concerning the preachers of the second century, Mosheim says, ' The Christian system, as it was hitherto taught, preserved its native and beautiful simplicity, and was comprehended in a small number of articles. The public teachers inculcated no other doctrines than those that are contained in what is commonly called the *Apostles' Creed;* and in the method of illustrating them, all vain subtilties, all mysterious researches beyond the reach of common capacities, were carefully avoided. This will not appear surprising to those who consider, that, at this time, there was not the least controversy about those leading doctrines of Christianity, which were afterwards so keenly debated in 'the church.' [1]

In the third century, the same historian says, 'The principal doctrines of Christianity were explained to the people in their native purity and simplicity. But the Christian teachers, who had applied themselves to the study of letters and philosophy, soon abandoned the frequented paths, and struck out into the devious wilds of fancy. Origen was at the head of this speculative tribe;' and though he handled this matter with modesty and caution, his disciples, breaking from the limits fixed by their master, interpreted in the most licentious manner, the divine truths of religion, according to the tenor of the Platonic philosophy.

Gregory Nazianzen, in enumerating the subjects commonly discussed in the pulpit, mentions,—' *The universal providence of God, the creation, fall, and restoration of man, the incarnation, passion, and second coming of Christ; the resurrection, judgment, and the final state of rewards and punishments;* and *above all,* he says, the *doctrine of the blessed trinity,* which was the principal article of the Christian faith.' Chrysostom, in his preaching to plain hearers, selected such subjects as these: ' *the benefit of afflictions; not seeking to know all things, is supreme wisdom; the reproach of this world is glory! death is better than life; it is better to suffer, than to inflict injury.*' In his twenty-fourth homily, on the baptism of Christ, he reminds his hearers, that the scope of his preaching had been concerning, ' *immortality, heaven and hell, the long-suffering of God, pardon, repentance, true faith, mystery, heresy.*'

I need not trace the regular and lamentable degene-

[1] Ecclesiastical History 1, 180.

racy of the pulpit from this time, onward to the reformation. Ferrarius, though when he wrote, the day
of better things had dawned, described some preachers,
who, during the darker periods of the church, discussed
the most frivolous questions, such as " Whether Abel
was slain with a club, and of what species of wood ?—
from what sort of tree was Moses' rod taken ?—was the
gold which the Magi offered to Christ, coined, or in
mass ? ' Hattinger says, that in a collection of sermons,
composed by the theological faculty of Vienna, A. D.
1430, a regular history is given of the *thirty pieces*,
which Judas had for betraying his master. These pieces
were said to be coined by Terah, father of Abraham;
and having passed through a succession of hands, too
ridiculous to be named, they came into possession of the
Virgin Mary, as a present from the Magi, and went into
the temple as an offering for her purification. At the
same period, Ferrarius complains that some preachers
made a great ostentation of their acquaintance with
ancient languages, versions, paraphrases, and manuscripts.
For a considerable period before the reformation, the
prevailing topics of the pulpit were, ' the authority of
the mother church; the merits and intercession of departed saints; the dignity of the blessed virgin; the
efficacy of relics; and above all, the terrors of *purgatory*,
and the utility of *indulgences*.' Sermons consisted of
quibbles, fables, and prodigies; and religion consisted
of external ceremonies. And be it remembered for ever,
that this prostitution of the pulpit was followed by the
reprobation of heaven on a church, which for centuries
has been gasping under the hand of death.

The meridian splendor of that light which shone at
the reformation, was soon obscured in different countries
by the combined influence of worldly policy and reli-

gious controversy. When the Baxters and Howes of the English pulpit were denounced in the days of Charles the Second, its glory departed. The rich and fervid instructions of the preceding age, were superseded by dry and speculative disquisitions; and the cardinal doctrines of the gospel, by the precepts of a cold and decent morality. And be it remembered again, that when real Christianity was thus supplanted in the pulpit, by a spurious and secular theology, the door was opened, at which entered the various forms of Arian and Socinian error, and finally of the most unqualified infidelity.[1]

## INTERPRETATION OF THE SCRIPTURES IN SERMONS.

I have adverted to the influence of Origen in corrupting the primitive simplicity of religion. Guided, not by a sober judgment, but by a wayward fancy, he laid down the broad principle, absurd as it is bold, ' that the scriptures are of little use to those who understand them as they are written.' Hence he maintained that the Bible is to be interpreted as the Platonists explained the history of their gods; not according to the common acceptation of the words, but according to a *hidden sense*. This hidden sense he divided into *moral* and *mystical;* and the latter he subdivided into the *inferior* or *allegorical* sense, and the *superior* or *celestial* sense. This machinery, when put into full operation, and recommended by the genius and learning of Origen, degraded the Bible at once from its paramount authority, as the standard of faith ; and made it subservient to the dreams of every visionary interpreter. Under the cover of this *mystical*

[1] Note (4.)

*meaning*, little ingenuity was necessary to elicit from the scriptures support for any opinion, however repugnant to Christianity and common sense.[1]

Among the Greeks, Gregory Nazianzen, and Augustine among the Latins, became zealous supporters of scholastic theology; combining in a most incongruous union, the doctrines of the gospel, with those of the Platonic philosophy; and drawing conclusions the most absurd. Every coincidence of phraseology, was fraught with important meaning. Augustine regarded the plagues of Egypt as a most pointed testimony against the sins of the Egyptians, because the ten plagues corresponded exactly in number with the ten commandments which they had broken. No doubt the commentator forgot that these ten commandments were given long *after* the plagues; and not given to Egyptians, but Jews.

If I were to indulge a single reflection here, it would be this, that the whole superstructure of doctrinal and practical religion depends on the principles adopted in

---

[1] From the endless examples of fanciful interpretation, furnished in the pages of Origen, I select but one. The prophet Isaiah, having rebuked the spendor and luxury of the Hebrew women, declares, that in the approaching havoc of war, such would be the slaughter of *males* that only *one* would be left to *seven* females. These latter, to escape the dread reproach of celibacy, would beg for the mere name and credit of wedlock, renouncing all its legal privileges. 'And in that day seven women shall take hold of one man, saying, we will eat our own bread, and wear our own apparel, only let us be called by thy name, to take away our reproach.' Let us see how this plain and vivid description of a great public calamity, is metamorphosed by the magic of a *hidden sense*.

These seven women, Origen says, are 'seven operations of the divine spirit; viz. a spirit of wisdom, of intelligence, of council, of virtue, of knowledge, of piety, and the fear of the Lord.' The *man* they take hold of is Jesus Christ, that he may take away the reproach, which the world heaps upon true religion.

interpreting the scriptures. Origen and a few other distinguished men were responsible for all the absurdities of transubstantiation, and all the fooleries of superstition that deluged the church, ages after they were dead.

From the sixth to the twelfth century, public instruction consisted of arguments and authorities drawn, not from the Bible, but from the writings of the fathers. So servile was the veneration for those infallible guides, that it was deemed impious not to submit, implicitly, in every article of faith, to their decisions. In the twelfth century, Christian teachers were divided into two classes. The former were called *biblici* and *dogmatici*, or expository and didactic divines. These professed great reverence for the Bible, and gave insipid explications of what they called its ' *internal juice* and *marrow.*' The latter were called *scholastici*, and avowedly subjected all articles of faith to the decisions of philosophy. The grand point of religion, however, through these dark ages, to the time of Luther, was, to know the decision of the sovereign Pontiff, and then to believe and act without examination.

## REASONING IN SERMONS.

Chrysostom, in his treatise Περὶ Ἱερωσύνης, requires the Christian preacher to be skilful in *dialectics*. The utility of this he shows at some length, from the argumentative powers of St. Paul. The reasoning of this father, though it is sometimes perspicuous and cogent to a high degree, is rather of the *rhetorical* kind than the *logical ;* in other words, it is characterized rather by the vivid illustrations of oratory than by the regular inductions of argument. But with the exception of Chrysostom and a few others, very little that deserves the name of reasoning, is to be found among the fathers. They were not accustomed to define terms and anatomize the subject, by investigating elementary principles. Their sermons, even when rich in thought, were commonly destitute of precision and skilful arrangement; and too often what were called demonstrations, consisted of incoherent allegories and conceits, more adapted to amuse the fancy, than to convince the judgment.[1]

## PREPARATION OF SERMONS.

How far the practice of preaching extemporary discourses prevailed among the fathers, cannot be determined with certainty. Origen is supposed to be the first who introduced this method. This, however, he did not attempt, as Eusebius affirms, till he was more than sixty years of age, and had acquired by experience, great freedom in the pulpit. That Augustine did sometimes preach without any preparation, is unquestionable; for, in one instance, he tells us that the reader, instead of reading the passage of Scripture, prescribed as the subject of the sermon, gave out another by mistake; which compelled him to change his purpose, and preach without premeditation. Ferrarius quotes Suidas, as saying that Chrysostom had a tongue flowing like the Nile, which enabled him to deliver his panegyrics on the Martyrs, extempore. The versatility of powers possessed by this great preacher, appears from innumerable instances, in which he dropped the main subject, and with the utmost pertinence and fluency of language pursued any accidental thought suggested at the moment.

[1] Note (5.)

But though there were in the primitive ages many exceptions, it seems plainly to have been the general usage, that sermons were written.  No other proof of this is necessary, if we advert to the indisputable fact that some skilful writer often composed homilies, which other preachers, and even dignitaries in the church, delivered as their own.  Ferrarius alludes to discourses as still extant, which were written by Ennodius, for the use of others.

This practice, Augustine not only recognizes, but formally justifies, in behalf of those who are destitute of *invention*, but can speak well; provided they select well written discourses of another man, and commit them to memory, for the instruction of their hearers.

In different countries and periods, there has been considerable diversity in the custom of preparing sermons. Before the civil wars in England, preaching without notes had become common.  During those commotions, when each pulpit was surrounded with spies, and each word of the preacher liable to be the ground of civil indictment, personal safety required him to *write* and *read* his sermons with care.  Hence this singular official order of Charles the Second, addressed to the University of Cambridge, forbidding, absolutely, that sermons should be *read;* and requiring that they should be delivered by memory, without book, and that the name of every preacher disregarding this requisition, should be forthwith reported to his Majesty.

There can be no doubt that sermons among the fathers were generally precomposed, and delivered, sometimes with, but more commonly without the aid of written notes.[1]

[1] Note (6.)

C 2

### ELOQUENCE OF SERMONS.

The two most distinguished ancient treatises on this subject were that of Chrysostom,—*De Sacerdotio*, and of Augustine, *De Doctrina Christiana;*' from which we learn that these luminaries of the Greek and Latin church had exalted views of Sacred eloquence. Their sermons, too, especially those of Chrysostom, furnish many examples of an elegant, fervent, and even sublime oratory. His accurate acquaintance with the human heart, his varied learning, and vivid fancy, furnished him with inexhaustible stores of argument and illustration. Yet he did not seek to *appear* learned; and never descended from his noble simplicity, to adopt those affected beauties of style, which sometimes debased the eloquence of Augustine.

Among the Latin fathers, *Jerome* of the fourth century, might be mentioned as one of the most distinguished for learning and eloquence. During his education at Rome, he devoted himself to the art of oratory, that he might successfully defend Christianity.—Erasmus pronounces him ' the greatest scholar, the greatest orator, and the greatest divine, that the church had produced,' including his predecessors of the three centuries before. His writings are valuable, not only for vigour and elegance of style, but for biblical learning.

Lactantius of the same century, though less sound as a theologian, was eminent as a Latin writer. He was a professed *rhetorician*. The beauty and eloquence of his writings acquired him the title of ' the Christian Cicero,' and induced the Emperor Constantine to choose him as teacher to his son.

---

[1] Lib. IV.

Among the Greek Fathers, the homilies of *Basil*, while they are preferred, by some competent judges, to those of Chrysostom, in classical purity of style ; are second only to his, in point of eloquence ; and the two Gregories occupy the next rank. That these men possessed real eloquence, might be inferred from the effect of their preaching on the hearers. When Chrysostom was banished, the people said, with one voice, " it were better that the *sun* should cease to shine, than that his mouth should be shut ; " and this, notwithstanding he often bore down on his hearers, in a torrent of bold and pointed reproof, such as is seldom heard from any modern pulpit. Take an example from his reprehension of those who were averse to reading the scriptures, but zealots for hearing sermons, and who demanded novelty and pomp in the pulpit. ' Tell me,' said he, ' with what pomp of words did St. Paul preach?—yet he converted the world. What pomp did the illiterate Peter use? You say, we cannot *understand* the things that are written in the gospel. Why so? Are they spoken in Hebrew, or Latin?—are they not spoken in Greek, to you who understand Greek ? But they are spoken darkly. How darkly? Are the histories obscure? There are a thousand histories in the Bible: tell me one of them. You cannot tell one. Oh! but the reading of the scriptures is a mere repetition of the same things ! And are not the same things repeated at the theatre, and at the horse-race. Does not the same sun rise every morning ? Do you not eat the same sort of food every day ? If we ask, why do you not remember our sermons ?—you answer, how should we, seeing they always change, and we hear them but once ?—If we ask, Why do you not remember the scriptures ? You answer, they are always the same. These are nothing but pretences

for idleness.' · I had selected an extract from the same
father, on the advantages of eloquence in a preacher, but
my limits forbid its insertion.[1]

<br>

### LENGTH OF SERMONS.

Cicero and Pliny allude to an instrument called
*clepsydra*, used by Greek and Roman orators to measure
time, by drops of water.   Ferrarius says that Italian
preachers of his day, used an hour-glass, with sands, for
the same purpose ; though there is no certainty that any
such usage existed among the fathers.   He affirms, however, upon what I think, inadequate evidence, that the
customary length of their sermons, was about *one hour*.

This point cannot be determined from the expressions
so common in preaching ; 'allotted hour,'—' hour of
sermon,' &c. which may denote merely that there was
a stated time of public worship.   Nor can it be known,
from the published sermons of the day, for two reasons.
One is, that when the same audience was addressed by
several preachers, in immediate succession, as was frequently the fact, sermons would, of course, be more
brief, than when the whole time was appropriated to one
man.   The other reason is, the impossibility of dis-
tinguishing homilies, preserved by the original manuscripts
of preachers, from those taken down by short-hand
writers, called ταχυγράφοι by the Greeks, and *notarii* by
the Latins.   The custom which Chrysostom applauds,
of *repeating* sermons in families, after they returned from
church, introduced the practice of note-taking.   These
notes of hearers, were sometimes published, after a

---

[1] See works Vol. 1. page 408.

revision by the preacher, and sometimes without his consent. In this way many homilies transmitted to us, are mere scraps of those which were actually delivered. For example: Chrysostom's first sermon on Lazarus, must have occupied nearly sixty minutes in delivery: Whereas others, as they appear in his printed works, and the same is true, concerning those of Augustine, would have required scarcely a tenth part of this time. On the whole, it is evident that sermons, as delivered by Christ, and the Apostles, and the primitive fathers, varied in length with circumstances :—that after Origen's time, they became longer, less desultory, and more conformed to the rules of Grecian eloquence; but that, in Chrysostom's day, they must have been less than an hour in length, as this was the customary time of the whole religious service.[1]

### EFFECT OF SERMONS.

The silence and order which decency demands in a modern Christian assembly, did not prevail in the ancient church. To prevent passing in and out during sermon, different measures were adopted; such as severe church censures, placing officers at the entrance of the church, and sometimes locking the doors.

The best preachers often reproved their hearers for talking and jesting in time of worship. In imitation of

---

[1] In some cases it would seem that what is given to us as one continued sermon, must have been delivered at several times. The sermon of Erasmus on the Fourth Psalm, is as long as *five* modern sermons. Editors probably took the same liberty as that by which several discourses of President Edwards have been embodied into a continued treatise.

the pagan theatre, it became an extensive custom for hearers to express their approbation of a sermon, by tumultuous applauses, such as stamping, clapping, waving of handkerchiefs, and loud acclamations. Thus the hearers of Cyril cried out, in the midst of his sermon, *orthodox* Cyril ! And Chrysostom's in another case exclaimed, ' Thou art the *thirteenth Apostle !*' These applauses were in many cases, mere matter of form, and were uttered without any intelligent apprehension of what the preacher had delivered. Thus Augustine reproved his hearers, in one instance, for interrupting him with their acclamations, when he had only begun to speak, but had not expressed a single thought. But many other preachers *encouraged* these disorders, from motives of vain glory. They had their reward,—while the illustrious men whose simple aim was to feed their hearers with the bread of life, saw their faithful ministrations blest, to the saving conversion of many souls.

The sketch which I had designed to give of the *modern pulpit*, in Great Britain, on the continent of Europe, and in the Greek church, must be omitted, except so far as it will be incorporated of course into the various topics of subsequent lectures.

# LECTURE IV.

## CHOICE OF TEXTS.

THE practice of expounding parts of the sacred Scriptures in public worship, as I have stated in the preceding
lectures, was common in the Jewish synagogue, and in
the early Christian churches. From this origin is derived
the usage, which for ages has prevailed in Christendom,
of selecting.from the Bible a few words or sentences,
called a *text*, from which the preacher deduces the subject of his discourse. It can be no valid objection to
the propriety of this custom in the pulpit, that nothing
analogous to it is found in the modern senate or forum,
nor among the great fathers of ancient eloquence. It is,
not the province of secular oratory, as Dr. Campbell has
properly remarked, to expound any infallible code of
doctrines or laws. But a sermon purports to be a perspicuous and persuasive exhibition of some truth or duty,·
as taught in the word of God. It is, therefore, with
great propriety, founded on some specific passage of this
sacred book.

The principles which ought to be observed in the choice
of texts may be included, perhaps, in the following

## RULES.

1. *A text should never be chosen as the mere* MOTTO

C 5

of a sermon. This is not sufficiently respectful to the Word
of God. Our authority to preach at all, is derived from the
same sacred book which prescribes what we shall preach.
It is not enough that what we speak is truth;—it must
be truth taught in the Bible; or else the declaration of
it deserves not the name of a Christian sermon. I do
not say that an elaborate explication, or *any* explication
is invariably necessary to show that the subject of discourse is contained in the text. When this is so obvious
as to be seen by every hearer; especially when it is
obvious without recurrence to the connexion of the context, or when there is no such connexion, explanatory
remarks are superfluous. This point will be resumed in
another place.

But here a question arises which demands some attention, as to the *order* to be observed in choosing a subject
and a text. Dr. Campbell[1] lays down the broad position, that ' the text ought to be chosen for the subject,
and not the subject for the text.' His reason is, that in
the opposite course, the preacher is tempted to descant
upon the words and phrases of a text, while the sentiment
becomes only a secondary consideration.

In point of fact, doubtless, every wise preacher often
fixes on some prominent doctrine or duty, which he
wishes to discuss, and then goes to the Bible to ascertain what it teaches on this subject, selecting some single
passage as a text, that is especially pertinent to his purpose. This, I presume, is the common process of preparation, where a sermon is to be adapted to any special
circumstance or occasion. The ordination of a minister,
for example, requires a discourse on an appropriate subject; and the selection of a text adapted to such a

---

[1] Lectures on Pulpit Eloquence.

subject implies no disrespect to the Bible; for the occasion itself, and all the instructions which it demands, are founded on the authority of this sacred book. Or, when there is some special reason for the preacher to discuss the doctrine of atonement, or of progressive sanctification, he adopts the same process in choosing a text.

But here is a danger to be guarded against, much more serious than the one mentioned by Dr. Campbell, on the other hand. Suppose you fix on your subject, and arrange your matter, and even write your sermon, as has often been done, and then go to the Bible in search of a text. Probably, your text will either not contain your subject; or contain it only by inference or remote analogy; or combine with it other subjects, which must entirely be neglected. I do not say that there can be no case in which it is admissible to arrange the plan of a sermon, and even execute it without having determined on a text. But from the specimens of motto-preaching which have fallen under my observation, I cannot doubt that the tendency of the above process is to sink the reverence due to the Bible; and hence it too often happens in point of fact, that, in what are called polite sermons, there is nothing but the *text* to remind the hearers that there *is* a Bible. The text is obviously chosen from respect, rather to the usage of the pulpit, than to the authority of the divine word; and it would better accord with the ends of the preacher in such a case, to choose no text; or, like him whom Melancthon heard preach in Paris, to choose one from the Ethics of Aristotle.

2. *In the choice of a text there should be* NO AFFECTATION OF PECULIARITY.

Some preachers have endeavoured to awaken the curiosity of their hearers by an artifice of this sort, altogether unbecoming the dignity of the pulpit. They select, perhaps, from a passage, a *scrap*, or a *single word*, that vulgar minds may admire the sagacity which can elicit so much meaning from a text, in which they perceive *no* meaning, and in which there truly *is* none.

I have heard a sermon from a clause of the passage Isaiah xlv. 11. " *Command ye me.*" The leading proposition was to this effect,—' that such is the condescension and faithfulness of God, in fulfilling his promises, that he consents to be addressed as a *servant*, in the language, not of supplication, but of *command*. It seems to me plain, that this is not at all the sense of the passage; but that it is to be read interrogatively,—' do ye command or dictate to me?'—and understood as a pointed rebuke of Jehovah, to those who assumed to meddle with his prerogatives. No other investigation, than to look at the context, is necessary to settle this point. But supposing the other sense to be the true one, the air of conceit and peculiarity in choosing this detached clause for a text, would be avoided by the preacher of sober judgment; when all becoming freedom and confidence in approaching the throne of grace, is encouraged in so many simple passages of the Bible.[1]

---

[1] Dr. Campbell mentions one of those declaimers, ' who will rather take the most inconvenient path in the world, than keep the beaten road, who chose the words, *a bell and a pomegranate, and a bell and a pomegranate*,—as the ground of a discourse on this topic, that faith and holiness in the Christian life, do ever accompany each other.' It would not be easy, he adds, ' to conceive a more extravagant flight. But where, you say, is the connexion in the subject? It requires but a small share of fancy to make out a figurative connexion any where. Faith cometh by hearing: and could one desire a better reason for making the *bell* which is *sonorous*, an emblem of faith? Holiness is *fruitful* in good works:—how can it be better represented than by a pomegranate, which is a very pleasant fruit?'

Now I protest against all whim and eccentricity, in ransacking the Bible for some odd word or phrase, to be the basis of a discourse. I would as soon adopt at once the recommendation of Sterne, that, when a preacher is much at loss to find a text for his sermon, he shall take this; '*Parthians, and Medes, and Elamites;*' or even as soon propose this same fantastical Sterne as a pattern of Christian decorum in the pulpit. But there is a kindred fault, which, though it may not arise from affectation, shows want of good taste.

3. *A text should contain a* COMPLETE SENSE OF ITSELF.

I do not mean that it should contain *all* the sense, of which it is susceptible, when viewed in relation to the *context*. In many cases, this would be impossible. But I mean that it should, generally, consist of at least one grammatical sentence, simple or complex, containing the distinct relations of subject, attribute, and object. The propriety of this is suggested by the primary end of preaching, the elucidation of thé scriptures, as the fountain of religious instruction.

When this principle is violated, it is commonly from the desire of *brevity*. Almost innumerable examples of this sort might be mentioned; and many from preachers of respectable rank. In some cases, a mere member of a sentence, amounting to no affirmation, and expressing no complete thought, whatever, is violently disjoined from its grammatical connexion, to stand for a text. Bishop Horne's sermon, entitled; 'The beloved disciple,'—has this text, "that disciple whom Jesus loved." The whole sentence is, "Therefore, that disciple whom Jesus loved, said unto Peter, It is the Lord." His sermon entitled 'the Tree of Life,' has this text: "The Tree of Life also in the midst of the garden." Each of these clauses is only a nominative case, with an adjunct.

In other instances, a few words are so selected as to express a complete sense; but the brevity at which the preacher so fondly aims, is attained by the omission of intervening words or phrases. The prelate just mentioned, in his sermon on patience, has this text, " Follow after patience; " which is a mutilation of St. Paul's injunction to Timothy, " Follow after righteousness, godliness, faith, love, patience, meekness."

Dr. Blair in his sermon ' on the importance of order in conduct,' thought proper to make his text exactly. pertinent to his subject, by omitting an adverb and a conjunction, in the middle, thus; " Let all things be done —— in *order*." In his sermon on ' Gentleness,' his text, by a similar modification, reads thus: " The wisdom that is from above, is —— gentle ——." In his sermon on ' Candour,' the text is " Charity —— thinketh no evil; " four members being omitted between the two parts of this clause. But the most singular example of this sort in Blair, is his choice of the words, " Cornelius, a devout man," as a text to his sermon on ' Devotion.' The passage is given as in Acts x. 2, where, indeed, three of its four words are found, while the other word occupies a remote place, in the verse preceding. The entire passage is this; " There was a certain man in Cesarea, called Cornelius, a Centurion of the band, called the Italian band, a devout man, and one that feared God with all his house, which gave much alms to the people, and prayed to God always." This is a sketch of a devout man, in one sentence. Why should four words be culled out of this sentence, and put together, containing a nominative case, without any grammatical correlatives, or any distinct sentiment?

*Brevity* is the object, but why should a preacher of good taste, why, especially, should a preacher of the Scotch church, whose stated duty it is to read portions of the Bible as a part of public worship, be so reluctant to read *one* complete sentence of this sacred book, as the basis of a long discourse. I admit that there are some special advantages in a concise text, provided it is perspicuous and appropriate. A long one is less likely to be remembered; and when it involves distinct subjects, is more likely to withdraw the preacher from the simplicity and unity of design, which ought to prevail in sermons. But when our choice falls upon a text containing more matter than we wish to discuss, the plain course is, to select our *one* topic, after reading and, if we please, briefly commenting on the whole, rather than to select a word or two, which suggest no subject whatever.

4. *A text should express* A COMPLETE SENSE OF THE INSPIRED WRITER, *from whom it is taken.*

This it *may* do, though it is but a single clause, selected from the members of a compound sentence; as, " Rejoice with trembling,"—" The time is short."— " Awake, thou that sleepest." Such a clause, however, by being severed from its connexion, is often wrested from its true meaning. You might take, for example, as a text, this complete and independent proposition, " There is no God." But you would use a liberty forbidden by all established laws of language; you would make the Bible contradict itself, unless you also take the previous clause, " The fool hath said in his heart, there is no God." " John the Baptist was risen from the dead,"—is a distinct proposition. But it does not express the sense of the inspired writer, and is not true without including more words : " And King Herod heard of him, and he *said*, that John the Baptist was risen from the dead."

A text is not to be hung upon a Sermon as an amulet; nor, like the nostrum of an empyric, is it to be taken up and applied at random. It should always express the *true* sense, and, as far as possible, the *complete* sense of the sacred writer.

5. *This should be the* PARTICULAR SENSE WHICH CONSTITUTES THE SUBJECT OF DISCOURSE: so that the text is pertinent to the subject; in other words, the subject should be directly expressed, or fairly suggested, by the unperverted meaning of the text.

Now this rule is violated in three ways. It excludes, in the first place, all those texts which are chosen from some fanciful connexion of *sound* with the occasion or subject in hand.

Archbishop Fenelon censures a sermon, delivered on *Ash*-Wednesday, from the words, " I have eaten *ashes* like bread." Here the correspondence between the text and the subject, lies not at all in the *sense*, but in the *sound of a single word*, which the preacher perceived to be related to the ceremony of the day.

Still less excuse is there, in the second place, for that affected eccentricity which lights on a text by accident, without any connexion of either sound or sense, with the point to be discussed. It is said of Latimer, that in his advanced age, he had a text which served for any subject; " Whatsoever things were written aforetime, were written for our learning."

I observe again, in the third place, that a text is not pertinent, when so disjoined from its connexion, that its apparent meaning, though it is truth, and *revealed* truth, is not the real meaning of the passage. Suppose you take, as the foundation of a sermon, the words, " What-

soever is not of faith, is sin;" and without examining
the connexion, make this your doctrine, that, *nothing
is true obedience which does not result from a principle
of faith*. This false sense of the passage, the authority
of Augustine made the classical one for a long period.
Doubtless, this sentiment is taught in the Bible, and
*seems* to be taught in this text; but examining the scope
of the whole passage, you perceive the Apostle's affirmation to be simply this; "Whatsoever is done without
a conviction of its lawfulness, is sinful;"—a conclusion
from his preceding remarks about conscientious scruples
as to meats and drinks.

I have heard the text, Psalm xlix. 8, "The redemption of the soul is precious," &c.—made to furnish the
doctrine, that "the salvation of man is procured at
great expense;"—and this, illustrated by various topics,
exhibiting the worth of the soul, and the love of God.
This is all true;—and it is truth often taught in the
Bible; but the primary, and obvious sense of the text,
as the whole connexion shows, is overlooked, by a mis-
understanding of the word *soul*, which in this place
means the life of the body.—Cecil says, "The *meaning*
of the Bible, is the Bible."

Dr. Blair's sermon on the duties belonging to middle
age, has this text,—"When I became a man, I put
away childish things." Was it then the design of the
Apostle to inculcate the duties of the middle age? Not
at all. He merely said, by way of illustration, that, as
the scenes of full manhood surpass the feeble comprehension of a child; so the grand concerns of the heavenly
state transcend our dark conceptions in this world. In
the next verse, the same sentiment is expressed by
another figure; "Now we see through a glass, darkly;
but then face to face." Every one perceives how absurd,

in this case, it would be to pass over the *thing illustrated*, and fix on the *illustration*, as a subject of discourse.

I am aware that the best of men have sometimes taken great freedom, with the plain meaning of the Bible, under the license of what they call *accommodation*. Thus Dr. —— from the words, " Speak to the children of Israel, that they go forward," preached on the doctrine of progressive sanctification. And the language poetically ascribed to Sisera's mother, waiting the return of her. heathen son, " Why is his chariot so long in coming ? " has often been made to express the aspirations of a dying Saint, for the perfect vision of his Saviour. How much more appropriate, in the former case, is the simple language of the New Testament, " Grow in grace," and in the latter, " I desire to depart, and be with Christ."

It is not enough, that the chief sentiment of a sermon is true, nor that it is important, nor that it is contained in the Bible; it must be contained in the *text*, or properly deduced from it. There is, I admit, a justifiable accommodation, if you please to give it that name, where a scriptural declaration or precept, or fact, special and limited in its original application, is made the basis of general instruction. " Son of man, I have made thee a watchman to the house of Israel," was an address to Ezekiel, as a minister of God in the ancient church. But there is no violence in considering the solemn charge to that prophet, as applicable to the ministers of the christian dispensation. " I have nourished and brought up children, and they have rebelled against me,"—though spoken of the Jews, would be a proper text for a sermon, on the general subject of ingratitude. So a passage of sacred *history*, exhibiting the character or obligations of man, the perfections of God, or the principles of his

government, furnishes instruction, profitable and pertinent
to men of whatever age or country.

6. *The only remaining quality which I would recommend in the choice of a text, is* SIMPLICITY.

The importance of this is implied in the remarks
already made : but it may be more apparent by some
distinct illustrations.

The simplicity to which I refer, is violated, in the first
place, by the choice of a text so obscure, as to require a
long *critical commentary* to prepare the way for the subject. It is certainly not my design to condemn such
critical remarks, as wholly inexpedient in the pulpit.
The judicious exposition of a paragraph or chapter, at
stated times, is an invaluable method of enlightening a
congregation, as to the contents of the sacred oracles :
and it is to be lamented that this ancient usage is so far
fallen into desuetude, in the churches of modern christendom. But, in these exercises, the steps of a philological investigation, are by no means to be exhibited
before common auditors. Much less is this proper in a
*sermon*, where men should be called to contemplate an
interesting subject, without having been first led through
a chilling and perplexing maze of critical speculation.—
On the same principle,—

Simplicity is violated, in the second place, by the
choice of a text which promises *great efforts in the
preacher*. This is especially the case, with such passages as present images distinguished for vivacity and
sublimity. Of this sort are the following ; " He bowed
the heavens also and came down, and darkness was
under his feet. And he rode upon a cherub and did fly,
yea, he did fly upon the wings of the wind." " I beheld
a great white throne, and him that sat on it, from whose
presence the earth and the heavens fled away." How-

ever grand or awful your subject may be, if you would
not disappoint your hearers, introduce it with a simple
text.[1]   Whenever this contains a figure, explain it, if
necessary ; and then, as a general rule, drop it, that you
may confine your attention to the thought.   It will
seldom be proper to follow a figure through your sermon,
and never to run it down, into a thousand fanciful points
of resemblance.[2]

[1] Note (7).

[2] The Christian Observer, vol. v, 493, recommends what it calls
the good old practice of announcing a text *twice*.   When a text is
very long, this may be inconvenient ; when very short, unnecessary.
It may be best, however, as a general rule, for the preacher to do
this, in cases where he is aware that the hearers expect it.   Probably
it would be well to do it, in all cases, where the text is of moderate
length.

# LECTURE V.

CHOICE OF SUBJECTS.—GENERAL PRINCIPLES.—FOUR
CLASSES OF SUBJECTS,—DOCTRINAL, ETHICAL, HIS-
TORICAL, HORTATORY.

WE proceed now to consider the choice of *subjects*.

In giving a brief survey of the pulpit, at different periods, I have already remarked, that this single article, the subjects of sermons, would furnish matter for a more complete history of preaching, than any which has been given to the world. Indeed, such is the influence of the pulpit on public sentiment, and such the reaction of public sentiment on the pulpit, that in the most important respects, the state of the church in any given period, may be determined from the prevalent strain of preaching, during that period.

Were we to make this principle the ground of a general estimate, and divide the history of the church since the Christian era into four periods, we might perahps denominate the first *simple* and *evangelical*; the second, *allegorical* and *mystical*; the third, *controversial*; and the fourth *mixed*. The first period may perhaps be considered as extending about to the time of Origen; the second, to the Reformation; the third to the commencement of the eighteenth century, and the last, to this time. It scarcely need be remarked, that this would be correct, only as a very general classification, admitting many exceptions in each period. The third, I denominate

*controversial*, as embracing not merely the mighty strug-
gle between the Romish and the Reformed churches, but
also the intolerant, and often sanguinary contests among
Protestants of different sects.    During this lamentable
season, while the pulpit was the theatre of acrimonious
attack and recrimination, the greatest question that has
ever agitated the church, namely, whether the Bible is,
or is not, the supreme standard of faith, may be considered as finally put to rest.

The fourth period I call *mixed*, because, at different
times and places, it has exhibited an endless variety in
the character of sermons, from the extreme of fanatical
declamation, to that of the frigid and courtly essay.

The selection of subjects, which any preacher will
make for his public discourses, will correspond with his
principal *end* in preaching.  If this is personal emolu-
ment or fame, his sermons will be modelled in matter and
spirit, according to the prevailing taste of the time.
His object may be to establish some point of technical
orthodoxy; or to confute some heresy; or to elucidate
some doubtful text from the resources of criticism; or to
promote good morals, by enforcing some duty or repro-
bating some vice; or finally, to amuse his audience, by
the exhibition of an elevated taste, or a splendid oratory.
If the preacher's end is to glorify God, and save his
hearers, the peculiar truths and duties of the gospel will
constitute the principal topics of his public discourses.

The pulpit, like all other things in which human agency
is concerned, has always been more or less subject to the
influence of local and temporary causes.  At one time,
all its powers have been directed, perhaps for half a
century, according to an impulse given by a few celebrated models of preaching.  At another time, an overwhelming current of public feeling and opinion has been

occasioned by some great subject of duty or danger, involving the common interests of the church. For a hundred years after Luther's time, scarcely a sermon was delivered in any Protestant pulpit, without alluding to the usurpations of the papal hierarchy.

But aside from caprice and passion, and the occasional excitement of great emergencies in the religious world, there must be circumstances in the view of every judicious preacher, affecting to some extent his own choice of subjects for the pulpit. He will take into view the capacity and cultivation of his hearers ; their attainments in religious knowledge ; their prejudices; and their intellectual and moral habits. He will have regard also to time and occasion. By this, I do not chiefly mean the periodical solemnities of religion, such as the Christian sacraments, days of fasting or of thanksgiving ; nor other special, public occasions, which usually prescribe their own limits to the preacher. But I refer to that general coincidence of things, which may render the discussion of a particular subject more. or less seasonable at any one time or place.[1]

The wise preacher too, will have some regard to his own talents, and taste, and age, in determining upon the topics to be discussed in his public instructions. I mention *age*, because a sermon designed to investigate some abstruse point in religion, or to arraign some vice which calls for the reprehension of the pulpit, will be much more likely to meet a favourable reception from the hearers, if the preacher is supposed to possess that maturity of judgment, and extensive knowledge of his subject, which nothing but experience in his sacred work can give. The relation which the preacher sustains to

[1] Note (8.)

the hearers, is connected with a distinct class of circumstances which good sense will not fail to take into the
account. That may be a fit discourse for a stated pastor, which would be very inappropriate if discussed by a
stranger : and that which might seem affectation of zeal,
or learning, or orthodoxy in a single sermon, from an
itinerant, might be unexceptionable as connected with a
series of addresses to the same audience.

There is one kind of public discourse, called Exposition or Lecture, which is distinguished rather by its
form than its subject, and the importance of which claims
for it a distinct consideration in another place. The
subjects of sermons, in the more appropriate sense of this
word, may perhaps be included in the following general
classes.

1. DOCTRINAL.—This head comprises that whole
circle of truths, which appertain to the system of revealed
religion. A sermon which discusses one or more of
these truths, as its principal subject, is called a *doctrinal*
sermon. Its professed object is to enlighten the understanding, confirm the faith, and obviate the mistakes
of the hearers. Of course, it is in the didactic strain;
as it is intended to exhibit, explain, and establish the
views which the preacher entertains on the point in
question. The absolute importance which he will attach
to this class of subjects, collectively, and the relative
importance of each, compared with the rest, will be
according to his general system of religious opinions.
Some of the doctrines above alluded to, have been denominated *essential* or *fundamental*. By this it is not
meant merely, that they are taught with so much distinctness in the Bible, that to deny them is to call in
question the authority of this book as a divine revelation ; but also that they are constituent parts of an entire

system, none of which can be taken away, without the virtual renunciation of the whole. On this ground, it is maintained, that the deliberate denial of these doctrines, by any one who understands them, is inconsistent with love to the truth, and therefore inconsistent with salvation.

It is foreign from my present purpose, to examine the views of those who discard the above distinction between essential and nonessential truths; and allege that error of opinion is not, in any case, either criminal or fatal. I shall only remark in passing, that to say there are no essential principles in theology, while we admit such principles in all those sciences which are secondary and subservient to this, is absurd. To say that error in opinion is never owing to obliquity of moral temper, is to contradict all experience. And to affirm, that while the Bible is our only guide to salvation, we may yet be saved, though we reject the most important truths which it reveals, is to charge absurdity on its contents, and folly on its author.

Taking it for granted then, that the Bible reveals truths essential to be understood and believed, it is clear that the preacher who is wise and faithful, will often make these truths the topics of his public discourses. Indeed, these are the grand basis of all profitable instruction. The character of God, the character of man, the way of salvation by Christ, and the kindred doctrines involved by necessary connection with these, are subjects which our hearers must be brought to understand, or they are taught *nothing* to any valuable purpose. The man who avoids these doctrines in his sermons, from a perverted taste, or a false delicacy, or a servile complaisance to the prejudices of others, forgets the chief end for which the Christian ministry was instituted. " The sword of the spirit is the word of God." Let the

D

doctrines preached by Christ and his Apostles, the
doctrines which constitute the glory, the efficacy, the
essence of the gospel, be generally excluded from the pulpit for one half century, and the night of paganism would
again spread its gloomy shades over Christendom: The
*manner* in which these doctrines are to be preached, will
claim our attention hereafter. I have only to add here,
that this class, including the primary and the subordinate
truths of revelation, afford the preacher a rich *variety*
of subjects for discussion in the pulpit.

2. *The next class of subjects to be noticed, may be
called* ETHICAL. —I prefer this term to the more common
ones, *practical* and *moral*, not on account of any primary
difference in the sense of the terms, but because these
latter are wont to be associated with views of Christian
duty, very indefinite, and often erroneous. In respect to
the motives, the consolations, and indeed all the essential
characteristics of a truly religious man, the doctrines of
the Bible are eminently *practical*. To give one example
of my meaning. Any minister of experience in his work,
knows that the most direct way to administer consolation
to a pious husband, mourning for the death of his wife,
would be to dwell on the holy perfection of God, and of
his providential government.[1] No system of morals,
indeed, that is not founded on these, will receive any
countenance from the ministrations of a public teacher,
who understands and loves the Gospel. He cannot for a
moment sanction the spurious morality which attaches
moral qualities to actions, independent of the temper and
motives of the agent. It may be said, and said truly
perhaps, that no respectable man does avowedly plead

---

[1] On the practical influence of Christian doctrines, see Erskine's
Discourses, 1798, page 54, and Bridges on the Christian Ministry.

for a principle, so repugnant to sound philosophy and to common sense. But unquestionably, thousands of sermons are every year delivered in Christendom, which contain no more recognition of this obvious principle than if it were self-evident that the heart has no connection with the conduct, but is altogether exempt from the claims of the divine law. Such sermons pervert and prostitute the first principles of Christian morality. They set up custom, convenience, or expediency, as the standard of human duty; and substitute mere external conformity to divine commands, for that love which is the essence of all acceptable obedience. Though such morality may assume the name of religion, it is a religion which the Bible disowns. It is completely at variance with the gospel, and with the law, which it is the great design of the gospel to honour and fulfil. Accordingly it deserves to be remembered, that the system which is thus termed morality, invariably fails of itself to make men *moral*. When this constitutes the prevalent strain of preaching, its influence falls far below the proper effect of Christian instruction.[1]

With these things in view, I need only add that the class of subjects denominated ethical, which the preacher is called to discuss in sermons, includes all those external duties which man is required to perform, resulting from his relations to other beings, especially to his fellow men. It includes prayer, observance of Christian institutions, fidelity, charity, &c. to our neighbour. Whenever these subjects are to be brought into the pulpit, three things at least ought to be remembered. One is, that the precepts of Christianity require the same conduct, as those of the moral law, extended, indeed, to greater particularity in

[1] The best illustration of this topic that I have ever seen, is contained in Dr. Chalmer's Address to the people of Kilmany.

D 2

detail, and enforced by stricter requisitions as to moral temper, and greater elevation of motive: while both possess, in all these respects, a vast superiority to every human system of morals. Another thing is, that good works, however unexceptionable in character, can never be the ground of justification before God, so as to supersede the dependence of a sinner on the atonement and grace of Christ. The last thing is, that while we cannot admit morality, without piety, to be acceptable obedience, nor with piety, to be meritorious; we should insist on the indispensable necessity of a good life; as commanded by God; as essential to the relations subsisting among moral beings; and as the only proper fruit and evidence of a holy temper.

3. *Another class of subjects for sermons, is the* HISTORICAL.—This includes a statement of facts, which is limited to the character of an individual; or which relates to some particular period, or to some community of men. In the former case, it is the object of the preacher to exhibit the traits of some distinguished character, good or bad, as the basis of practical instruction. Such descriptions, so far as the pulpit is concerned, have commonly been restricted to the character of persons deceased, and to their excellences rather than their defects; according to the long received maxim; "De mortuis, nil nisi bonum." To this maxim, in its full extent, I can by no means accede. If it is understood to imply merely that death imposes an awe on the licentiousness of the tongue, because it extinguishes those little antipathies which often affect our estimate of *living* persons; no enlightened mind will question its correctness. But if the meaning is, that when men die, their errors and faults cease to be the occasion of warning or instruction to the *living;* and that in all such cases,

where we cannot truly speak good, we must of course speak *nothing* or *falsehood;* the principle has no sanction from reason, none from the Bible, and it will have none from the scrutiny and the retributions of the final judgment.

Shall the preacher then revolt the sensibilities of his hearers, by exactly portraying the imperfections of departed friends?—I answer, no. But he is not to escape this difficulty by indiscriminate panegyric. Did we *know* the man whose character is represented as perfect? Of course we know that it is overdrawn, for he was *not* perfect. Was he a stranger to us? Still we know, from revelation and from analogy, that he was not perfect. In general, therefore, unmingled eulogy of the dead, however it may gratify the partial sympathies of friendship, or promote the interest of the preacher, is beneath the integrity and dignity which belongs to his sacred office. His true course then, is to avoid describing the character of persons recently deceased, except in a few cases of conspicuous and acknowledged excellence. And while these are drawn in colors not too bright to present the likeness of any human being, the qualities of an eminently good and useful man, exhibited in one consistent view, furnish to others, very powerful motives to imitate an example so attractive. So much it seemed proper to say on a subject which occasionally claims the consideration of every preacher : and more, I presume, need not be said, since modern usage excludes from the pulpit the extravagant panegyrics of former days. At this period, even in Roman Catholic countries, it would hardly be admitted as an apology for such servile flattery, as that exhibited by Bossuet, in some of his *Funeral Orations*, that it was addressed to the ears of royalty. [1]

[1] Note (9.)

But under the head of historical subjects, the Bible affords an ample range, free from all the above difficulties. From individual characters there delineated, and from facts exhibiting the providence of God, and the agency of man, in the history of communities, the preacher may derive the most interesting topics for sermons.   As these have been very much overlooked, in preparations for the pulpit, it may be useful to inquire whether they are attended with any peculiar *inconvenience* or *advantage*. There are certainly some *inconveniences*.

The common method adopted in describing a character, an event, or a series of events, is to follow a chronological order, and relate occurrences as they stand connected in time.   Here, the first difficulty arises from a tendency either to undue brevity or prolixity in the narrative.   It is peculiarly the province of good taste, to fix on the medium between a naked outline, and that particularity of detail, which disgusts by excessive minuteness.

Another and greater difficulty arises from the miscellaneous train of remarks, commonly suggested by an historical subject.   In some cases, I know, a single point may be selected for discussion ; but a sermon founded on facts, almost of course, takes into view various reflections resulting from the narrative.   Though this sacrifice of unity is not consistent with the highest effect of a sermon, it is, in my opinion, fully justified on proper occasions, by the advantages with which it is attended.   What then are these *advantages ?*

The first is, the *familiarity* and *precision* which attends the evidence of facts.   Men instantly *understand* reasoning of this sort.   It corresponds with their customary modes of conception.   When an argument depends on the investigation of criticism, or the deductions of logic, few possess that intellectual discipline and patience of thought, which are necessary clearly to perceive its force. But a plain historical statement, if the facts are unquestionable, is a kind of argument which it is perfectly easy to comprehend. It is on this account, probably, that the instructions of the Bible are so much thrown into the form of narrative. And it is especially to our purpose here to remark, that the public discourses of our Lord, more particularly his parables, which are only a peculiar species of narrative, are adapted to this common principle of the human mind. Hence this kind of evidence more readily commands assent in common minds, than any other. In its power it is complex, though without obscurity. With a felicity peculiar to itself, it unites the evidence of sense, of experience, and of testimony; while the combined influence of these is strengthened by the simple light in which this evidence is presented to the understanding.

A *second* advantage is, the *vivacity of impression*, with which this species of discourse is attended. Every preacher knows how difficult it is to keep up the interest of a common assembly in the discussion of an *abstract* subject. Their feelings demand something of that variety in illustration, which attends the concerns of real life. Hence it is, that a metaphor or comparison, founded on some familiar object of sense, is so striking in its effect. Hence, too, a statement of *facts*, delineating human character, and tracing human passions and principles in their various operations, invariably commands the attention of common hearers, especially of the young. It accords with the manner in which they are accustomed to receive instruction from the book of *Providence*, and of *Creation* around them. We readily feel the difference between the description of a man's person, and the sight of his picture; or between the sight of his picture, and that of his living face. Analogous to this, as to vivacity of impression, is the difference between instruction of *doctrine* or *precept*, and the instruction of *facts*. When the baseness of envy, or the obligation of filial affection, and religious integrity, is set before us, in the form of didactic representation, we readily assent to its correctness. But how different is the thrilling interest with which we contemplate the same things in the simple story of Joseph! We are convinced by the logical discussion which proves the vanity of earthly distinctions, and the certainty of an eternal retribution. But we are impressed, arrested, agitated with awful emotion, when we view these truths in the parable of the rich man and the beggar. In what way do we form the most striking apprehension of faith, repentance, devotion? Not by viewing these in the light of precept or reasoning; but as they are seen in the example of Abraham offering up Isaac; of St. Peter, weeping bitterly for the denial of his Lord; of Daniel, braving the terrors of the lion's den. And the excellence of humility we perceive not so strongly, from an abstract dissertation on the greatness of God, or the meanness and guilt of man; as when we see the publican smiting on his breast; or the Saviour, in the majesty of condescension, rising, and girding himself, and washing the feet of his disciples.

In these remarks, I cannot be understood to recommend that historical subjects should supersede others in the pulpit. My meaning is, that this class of subjects has some peculiar advantages, which have not been duly considered by public teachers.

4. *There is one more class of subjects which ought to be mentioned, namely, the* HORTATORY.

Upon this head, there is no occasion that I should enlarge, though the topics which it includes are endless in variety and extent of interest. Among these are to be reckoned all the points on which the preacher considers his hearers both to *know* and *acknowledge* the truth, in speculation; while they neither feel nor obey it.

The defect which is far more common than any other in the hortatory discourse, consists in a reliance on the *subject itself*, to produce impression, while it is exhibited only in the feeble dress of common-place illustration. Upon a subject which demands deep emotion, the preacher perhaps displays an artificial animation; and *declaims* merely, where he ought to speak " in demonstration of the spirit and with power." *Conviction* is the basis of persuasion; and to address men with epithets of *terror*, to assume the attitude and aspect of *denunciation*, in pointing the thunderbolts of heaven, when no light has been presented to the understanding, though a very common defect of comminatory sermons, is one of the most unprofitable efforts in which a minister of Christ can employ his powers. To preach the *truth* on some subjects, and to some descriptions of men, is unavoidably to preach *terror*. But if we follow the example of Christ and the Apostles, the terror will consist in the *thought*, rather than the *language*. They never, indeed, avoided the use of figures the most awful, nor of such words as *damnation*, *hell*, &c. when *necessary* to express the sentiment they wished to utter; nor did they ever employ these forms of expression unnecessarily. On the contrary, without using them at all, they sometimes preached the gospel in the most alarming manner. It deserves to be remembered that such was the fact with St. Peter's sermon on the day of Pentecost, the most pungent and powerful one that ever was delivered. The sermon of President Edwards, entitled, " Sinners in the hands of an angry God," was one of the most awful exhibitions of truth, as to both sentiment and language, that has been made in the modern pulpit. Its effect on the audience, as to deep and solemn impression, was perhaps greater than that of any other sermon that can be named within a century past. But terrific phraseology was used no farther than was necessary to express the thoughts. So Whitfield often employed words and figures full of terror; but he did this with tenderness, and often with tears; instead of that unfeeling severity of denunciation so often witnessed.[1]

When we choose a subject from this class, we ought to do it with the full conviction that our success, so far as it depends on ourselves, depends almost entirely on that sort of ethereal simplicity, sincerity, affection, and fervour, in the spirit and execution, which commend the truth to the hearts of the hearers.

*Three remarks will close this Lecture.*

1. In selecting subjects for sermons, the Christian teacher should *aim at variety.* To preach month after month, on a single subject, or a contracted circle of subjects, is to depart from the grand model of instruction as contained in the book of Revelation, and the book of Providence. *Diversity* in the course of events, in the condition, taste and attainments of different hearers, and of the same hearers in different circumstances, demands a correspondent *diversity* in the instructions of the pulpit. Let the preacher then seize upon *occasions,* as they rise. Let him follow Providence; and always turn to good account, every interesting occurrence among his flock. Yet,

2. The preacher should never, to gratify *a vain love of novelty and amusement,* sink his ministrations to the rank of a dramatic exhibition. He should never forget that he is an ambassador of Christ; and that his main busi-

[1] Note (10.)

ness is, to turn the sinner from darkness to light; and to build up the believer in his most holy faith. The exact limits within which he shall keep, cannot indeed be prescribed. But when he descends, as some preachers of our time have done, to discourse upon " vaccination"— " upon the popular dread of apparitions,"—" the beauties of a New England autumn, and the charms of its Indian summer; " it is no great stretch of preciseness to say, that he occupies ground which better accords with the objects of a novel or gazette, than with those of a Christian sermon. The incidental allusion to such topics by way of illustration, is by no means improper ; but they cannot be made the chief subjects of discourse, without wresting the pulpit from ' the sober use of its legitimate peculiar powers.' ' Insist,' said the venerable Archbishop Usher, in his directions to young ministers,— ' insist most on those points, that tend to produce sound belief, sincere love to God, repentance for sin, and a life of holiness.'

3. That preacher who *is perplexed through want of subjects for sermons*, should suspect that something is wrong in himself; at least, that he is very imperfectly qualified for his office. His religion furnishes topics, inexhaustible in variety, and beyond all comparison, superior in richness, elevation, and sublimity, to those which any other public speaker is called to discuss. In the character of God, he contemplates all that is profound in wisdom, awful in holiness, and attractive in mercy. In the character of man, he sees a combination of dignity and misery ; the dignity of an immortal soul, polluted and degraded by sin. He sees majesty and meekness, glory and ignominy, strangely united in the character and sufferings of Christ. He sees in the gospel provided for fallen man, at infinite expense, a rescue

from his ruin, ‘a remedy for his maladies, and a rule for his guidance.’  He sees heaven with all its blessedness inviting to a life of piety, and hell with all its miseries awaiting the ungodly.  Is it possible that with a field before him, absolutely boundless, a man can want sub- jects for sermons?  In selecting among these one that shall be most appropriate in given circumstances, I allow he may hesitate.  But, with the profusion of interesting matter, displayed in every page of the Bible, if he is perplexed to find any topic of discourse, he has mistaken his profession.  The fact that he wants a *subject*, is demonstration that he wants either the *understanding* or the *heart* of a minister.

# LECTURE VI.

STRUCTURE OF SERMONS,—PRELIMINARY REMARKS,
—NECESSITY OF SOUND JUDGMENT, AND A PIOUS
SPIRIT IN A PREACHER.—EXORDIUM.

OUR attention will be directed through several following
lectures, to THE STRUCTURE OF SERMONS. In entering
upon this large class of topics, some preliminary suggestions seem to be required.

The composition of a sermon calls into exercise both
the *intellect* and the *heart.* As a work of intellect, the
preacher's success in selecting and arranging his materials,
depends in no small measure on the soundness of his
judgment. Through an infelicity of taste or habit, some
men treat all sorts of subjects in one precise method.
They have just so many principal heads, just so many
subdivisions, and so many inferences in each discourse,
following in exact succession, like the strokes of the
clock, which mark the hours of the day. The hearers
easily anticipate the particulars of this unvarying round.
Now this rigid uniformity is not applicable to any important business, depending on the agency of mind.
What should we think of a general, who should plan a
battle or a siege according to books, without regarding
the character of his troops, the circumstances of his position, or the strength of his enemy? He might spend the
time of a campaign in drawing lines of circumvallation or
contravallation, and with all his mathematical exactness,

he might prove a harmless enemy to those who would have trembled at the prompt use of bayonets and heavy artillery. Should the lawyer treat all causes of his clients, or the physician all diseases of his patients, in one technical method, without regarding the endless variety of circumstances, what should we say of their skill in their several professions? Certainly a mode of proceeding, which is absurd in all other cases, is not less absurd in the pulpit.

But the reasonable disgust which we feel at a mechanical uniformity, should not push us into the opposite extreme. Oratory, like other arts, has settled principles. The barrister when he speaks, has some *end* in view; and applies his powers to attain it, not at random, but according to some plan, adapted to his purpose. He states facts, adduces testimony, cites authority, reasons, obviates prejudices, rouses emotion. To gain his cause, he combines more or fewer sources of argument, and directs his efforts to a given point of attack or defence, as a versatile invention, and a skilful judgment may dictate. He adopts a particular course, not by accident, but because his knowledge of men and of his profession, induces him to prefer this, as most likely to be successful.

The wise *preacher* too, will proceed according to the *subject* and *design* of his discourse; and will not be so afraid of rules, as to determine that a sermon should have *no* subject nor design. Without using judgment, every rule indeed will be unavailing, even to teach him the meaning of his text. Does it therefore follow that the system of sacred interpretation can give him no aid in understanding the Bible?—or that he is to ascertain the sense of a single text only by chance, without any principles to guide him? No more does it follow, because mere rules cannot enable him to compose a good sermon, that therefore he can never hope to make such a sermon, except by chance. The thought, the method, and the expression, all demand pains and skill. Writing is a fine art, and has elementary principles. Accident might as well produce the Messiah of Handel, as the Paradise Lost; might as well guide the chisel of Praxiteles, or the pencil of Raffaelle, as the pen of Addison.

I am aware that a random effort in the pulpit, is sometimes successful. But when it is so, if it was occasioned by affected peculiarity, or careless neglect of regular preparation, it requires apology rather than commendation.

This leads to another remark, viz. on the necessity of *pious feeling*. The preacher's success in composing a sermon, depends pre-eminently on the state of *heart* with which he comes to the work. Suppose he engages in it with the same frigid calculation, with which a mechanic sits down to the construction of a clock. His object is to amuse his hearers; to make an advantageous display of his own genius, or learning, or eloquence. With this view, he chooses his subject and his method; adopts some novel interpretation of his text, becoming a man of erudition; calls to his aid all the resources of profound theological research; adjusts all his topics of argument and of address to the passions, according to the best canons of taste;—and when the sermon is finished, what is it?—a body with fair proportions, elegant, splendid, perhaps, in its decorations, but a body without a *soul*.

But let the preacher commence his preparation for the pulpit with the heart of a devout Christian; a heart that regards as the great end of preaching, the glory of God and the salvation of man; a heart that feels the worth of souls, glows with holy affection to the Re-

deemer, and anticipates with trembling hope, the day
when he shall come to be glorified in them that believe;
and this spirit will diffuse a savour of godliness through
the sermon, that will warm, and impress, and penetrate
his hearers. Luther's maxim, ' Bene orasse est bene
studuisse,' should be graven on the memory of every
preacher. None but God can effectually teach *us* how
to teach *others*. A heart devoted to him in the study,
will stamp its own character of sanctity and energy on
every preparation for the pulpit. And let it never be
forgotten, that no fund of knowledge, no rhetorical skill
in the selection of matter, or in the arrangement or embellishment of a discourse, can make it in any measure
what a Christian sermon should be, if it wants that vital
impulse, which nothing can impart but a spirit of fervent
piety.[1]

With these general remarks in view, we may proceed
to consider that arrangement of parts, which is most
usual in a regular sermon. To every such sermon,
some of these parts will of course belong. You will
readily perceive that it is not my object to designate the
cases in which more or fewer of them may be dispensed
with; but to lay down some principles in respect to each,
that may assist the young preacher in his preparations
for the pulpit; taking it for granted, that he will endeavour to make such an arrangement of parts, in any given
case, as is best adapted to the subject and design of his
discourse. The principal parts of a sermon which now
demand our consideration are these five, *exordium, exposition and proposition, division, discussion or argument,
and conclusion*. The observations which I shall make
on these particulars, will necessarily bring into view
some of the great principles of preaching; and instead

[1] See Erskine's Discourses on Ministry, Ser. I.

of exhausting the subject, will only prepare the way for examining, more fully, the general characteristics of sermons.

## EXORDIUM.

The only valuable purpose for which any public speaker can address an assembly, is to make them understand, and believe, and feel, the sentiments which he utters. The chief object of an introduction then is, to secure that attention which is most favourable to the attainment of this purpose; and the obstacles which prevent this favourable attention, are commonly found in the *prejudice*, the *ignorance*, or the *indifference* of the hearers. They may have a low estimate of the talents or the moral character of the preacher. In such a case, however, the remedy lies not in any effect which he can hope to produce by a few prefatory sentences at the opening of a sermon, but in his becoming better *known* to his hearers, if he *deserves* their respect, or becoming a *better man*, if he does not. If the prejudice is directed against *general opinions*, which he holds, or is supposed to hold, no benefit can arise from attempting, in an exordium, to defend those opinions; nor from alluding to them in any form, except in some rare case, where a prompt disavowal may remove at once some injurious mistake. But if he is aware that the hearers are preoccupied with unfavourable impressions, as to the particular *subject* he is about to discuss, his first aim evidently should be, so to present that subject, if possible, as not to strengthen, but to obviate those impressions.

Supposing, however, the preacher to be satisfied, that no *prejudice* of the hearers exists to frustrate the effect of his discourse, still he is to presume that their *ignorance*, or at least their *indifference* to divine things, will present powerful obstacles to his success.  He must therefore introduce his subject, so that it shall promise to be intelligible to them, and interesting; so that they shall be attracted to listen, and gradually disarmed of that deadly insensibility, which bars up all the avenues of profitable instruction from the pulpit; so in short, that they shall become prepared spontaneously and earnestly, to "give heed to the things that are spoken." An exordium, then, should possess the following properties:

In the first place, SIMPLICITY.

Here there is no room for artificial structure, and studied ornament of diction.  Good taste absolutely forbids both the stiffness of aphoristic brevity, and the elaborate harmony of the stately and periodic style.  It is an ancient precept, that no discourse should commence with a long sentence.  All pompous allusions, Horace condemns as splendid patches on an introduction, which render it ridiculous; such as ' the grove and altar of Diana; the stream winding through beautiful fields; the majestic river, and the rainbow.'

All those warm *appeals to the passions* or imagination, which may be highly proper in the sequel of a discourse, are entirely out of place at the beginning.  The obvious reason is, the hearers come together with their hearts cold, and their thoughts dissipated by intercourse with a thousand minor objects.  They can no more be started into high emotion by a fervid stroke of eloquence, than a mountain of ice can be dissolved in a moment, before the blaze of a taper.  Besides, were it practicable to awaken this sudden ardour of feeling, it would not be desirable.  High emotion is necessarily transient.  He who thinks himself able to keep up its full intensity through a long discourse, needs only a few lessons from experience to undeceive him.  By striking his highest

string at first, he compels himself to sink as he proceeds; and thus very unskilfully excites expectation,
only to disappoint it. The discourse that begins in
ecstasy, to be consistent with itself, must end in phrenzy.
A good judge on this subject says, ' reserve your fire :
bold thoughts and figures are never relished, till the
mind is heated and thoroughly engaged, which is never
the case at the commencement. Homer employs not a
single simile, in the first book of the Iliad, nor in the
first book of the Odyssey.'

Under the head of simplicity, I remark too, that an
introduction should not exhibit a *display of learning*.
Grammatical and philological observations, the names
and opinions of celebrated men, and in general, whatever
looks like ostentation of extensive reading, is to be
avoided as much as possible in this part of a sermon.

It should not be *abstruse*. Controversial speculation,
metaphysical subtleties, protracted and profound argumentation, abstract thoughts and language, are entirely
unsuitable while as yet the minds of those we address are
prepared only for that which is perspicuous and familiar.

It should not be *abrupt*. The general reason is, that a
bold dash upon the hearers at first, is not congruous with
the cool state they are in, nor with the steady and
increasing interest, which we wish to preserve in their
minds. Extraordinary circumstances may justify the
departure from any rules, which common sense prescribes
for common cases. Such was the sudden and vehement
attack on Catiline, with which Cicero opened his first
oration against that conspirator. Chrysostom, after an
earthquake, began a sermon thus : ' Do you see the
power of God? Do you see the benignity of God ?—
Power, because the firm world he has shaken ; benignity,
because the falling world he has sustained.' And

Flecher commenced a funeral discourse thus: ' With
what design, Sirs, are you assembled here ?   What view
have you of my ministry ?   Am I come to dazzle you
with the glory of terrestrial honours ? '

But those abrupt exordiums which denote a studied
eccentricity in the preacher, are without apology.   The
most faulty examples of this kind, that I have seen, are
in the sermons, (as they are called,) of Sterne.   On the
text " His commandments are not grievous ; "—he
begins—' No,—they are not grievous, my dear auditors.'
After the text : " For we trust that we have a good
conscience ; " he exclaims—' Trust! *trust* we have a
good conscience ! '—On the text : " It is better to go to
the house of mourning than to the house of feasting ; " his
first sentence is : ' That I deny.'   The first of these
examples is tolerable; but the others, especially the last,
are a puerile effort at witticism, which a man of good
taste might excuse in the tavern or circus, but which he
must reprobate in the house of God.

In the second place, another quality requisite in an
exordium, is PERTINENCE.   It should correspond with
the subject, and the occasion.   Writers on oratory have
often adverted to the fact, that both Demosthenes and
Cicero were accustomed to compose introductions beforehand, from which they might make a selection in case
of an emergency.   The reason assigned for this, is the
importance, and at the same time the difficulty, of beginning well an address, when there had been little opportunity for preparation : and while neither the speaker nor
the hearers have as yet become deeply interested in the
subject.   Unquestionably these great masters of oratory
might devise a few sentences, adapted to the general
state of affairs, which might be made the preface to the
discussion of almost any topic.   But the preacher is

seldom called to an unpremeditated effort; and so constant is the repetition of his public services, that he would soon find an expedient like the one just mentioned, utterly fallacious. It is an indispensable quality of an exordium that it should be engaging. This it cannot be, if it consists only of thoughts which are trite or trivial. The preacher may begin by descanting on some such point as,—the *vanity of the world*,—the *brevity of human life*,—the *worth of the soul*,—the *calamities of the fall;* but it requires no common skill and vivacity to give interest to an assembly, in that which they have heard a thousand times repeated.

Now *pertenence* promotes *variety*. The important difference as to variety between general subjects and those which are particular, is this; the former are few, obvious, and to all men who reflect at all, familiar. While particular subjects are as various as the endless diversity that exists in the properties and relations of things. So far then as interest depends on *variety*, we have only to select various subjects for sermons, and to make the exordium of each appropriate, and the end is accomplished. I am aware that there is one kind of introduction, which, though limited to the subject in hand, is void of interest, because it recurs in formal routine, on every Sabbath. It consists in a strain of indefinite remarks, bespeaking attention to what shall be delivered, on account of its *immense importance*, and the *momentous consequences* connected with the manner in which it shall be received.

Those Introductions which cast a preparatory light on the subject from the context, may easily unite the advantages of simplicity and pertinence. And there is a peculiar felicity in this connexion, where it can be exhibited in the form of narrative.

In the third place, DELICACY is another indispensable quality of a good exordium.'

There is a becoming congruity between the preacher's work, and the air of religious sensibility and reverence with which he should engage in its appropriate duties. When he enters the place consecrated to Jehovah, the reflection, " This is none other than the house of God, and this is the gate of heaven," should repress all feelings that do not accord with the dignity and sanctity of his business. The same Luther who braved the anathemas of the Roman Pontiff, always ascended the pulpit with trembling knees. But besides this aspect of religious awe, which a deep feeling of divine things will certainly impart to the preacher, there is a decorum of manner, which will arise from a proper respect to his hearers. Where this is wanting, they will not fail to perceive it, and to be instinctively prepossessed against what he shall deliver.

But we must not mistake the character of that modesty which is becoming in a preacher. It is not a timid, tremulous manner of saying things, which seems to imply that he does but half believe his own sentiments. The divine commission to Jeremiah was : " Arise and speak unto the people all that I command thee ; — be not afraid of their faces." And St. Paul besought his brethren to pray for him, " that he might speak boldly as he ought to speak." Certainly no commendation is due to that modesty in a preacher, which makes him " ashamed of the gospel of Christ."

Nor does real modesty require those formal *apologies*, with which sermons are often introduced. When a preacher compliments an assembly with the assurance, that he considers them as *very enlightened* and respectable ; that through the weakness of his powers, or the want of preparation in the present case, he is conscious that what he shall deliver will be unworthy of their attention; it may seem to result from an amiable self-diffidence. But judicious hearers will suspect, and often suspect truly, that pride is speaking under the cloak of humility.

At the bar, or in the senate, the public speaker may with happy effect sometimes allude, by way of apology for himself, to his want of health, or want of time for preparation, to the inexperience of youth or the imbecility of age. But the same indulgence is by no means allowed to the Christian preacher. The exhibition of himself in any form, is so inconsistent with the sacred delicacy and elevation of his work, that it rarely fails to excite disgust.

Before I dismiss the article of delicacy as a becoming property of an introduction, allow me to say, that it absolutely forbids an angry, austere, or querulous manner of address. He knows but little of men, who does not know that harsh and acrimonious language is adapted to produce unsanctified resentment, rather than evangelical repentance. He may imagine that fidelity to the truth requires him to assume a frowning front; to arraign his hearers with a *magisterial* air, and bid defiance to the sentiments they may entertain of him and his doctrines. But while they may be satisfied perhaps, that his religion has made him fearless and honest, they will hardly be persuaded that it has made him either an amiable man, or a wise preacher. Love and gentleness win upon the affections, while asperity and threatening fortify the heart against persuasion. A sermon, however excellent in other respects, will be lost to the hearers, if it assails them with an angry commencement.

In the fourth place, an exordium should be JUDICIOUS AS TO LENGTH.

I say *judicious*, because what is proper in each case, must be determined by the subject and the circumstances. Many of the old divines extended this part of their discourses to a tedious prolixity; while others, in modern times, both among the English and the French, have adopted the opposite extreme, and have passed from the text to the discussion, with only a sentence or two of introduction. This matter, however, should be regulated by sober principles, and not by caprice. The wise traveller will adjust the rapidity of his first movements, and the length of his stages, to the extent of his whole journey. If the subject to be discussed by the preacher is very copious, the exordium should be brief, to make room for the subsequent matter. If the sermon, on the other hand, is to contain but few thoughts, it is a very inadequate remedy for the defect, to postpone the consideration of these, by an attenuated introduction. I have sometimes been pained at the want of skill, which leads a man to select a subject extensive enough for five sermons, and then to occupy in loose prefatory remarks, one third of the time allotted to his discourse. The most common characteristic of such introductions, is sterile and languid declamation. The preacher begins perhaps with the charms of Eden, the primitive innocence and felicity of man, his fatal seduction by the subtilty of the Tempter, his apostacy, and his expulsion from Paradise. Then follow, in regular gradation, the miseries of the fall, and the wonderful plan of redemption. Besides the disproportionate *length* to which these tame exordiums are apt to be extended, they are too miscellaneous, and too trite, to awaken interest. The preacher is so much at leisure, that every trifle by the way-side attracts his attention ; and his subject (if indeed he has one) is forgotten. In this case, no congruity of parts is maintained, no regard to the maxim :

" Primo ne medium, medio ne discrepet imum."

The fault indeed is not so much that subsequent matter is inconsistent with what had preceded, as that the sermon is a dull repetition of thoughts anticipated in the introduction, some of which might have been vivid and interesting, in their proper place and order.

Two hints, founded as I think on careful observation, will close this lecture. One is, that young writers of sermons are extremely apt to dilate all the first thoughts of a sermon, from an apprehension that their stock of materials to complete it will be too soon exhausted. The other is, that a similar diffuseness may be expected, when a man is too indolent or unskilful to look through his subject, and arrange its parts, before he begins to write. In this case, his introduction will almost of course be inappropriate, and tedious in length. [1]

[1] Note (11.)

# LECTURE VII.

As the *subject* is the basis of a sermon, this ought in the
first place, to be very distinctly apprehended by the
preacher, before he can be prepared to state it clearly,
to enforce it by argument, and to apply it with power to
the conscience. It ought also to be fairly contained in
the passage from which it is professedly deduced, as I
have shown at some length in discussing choice of texts.
It is this unquestionable principle, that the subject of a
Christian sermon ought to be derived from the *oracles of
God*, which often makes the *explication* of the text
necessary, before the subject of discourse is announced.
As very few remarks will be requisite on that part of a
sermon, which we call *proposition*, I shall defer these
till I have considered what is proper in explaining a text,
when this is required.

It ought then to be taken for granted, that no man
will attempt to discuss a text in public, while he does
not suppose himself to be possessed of its true meaning.
Not that absolute certainty concerning every passage, is
essential or attainable. A man of the clearest conceptions, with the best aids which learning can furnish, may
sometimes be in doubt, among the different senses that
have been attached to a passage, which is the true one.
But instead of obtruding his doubts on his *hearers*, pro-

fessing to enlighten their minds, while his own gropes in darkness, Christian discretion prescribes a shorter course, namely, to let that passage alone in the pulpit;—at least not to make it a subject of a sermon. ' A man,' says Claude, ' who needs to be told that he ought not to preach on a text before he *understands* it, needs at the same time to be informed, that he is fitter for any other profession than that of the Ministry.'

But when there is no real *difficulty* in the sense of a passage, it is often useful to notice the occasion and circumstances with which it is connected, for the sake of a more vivid *impression*. When this is done by allusion to the context, especially when a simple statement of facts is all that is required, such an explanation of the text very properly falls into the exordium. I may add, that in much the greater number of cases, this familiar preparation to announce the subject of discourse is the best that can be adopted. There must however, be instances in which a regular explanation of the text is necessary to show the hearers that it contains the sentiment which the preacher deduces from it. In such a case he must resort to those laws of sacred criticism, by which, as an interpreter of the Bible and a theologian, his inquiries should be guided. To give instruction in these, is not the business of Sacred Rhetoric. But as the great end of sacred philology is the elucidation of divine truth, and that for the benefit of common understandings, the *critic* and the *preacher* must to some extent be combined ; and it often becomes a question how far the *literary habits* of the *former* are to be modified by the *practical wisdom* of the *latter*. You sit down at your study table to investigate an interesting passage of scripture, with a view to bring forth its real import in a sermon. But there is an important difference between the process by which you examine that text to *ascertain* its meaning, and that by which you are to *exhibit* that meaning to plain hearers. In the first case, you act as an etymologist, and a critic ; in the other, as a " teacher of babes." It would seem, if we judge from facts, that there are extremes on different sides of this subject; and to guard the young preacher against these, by suggesting a few plain principles of common sense, is all that is required by the plan of these lectures.

1. *The preacher may err, by taking it for granted that some* GREAT DIFFICULTY *is to be encountered in every passage.* With this spirit he will come to the Bible, as the empiric does to his patient, resolved at all events, to find occasion for the display of his professional skill. He will magnify difficulties when they *exist*, and *create* them when they do not. The medical student must make it his business to investigate human diseases ;— shall he therefore presume that every man he meets is sick ? No more must the Biblical student take it for granted that every part of the sacred oracles is full of mystery, because critical research is necessary to elucidate passages that are *really* obscure. In all points that are essential to salvation, the Bible is a *plain* book. Should we admit that, as to its great purposes, it is so obscure that its meaning cannot be understood by common men, till it is explained by critics and commentators, and that these are entitled to exact from the unlearned an *implicit confidence,* then the grand principle of Protestantism, that ' the Bible is the only rule of faith,' applies merely to the initiated few ;—that is, the Bible is the rule to *critics*, and critics the rule to *common men*. What advantage then has the Protestant over the Papist ? If unlearned, neither has any Bible : from the one it is locked up in the arcana of *criticism* :—from the

other, in the arcana of an *unknown tongue ;* and to both, their authorised teachers are lords of their conscience. As Protestants therefore, we must maintain that the Bible in its great outlines is intelligible to plain men, in whatever translation, provided that such translation is a faithful one ; and provided also that it is studied with a candid and devout spirit.

The language of this sacred book is not technical nor philosophical, but more familiar than that of any other book, ancient or modern. It was written chiefly by *plain* men, unaccustomed to the abstract phraseology of science. It was written *for the use* of plain men, such as have always constituted and always must constitute the great majority of our race. It was written too, for purposes equally *important* to the *illiterate,* as to the *learned,* namely to be the foundation of their faith and hope, and the directory of their conduct, as candidates for eternity. From the benevolence of God then, in giving this book to men, and from the design for which he gave it, it would be reasonable to presume, that, in its grand characteristics as a guide to heaven, all who read it with humility, integrity, and common intelligence, as to its *principal* contents, must be able to understand its meaning. Accordingly we find that the body of plain, pious men, whose minds are unperverted by prejudice, *have correctly understood* the great outlines of religious truth contained in the Bible. In respect to these, the *coincidence* of views expressed in their *formularies of faith,* drawn up in ages and countries remote from each other, would be an absolute miracle, on any other supposition, than that one leading· system of truth, is stamped in characters of light, on the sacred pages. That such coincidence of views has existed, is a fact placed beyond all question by the evidence of history. The general *correctness* of these views is not invalidated, but confirmed by the profoundest investigations of criticism.

And why should we *expect* it to be otherwise ? The great Teacher, who came from God, was predicted as one " anointed to preach the gospel to the *poor*." In the best sense of the word, he was preeminently a *popular* preacher. " The common people heard him gladly," because his instructions were so simple and familiar, that they easily understood him. But I need not enlarge on this topic. It is preposterous for the preacher to treat plain declarations of the Bible, as though he considered them to be involved in mystery. Yet,

2. *The preacher may err by taking it for granted, that the most* OBVIOUS *sense of a text, is* ALWAYS THE TRUE SENSE. A little reflection will satisfy any one that this could not be reasonably expected. The *diversity* of *language* contained in the Bible must be somewhat correspondent with the diversity of individual taste and manner among its writers. Its *matter* too, consisting of history, poetry, prophecy, biography, precept, and doctrine, necessarily occasions great variety in its phraseology, The frequent allusions, especially in the Old Testament, to *local* usages, to customs of *different ages*, and such as were peculiar to *eastern* countries ; the *metaphors* taken from such local usages, or from local objects or facts, present many points of difficulty to those who read the Bible, in countries and periods *remote* from those in which it was written. I would by no means intimate that scriptural figures are of course obscure. So far from this is the fact, that when they are taken from familiar objects, and expressed in simple terms, the meaning conveyed is instantaneously and forcibly impressed on the mind. Still it is certain, that not figures merely, but allusions to oriental customs, are sometimes unintelligible,

except to men of reading. ◆To mention one brief example, in which a phrase according to the obvious import of its words, expresses no meaning at all;—Moses say to Israel : " The land whither thou goest in to possess it, is not as the land of Egypt, whence ye came out; where thou sowedst thy seed and *wateredst it with thy foot;* but the land whither ye go, is a land of hills and valleys, and drinketh water of the rain of heaven." Any plain man might see that here a difference is alluded to between two countries, in one of which the ground is watered by some artificial process, and in the other by rain. But he would attach no meaning to the phrase, "wateredst it with thy foot;" unless he happened to know that, on the borders of the Nile, large cisterns were provided, that the roots of vegetables might be refreshed by water, which was distributed from these cisterns, through small trenches ; and to which the gardener gave a new direction at any time, by turning the earth against it with his foot.

In some cases where no *figure* is used, the obvious literal sense of a passage, is not its true sense ; at least as it must be understood by modern readers generally. For example; our Saviour says, " When thou fastest, anoint thine head, and wash thy face." It is a simple injunction that his disciples, on such occasions, should appear in the *usual* manner ; in distinction from hypocrites, who, as a signal of special devotion, covered their heads, or wore ashes on their faces, that their sanctity might attract observation. But where there is no such *common custom* as anointing the head, a literal conformity to this precept would be a violation of its spirit; because the man who is keeping a private fast, would proclaim this to his neighbours, by an external sign; the very thing which Christ forbids.

These examples are selected, not as presenting difficulties to the critic, but as familiarly illustrating the
principle, that we must often look beyond the *phraseology*
of a text to ascertain its meaning. Of course the preacher
cannot take it for granted that the *common interpretation*
is right. A general and spontaneous concurrence of opinions, as to the meaning of a passage in the Bible, or in
any other book, would be presumptive evidence that
such opinion is correct. The weight of this evidence
however, would be great or small, according to circumstances in a given case. And in no case can it be sufficient to supersede a personal examination, in one who is
a professed interpreter of the sacred oracles.

Still it should be said,

3. *That it must not be his aim to find a* NEW *sense to
his text.*

Whatever danger results from a tame submission to
authority on this subject, the attractions of *novelty* are
still more dangerous to a man of sprightly genius, not
matured by experience and judgment. To exhibit the
points of difference between his opinions and those of
others, gives opportunity to display at once, the extent
of his reading, and the superiority of his discernment.
But how does such puerile ostentation accord with the
dignity of his office, who is " a servant of the most high
God, to show unto men the way of salvation."

No translation or commentary is to be regarded as
exempt from the scrutiny of criticism; nor need we
scruple to say, on any proper occasion, that the received
English version of the Bible has many inaccuracies and
defects. Yet to assail this version from the pulpit, on
all occasions, and thus to invalidate its authority with
common minds, while we admit its correctness, as to the
great outlines of divine truth, is a mistake, which no

preacher of good sense will commit. Besides, in this case it is oftener pedantry than learning, that is displayed. One of those venerable men, who assisted in forming this version, being afterwards on a journey, heard its defects pointed out, to an illiterate congregation, by a very young preacher, who, in one instance assigned three reasons why a word should have been differently translated. In the evening, the learned divine said to the young man, 'You might have preached a more useful sermon to these poor hearers. The king's translators considered well the *three* reasons which you have suggested for another rendering of that word; but they were induced by *thirteen* weightier reasons to prefer the rendering that was adopted.'

On this point, I am happy to express my own views in the language of Dr. Campbell, who was at once an enlightened scholar and a judicious preacher. 'Particular care,' says he, 'ought to be taken, in expounding the Scriptures, not to appear over-learned and over-critical. There is no occasion to obtrude on an audience, as some do, all the jarring interpretations given by different commentators; for this knowledge can serve no other purpose than to distract their thoughts. Before you begin to build, it is necessary to remove such impediments as lie directly in your way; but you could not account him other than a very foolish builder, who should first collect a deal of rubbish, which was not in his way, and could not have obstructed his work, that he might have the pleasure and merit of removing it. And do the fantastic and absurd glosses of commentators deserve a better name than rubbish? They are even worse than useless: where a false gloss cannot be reasonably supposed to be either known or thought of by the audience, it is in the preacher worse than being idly ostentatious of his learning, to introduce such erroneous gloss or comment.'

We must always remember too, the difference between a church and a college. In most Christian congregations there are very few, if any linguists. I do not say that we ought never to mention the original. Justice to the passage we explain, may sometimes require it. Nor is it necessary that our translators should be deemed infallible. But then, on the other hand, it is neither modest nor prudent in the preacher, especially if a young man, to be at every turn censuring the translators, and pretending to mend their version. It is not modest; as they over whom the corrector assumes a superiority, are allowed on all hands to have been men of eminent talents and erudition. And it is not prudent, as this practice never fails to produce, in the minds of the people, a want of confidence in their Bible. Indeed, in regard to every thing which may be introduced, either in the way of criticism or comment, it is not enough that such an observation is just, that such an interpretation has been actually given, or that such an opinion has been maintained ; the previous inquiry which the preacher ought to make by himself is, whether it be of any consequence to the people to be informed of the observation, comment, or opinion. If on other occasions, more especially on this, the apostolical admonition ought to be sacredly observed, that 'nothing proceed out of the speaker's mouth, but that which is good to the use of edifying, that it may minister grace to the hearers.'

On the literary vanity which employs an excess of criticism in the pulpit, I add one more remark, that it has no countenance from the highest of all examples, that of our Lord and his Apostles. The great body of primitive Christians had access to the Hebrew Scriptures chiefly through a *translation;* and one less perfect, unquestionably, than the common version in *our* language. Yet the first preachers of Christianity, qualified as they certainly were, to correct all mistakes, by gifts more adequate than those of scholarship, ' never perplexed their hearers with various readings and various renderings.'

You may say perhaps, of what value to me as a Christian teacher, or to my hearers, is my critical knowledge, if I am not to use it? I answer, of the same value with any other knowledge, if you have not discretion to use it aright; that is, of no value at all. You may have a knowledge of *grammar,* and make it subservient to the great business of the pulpit, without giving your hearers in every sermon, a disquisition upon etymology and syntax. Your *logic* may be made the instrument of instruction and conviction to sinners, without acquainting them with the ten categories of Aristotle, or the difference between abstract and concrete terms. Your *eloquence* may melt your hearers, while they know not that you have read Quinctilian or Longinus; and care not whether the figure that thrilled their bosoms, has been called *metonymy* or *apostrophe,* in technical rhetoric. Just so you may use your knowledge of sacred criticism, without abusing it. From its stores, humility and good sense may draw the richest instruction for your hearers, without ostentation on your part, or perplexity on theirs.

Having remarked at so much length on the practical principles to be observed by the preacher in explaining a text, when its meaning is doubtful, I shall be brief in noticing the other topic, which belongs to this lecture; namely, the *proposition* of the subject.

The term *proposition,* as used in *logic,* is applicable only to an assemblage of words, in which something is *affirmed.* As used by writers on *oratory*, it is not restricted to this sense, but applies to any form of expression, in which the *subject of a discourse is announced.* Thus, if my text were,—" There is not a just man upon earth, that doeth good and sinneth not," I might say, we are called to consider as the subject of this discourse, the ' *universal sinfulness of man :* ' or, I might reduce it to a logical affirmation, and say,—the doctrine of the text is, " *that all men are sinners.*" Either form amounts to what rhetoricians mean by a proposition of the subject ; though I would not say that in all circumstances, either form is equally good. If you take the former method, you have indeed a subject before you, but you feel at liberty to treat it in the way of discursive remarks. If you take the logical proposition, you are pledged to one course : you must *prove* the thing affirmed, before you make it the subject of inference or exhortation. A sermon written under such a necessity, is more likely to possess unity, and to combine to the best advantage, instruction with impression.

For reasons that are obvious to every mind, the doctrine or duty to be discussed in the sermon, should be announced in the proposition, with as much *brevity* and *clearness* as possible.

Two circumstances, in this connexion, deserve some regard. One is, that when you are prepared to state your subject, the form of expression employed, should be such, as to give the hearers a *momentary premonition* that you are about to do it.

For example,—' The doctrine which is taught in the text, and which I shall endeavour to establish in the following discourse, is this, that the only possibility of human salvation, consistent with the character and government of God, is suspended on the atonement of

Christ.' Now, if language like this is employed, every intelligent hearer will perceive that you are about to announce your subject *before* you have done it; and accordingly that sentence of your sermon, which it is more important for him to remember than any other, he will be more likely to remember. But many preachers would reverse the order of members, in the example given above, and consequently the hearers, being told in the end of a complex sentence, that the subject of the sermon *was* stated at the beginning of it, may recall the statement, if they can.

The other circumstance is, that the terms employed in stating the subject, should be such, if possible, as not to call for *explanation* after the proposition is announced.

# LECTURE VIII.

## UNITY.

WHEN the preacher has ascertained the sense of his text, and, after a proper exordium, has placed his subject distinctly before his hearers, he must proceed in some method to elucidate and apply this subject. The next thing that comes regularly to be .considered in the structure of sermons, is *division*. Many persons appear to object to divisions, especially to regular and explicit divisions, in a sermon ;--because, as it is said, they are inconsistent with *unity*. This objection is not merely the offspring of a fastidious or fanciful taste ; it has been made by men of respectable name. The Archbishop of Cambray, whose judgment is entitled to high regard, says—' There remains no true *unity* after such divisions ; seeing they make two or three discourses which are joined into one, only by an arbitrary connexion.' And Bishop Burnet, himself an excellent preacher, recommends that a sermon should have ' *one* head and *only* one, well stated and fully set out.'

The canons of rhetoric invariably require *unity*, not only in dramatic and epic poetry, but also in oratory. And every one who has learned his first lessons in sacred eloquence, admits without doubting, that unity is an essential attribute of a good sermon. Now, though the same precision of language is not demanded here, as in the abstract sciences, it is perfectly obvious that men of good sense seem to differ on this subject, because they have been accustomed to attach no definite meaning to their words. It becomes necessary then to examine the question, what *is* unity in a sermon? and the importance of this point to our main business, requires that the examination shall be extended through this lecture.

In entering on this subject, let me say, I do not mean by unity that *sameness* which excludes all interesting variety of thought and illustration in a discourse. If twenty pieces of coin, stamped with the same die, are spread before you, each is so perfectly like the rest, that though you turn them over and over, you see the same object still without variety. If you travel across an extended plain of arid sand, stretching around you in a wide, unchanging scene of barrenness, there too you have *oneness without variety*. But how soon do you long for a hill, a rivulet, a cottage, a tree, or even a shrub, to relieve you from this intolerable unity of prospect. If you stand on the deck of a ship, in mid-ocean, on the morning of a calm summer's day, you contemplate this vast expanse of waters with emotions of sublimity. But how soon does the eye become weary of a scene, which presents nothing but one immense, unvarying, unmeaning uniformity? Suppose now you sail down a majestic river; here on its banks a flourishing village meets your eye; there a rugged cliff, there cultivated fields, and there a tributary stream rushes down from the neighbouring mountains. Or suppose you travel on a great *road* leading through a fertile country, interspersed with meadows and forests, with the splendour of wealth, and the simplicity of rustic life. In these cases, the *unity* of the *river* or the *road*, is associated with an interesting *variety*. You glance at the changing scenery as you pass on, and feel the vivacity which it inspires, without being at all diverted from your chief object.

Now, to apply these illustrations to the purpose in
hand. There is a kind of unity in a sermon, which
indeed is in no danger of distracting the attention of
hearers, by the multiplicity of objects presented. It
consists in a constant recurrence of the same thought,
attenuated and repeated with undeviating uniformity.
The hearers pass on with the preacher, not from one
branch of the discourse to another, delighted with the
richness of matter and variety of illustration; but from
one topic presented again with some trifling changes of
representation. The above sort of taste, indeed, does
not always deign, in this last particular, to humour the
caprice of hearers. It gives them over and over the
same favourite thoughts, in the same favourite expressions, and often very consistently completes its claims to
their attention, by a favourite monotony in delivery.
Nor is this sameness limited to a single discourse of the
preacher; it extends, perhaps, through the whole range
of his instructions; so that whatever reason the hearers
may have to expect a new *text*, they have the advantage
of foreseeing essentially what the *sermon* will be, from
sabbath to sabbath. Now if this is the indispensable
quality in sermons which we call unity, it is one, as all
will agree, in which it is the province of dulness to
excel. But to suppose that our hearers are benefited by
such a sameness in the pulpit, is to suppose that when
they enter a place of worship, they cease to be men.
Correct views on this subject, are to be acquired only by
studying the human mind in its general operations.
That acute and able writer, the late Professor Brown,
in analyzing the philosophy of emotions, has the following remarks which I quote with pleasure, as strength-
ening the illustrations already given. ' Even objects
that originally excited the highest interest, if long con-

tinued, cease to interest, and soon become painful. Who, that is not absolutely deaf, could sit for a whole day in a music room, if the same air without variation, were begun again in the very instant of its last note? The most beautiful couplet, of the most beautiful poem if repeated to us without intermission, for a very few minutes, would excite more uneasiness than could-have been felt from the single recitation of the dullest stanza of the most soporific inditer of rhymes. How weary are we of many of the lines of our best poets, which are quoted to us for ever, by those who read only what *others quote*. What we admired when we read it first, fatigues and disappoints us, when we meet with it so often; and the author appears to us almost trite and common in his most original images, merely because these images are so very beautiful, as to have become some of the common places of rhetorical selection.

Notwithstanding our certainty that a road without one turn, must lead us to our journey's end, it would be to our mind, and thus indirectly to our body also, which is soon weary when the mind is weary, the most fatiguing of all roads. A very long avenue is sufficiently weary-ing, even when we see the house that is at the end of it. But what patience could travel for a whole day, along one endless avenue, with perfect parallelism of the two straight lines, and with trees of the same species and height succeeding each other exactly at the same inter-vals? In a journey like this, there would be the same comfort in being blind, as there would in a little tem-porary deafness, in the case before imagined of the same unvaried melody, endlessly repeated in the music room. The uniformity of similar trees, at similar distances, would itself be most wearisome. But what we should feel with far more uneasiness, would be the constant dis-

appointment of our expectation, that the last tree, which
we beheld in the distance, would be the last that would
rise upon us; when tree after tree as in mockery of our
patience itself, would still present the same dismal continuity of line."

I need not be more particular in applying these illustrations. As men are constituted, they demand *variety*
in intellectual subjects, as well as in material. And the
preacher of good sense, will never be anxious to attain
that unity in his public instructions, which excludes a
proper variety.

What then *is* the unity so important to be observed in
the composition of a sermon? I answer, it requires that
the sermon should be,

*In the first place,* ONE IN SUBJECT.

It will be unnecessary to dwell on this point, farther
than to explain my meaning. The preacher may have
but one chief subject in his eye, and yet manage so unskilfully as by way of preparatory remark, to suggest a
number of distinct subjects, which will preoccupy the
attention of the hearers, and leave a divided impression
on their minds. This is especially liable to be the case,
when a sermon commences with *critical discussions*,
extended to some length. As an example of this fault,
I mention Claude's plan on the text, Acts ii. 27. "Thou
wilt not leave my soul in hell, neither wilt thou suffer
thine Holy One to see corruption." The subject is, the
resurrection of Christ. Before entering on this, however, he would discuss two other points. In the first
place, he would show that the language of the Psalmist,
quoted in the text, was correctly understood by St. Peter,
as referring to Christ. In the second place, he would
refute the opinion of the Romish Church respecting
Christ's descent into what they call ' *limbus patrum,*' as

grounded on the word *hell* in the text, which in this case means the state of the dead. But with whatever propriety these several topics might be embraced in an expository lecture; a *sermon* on the resurrection of Christ would evidently be ruined by a formal, preparatory discussion of St. Peter's inspiration, and of a gross superstition, founded on a verbal mistake. The former should be taken for granted; and the latter, noticed in the briefest manner possible, while explaining the terms of the text.

There is another way in which the above principle is violated. The preacher, from an apprehension of falling short in matter, or from a false notion that his hearers will be edified, in proportion to the range of topics in each sermon, contrives to bring before them every sabbath, the *whole system of religion.* Every subject which has any affinity to the one in hand, comes in for its share of attention. Thus in considering the question of Pilate, " What is truth?" the hearers are gravely told that all truths have a common foundation, and a common connection one with another; and hence it comes fairly within the compass of the sermon, to speak of *every thing* which is *true*. In regard to the violation of unity by such a heterogeneous assemblage of matter, the preacher might often receive admonition, by attempting to fix on a brief *title* to his discourse; or even by searching for a *psalm* or *hymn, appropriate* to his subject.

*In the second place, unity requires that a sermon should be* ONE IN DESIGN.

The wise preacher will propose to himself some chief *effect* which he hopes to produce, by every discourse. This is a distinct thing from the *subject* of discourse; just as the same end in other cases, may be sought by various means. Thus, if you would make sinners feel

their guilt, your direct subject may be either their obligations or their transgressions.   If you would console a-
good man in affliction, your subject may be the perfection of God's providence, or the benefit of afflictions.   If
you would inculcate the obligation of children to love
their parents, you may do this by preaching on filial
affection, as a direct subject, or on the character of
Joseph, as an indirect one.   The good to be accomplished by a sermon, whatever is its subject, must depend
very much on its fitness to leave on the hearers' minds
some specific and predominant impression.   Whether it
bears upon insensibility, or error, or vice; whether it is
designed to alarm the carelesss sinner, or to strengthen
the wavering Christian, its bearing should be distinctly
seen and felt.   This requires not only that the sermon
should *have* a definite subject and a definite design, but
that these should be constantly *in the preacher's eye.*
' It is a favourite method with me,' said Cecil, ' to reduce the text to some point of doctrine.   On that topic
I enlarge, and then apply it.   I like to ask myself,
' What are you doing ?—What is your aim ?'

    This leads me to remark,

    *In the third place, that unity requires a sermon to be*
ONE IN THE ADJUSTMENT OF ITS PARTS TO THE
PRINCIPAL END, AND TO EACH OTHER.   And here I
lay it down as an elementary principle of great importance, *that a discourse should be adapted to produce
an effect as a* WHOLE.   This principle was substantially
stated above, but is here varied in form for the sake of a
more extended illustration.   It is not enough that there
is a succession of good words, or of striking sentences,
or of brilliant paragraphs, or even of weighty detached
thoughts.   The choice and arrangement of matter should
be such as to produce a growing interest in the auditors,

and to leave a strong impression of the *subject* on their minds. This supposes the preacher, before writing, to have examined well the materials of which the sermon is to consist, and to have settled with himself the *order* in which these are to be disposed, to the best advantage.

There is no work of art in which this principle of unity is not essential to perfection. The architect studies the *purpose*, for which a building is intended, while he adjusts its parts in his whole plan. He will employ what is called the prophetic eye of taste. He will anticipate just what the principal edifice, and the subordinate buildings will be when finished. It is not a fine column, or window, or gateway, that makes a beautiful seat, but the combined effect of symmetry and fitness, which strikes the eye, in the structure and its appendages, when viewed as a whole.

So with the *landscape gardener*. Give him a rude spot to transform into a beautiful garden ; and he sees by anticipation, how each part of the grounds must be shaped, where each avenue must pass, and each tree and shrub must stand, when the plan is completed ; and ' when he plants a seedling, he already sits under its shade.' So the *historic painter*, if he would represent a shipwreck, must not be satisfied to show you a broken mast or cable. Nor yet must he show you the mariners clinging to a tempest beaten ship, while other ships in the same prospect are becalmed. The heavens must frown with blackness, and the ocean swell in angry surges, and spread before you a *consistent* scene of terrific sublimity.

So the *portrait* painter must not exhaust his skill on a single feature, but must exhibit the united expression of all the features in the human face divine.

' 'Tis not a lip, or eye, we beauty call;
But the joint force and full result of all.'

So the epic or dramatic *poet*, must not set before you
an incongruous succession of characters or incidents,
violating all probability and consistency. He must show
you a *train* of things, growing in interest, and leading on
to some common result. Shakspeare, though he has
been called the stumbling block of critics, though he is
frequently inelegant, obscure, and ungrammatical in style;
and though he pays little regard sometimes to what are
called the unities of time and place,—shews you men
and things as they are. He not only pleases you with
here and there a speech, but arrests your attention to
the course of events; fills you with a restless eagerness
to keep up with his incidents; and leaves you at last
under some *strong impression*, that abides with you. Of
this great dramatic poet Johnson says, ' He who tries
to recommend him by select quotations, will succeed
like the pedant in Hierocles, who, when he offered his
house for sale, carried a brick in his pocket as a specimen.' When you have read Julius Cæsar, or Hamlet,
you may be unable to repeat a single line, but you
never can forget the *subject*.

I have extended these illustrations, to show that
preaching is not exempt from the common laws which
apply to all other things, where good sense and taste are
to be exercised. A sermon should have unity of plan.
The matter, length, and order of its parts should be so
adjusted, as to preclude anticipation, repetition, and
collision. Good judgment will not so much inquire,
whether a thought is *important*, as whether it belongs to
the subject in hand, and in what *place* it may be introduced, so as most to increase the general effect. That is
not useful preaching, which is a mere *collection of good*

*remarks,* without the scope, connexion and impression, which belong to a regular discourse. Nor is that a profitable sermon, which now and then startles the hearers with a vivid flash of thought, or makes them remember a few eccentric phrases;—but that which fixes their eye on a *single subject;* which holds their attention steadily to *that subject;* which gives them as they go on a clearer perception and a deeper feeling of *that subject;* and finally compels them to *remember that subject,* though they cannot repeat one expression uttered by the preacher.

To accomplish this end, *I only add, fourthly, there must be* UNITY OF ILLUSTRATION. No mixing of topics in argument, or of incongruous images should be allowed to impair the object of a discourse.

——————— ' Servetur ad imum,
Qualis ab incepto processerit, et sibi constet.'

Of a distinguished living preacher, it is remarked by a professed critic, that, ' exuberant as are his resources, little or nothing is introduced by him, without a distinct reference to his main design. Every additional figure or idea, illustrative of his chief topic, serves for the most part to convey it more distinctly to the mind; and though Pelion is sometimes heaped upon Ossa, in his gigantic sport, we do not view it as an useless exertion, when he appears himself to be reaching heaven by the process, and showing us a path to the same elevation.'

Such is that unity which is worthy to be sought in the pulpit. It is not a sterile sameness; but it requires that a sermon should be one in subject, one in design, one in the adaptation of its parts to each other, and to the common effect, and one in illustration. Of course, unity does not forbid *divisions;* it only requires that these should not exhibit several *distinct* subjects, but only that they should present several *parts* of the *same* subject, as one complete whole. Against such a fault as that just alluded to, it will be our business to guard still farther, in considering the characteristics of a perfect division.

# LECTURE IX.

DIVISION.—OBJECTIONS TO ;—UTILITY OF ;—KINDS OF ;—RULES.

THE objection that divisions in a sermon are inconsistent with *unity*, rendered it proper to consider, at length, in my last lecture, this most important principle in the sacred work of the preacher. Two other objections require a brief notice at this time.

It is sometimes said, that divisions give a stiff and mechanical appearance to a discourse ; that to announce its chief parts beforehand, is to take from it the charm of novelty, and to destroy the pleasure which an intelligent hearer would derive from discovering your method for himself.

But you must remember, that of those to whom the gospel is preached, only a small part are so intelligent, as to perceive that which is not very easily perceived. To adopt an occult method, because this is supposed to be most consistent with the rules of elegance, or because some obscurity furnishes exercise to the ingenuity of hearers, is a doubtful expedient, even in respect to *cultivated* minds ; but in respect to *plain* men, such as constitute the body of every congregation, it is, to say the least, a great error in judgment. If such hearers might be able to analyze an obscure train of thought in a *printed* discourse, this is not to be expected in one that

F

is *spoken*, where they have no opportunity to examine and compare different parts.

The other objection is, that divisions are a scholastic device, unknown in the best days of ancient oratory.

That the celebrated orators of old were less formal in this respect than has been common in the modern sermon, is certain; and perhaps a sufficient reason for this appears in the object of their orations, and the character of those to whom they were addressed. But the most celebrated of those orations have method, and some of them, method very distinctly expressed. Cicero, in his oration for the Manilian law, has three divisions; the nature of the Mithridatic war;—the greatness of it;—and the choice of a proper general. The first of these heads is discussed under four minor heads,—the honour of the state;—the safety of their allies;—the public revenue,—and the interests of private citizens. The third head, too, has four minor heads. Pompey is recommended as a consummate general, for his military skill;—his courage;—his authority; and his success. The same orator, in his seventh Philippic, dissuades the senate from making peace with Marc Antony, by three heads of argument, showing the measure to be base, to be dangerous, and to be impracticable. In his oration for Muræna, the division has been allowed by some critics to be perfect. 'The whole accusation, O judges, may be reduced to three heads; one consists in objections against his life; the second relates to the dignity of his office; the third includes the corruption, with which he is charged.'

His oration against Cæcilius has two, and that for Publius Quinctius three general divisions.

To mention no other examples, Quinctilian says, 'divisions may be too many, but ought not, as some think, to be limited to three.' So much for an objection, drawn from antiquity, against that method in a discourse which constituted so important a part of both theory and practice in ancient eloquence.

We proceed now to consider the *utility* of divisions,— the different *kinds* that have been employed—and the *rules* by which they should be conducted.

In remarking on the *utility* of method, let it be observed, that I mean to recommend a method, which is *obvious* to the hearers; and in general, one that is *announced* by the preacher, in entering on the discussion of his subject. Though his plan of thought may be distinctly marked in his own mind, and though every sentence he utters may be intelligible, the sermon, if the method is studiously *concealed*, will have only the aspect and effect of a smooth essay. He who aims to save rather than amuse his hearers, will not scruple to interrupt the polished flow of his composition, by dividing it into separate heads. Not that these should, of course, be named numerically at the opening of the sermon. It is not always best that so formal a distribution by first, second, third, &c. should announce the *main* heads beforehand; and seldom can this be properly done with the *subordinate* ones.[1] In regard to these latter, the speaker as he passes on, may, if he chooses to omit the numerical distribution, mark them sufficiently by *pauses*, by *antithetic distinction of words*, by change of *quantity* and *pitch of voice*, or by simple *emphasis*.[2]

Doctor Doddridge advises that more prominence still should be given to divisions, by the manner of *announcing* them. Thus his own practice was to mention the general heads *twice*, beforehand. At the opening of each head,

---

[1] Note (12.)

[2] Jay's Family Discourses, furnish a good pattern for short subdivisions.

if it was to have subdivisions, he announced these beforehand; and in the conclusion, he briefly recapitulated all
his topics, principal and subordinate.  So rigid an exactness, as an universal habit of a preacher, seems to me
undesirable; yet he will be compelled to study lucid
arrangement, by a frequent resort to such a practice.

Among the *advantages* of an obvious method, I remark
that *perspicuity* is promoted by it.  The understanding
is a faculty that delights in order.  It contemplates with
ease and pleasure, things that are placed before it in the
light of a just arrangement.  Hence Horace properly
calls such arrangement, ' lucidus ordo.'—Hence again,

*Beauty* is promoted by order.  Aside from those laws
of mind, agreeably to which method facilitates our perception of relations among things; according to our
principles of emotion, good taste is disgusted with confusion.  A fine library, promiscuously jumbled together,
without regard to connexion of volumes, or distinct
works, would offend the eye just in proportion to the
intrinsic worth, or the elegant appearance of the several
books.  The same sensation of incongruity is excited by
*thoughts* or *expressions*, however brilliant, which have no
connexion.

*Brevity* is promoted by order.  The poet above
alluded to says—' This will be the excellence and
beauty of method, that it will enable the writer just now
to say what just now ought to be said, and to omit every
thing else.'  He who *classes* his thoughts on a subject,
will see what to use, and what to refuse, among the
general mass of matter related to that subject.  Besides,
confusion of thought leads to repetition; and repetition
leads to undue length.

*Energy* is prompted by order, in two ways; the first
is by *concentration*.  The power of a discourse to im-

press the mind, depends not on the separate impulse of its parts, but on the combined effect of the whole. And often an argument derives all its strength from its standing in proper connexion with *other* arguments. The united strength of five men, might easily raise a weight, which the separate efforts of the five would be unable to stir. The regular phalanx, disposed in order of battle, so that each individual may support the whole line, is irresistible in its outset. But the undisciplined rabble is harmless in its movements, if not contemptible.

The other way in which order contributes to strength, is by promoting *vivacity*. Give to the traveller, who is to pass through a strange country, a chart, pointing out beforehand his road, with the chief objects that will demand his attention, and he pursues his way with increased spirit. Even the languor of a single day's journey is relieved by his being able often to ascertain what progress he has made, and what is the distance to the next stage. So *division* relieves heaviness in a discourse. Quinctilian supposes his orator to say, ' I will tell you what facts occurred before this transaction, what at the time, and what afterwards.' ' This,' he says, ' will seem to be three short narrations, instead of a single long one. The hearer is refreshed as he perceives the end of the last division, and prepares himself, as to a new beginning.' The advantage of such transitions, Cicero well understood. ' Hitherto, Cæsar,' said he, having advanced one stage in his defence, ' Hitherto, Cæsar, Ligarius appears to be free from fault,' and then commences another branch of his argument. Finally,

*Memory* is assisted by order. It were easy to show how important this consideration is to the preacher himself. But I refer especially to the memory of hearers. What is memory? It is that reflex operation of the mind, by which it recalls its past thoughts. The capacity of doing this, in a given case, other things being equal, depends on the strength of original impressions, and the circumstances which facilitate the voluntary *repetition* of those impressions. A succession of ideas must be understood, before it can be remembered; and perspicuous method is the vivid light, by which the mind clearly perceives, and deeply feels what is presented before it. But as few original impressions are so deeply imprinted, as to fix themselves in the adult mind, without *repetition*, the recollection of its thoughts depends much on its power to *renew* them, at pleasure. And this again depends on the associations by which they are connected. For example; suppose you were to enter, for the first time, a city with parallel streets, in one direction, marked according to the ordinals, first, second, third; and the intersecting parallel streets marked with the names of the United States, in their usual order. How easily would you remember the plan of this city, compared with that of another, where the streets are laid out at random, are crooked, irregular, and designated perhaps, by names which you never heard before. Suppose you were introduced to ten strangers, who should keep their seats in the same order, till you had recalled a few times the name of each successively. With how much more ease could you recollect them, than if they had been, all this time, passing about the room. The reason why *familiar* things are not forgotten is, that frequent *recurrence* stamps impression. The importance of method to memory, therefore, as an associating principle, lies chiefly in the fact, that method is the medium of spontaneous and instantaneous reflection. The incidents in the story of Joseph, for example, are so connected, that one reading fixes them in the memory of even a child. But that must be a miraculous memory, which could repeat, in the same manner, the genealogical lists of names in the Chronicles.

Witherspoon says, 'Suppose I desire a person going to a city, to do several things for me; to deliver a letter to one man ; to visit a friend of mine, and bring me notice how he is; to buy a book for me ; and see whether any ship is to sail for India soon.—It is very possible he may remember some of them, and forget the others. But if I desire him to buy me a dozen of silver spoons, to carry them to an engraver, that my name may be put on them, and to procure a case for them ;—if he remembers one article, it is probable he will remember all.'

In view of the foregoing illustrations, I will only add that the importance of method, by which I mean *obvious* method, in a sermon, is so unquestionable, that to affirm it, is only saying in other words, that the sermon of which the hearers *remember nothing*, is useless. The principle involved, in this case, may be tried by one simple, practical test. The custom of taking notes of sermons, as they are delivered, was common in the ancient church, and to some extent it prevails, in many congregations at this day.[1] Suppose then a sermon to be immethodical and incoherent, I do not ask whether an expert stenographer can record every word of it, from the mouth of the speaker? but can an intelligent hearer commit to paper a brief outline of the chief thoughts, in such an arrangement, that the review of these will enable him to recollect the substance of the whole sermon? If

---

[1] A practice which is highly objectionable on various grounds.— The mechanical act of writing must tend more or less to weaken the impression.—EDITOR.

not, an elementary principle of preaching has been disregarded, in the composition of the sermon.

The appeal may also be made to teachers of schools,
and to Christian parents, who are still in the good old
practice of calling their children to ' repeat sermons; '
what sort of sermons are those of which they can give
the best account? Without a single exception, the
answer will be, those sermons which are constructed on a
*simple, obvious* train of thought;—not those in which
there is an *occult* method, or *no* method. Let the
' teacher of babes,' condescend to be *taught* by babes,
in this thing.

# LECTURE X.

WE are to consider next the different KINDS of method. These are, the *textual*, the *topical*, and the *scholastic*.

1. The textual or verbal division is taken from the *words* of the text. An example of this sort we have in the exhortation of the Apostle, " Add to your faith virtue, and to virtue knowledge, and to knowledge temperance, &c." where the preacher follows these particulars, in a separate consideration of each *word*, as *faith, virtue, knowledge, &c.*

2. The topical division drops the *phraseology* of the text, and is grounded on its *sense*, as expressed in some distinct proposition. A sermon of this sort, on the text just mentioned, instead of treating five or six subjects, would illustrate perhaps this one theme, ' that all the graces of the gospel are united in the character of the consistent Christian.' The words of Christ, to the malefactor on the cross, " To-day shalt thou be with me in Paradise," the textual preacher would divide thus ; Consider first the person to whom this promise was made, " Thou," the penitent thief. Secondly, the matter of the promise, " shalt be with me in Paradise." Thirdly, the time of its accomplishment, " To-day." The topical preacher would perhaps divide thus ; ' First, the death of believers introduces them immediately to

eternal happiness. Secondly, God sometimes prepares
men for this happiness in the last moments of life.'

On such a text as this,—" What doth the Lord require
of thee, but to do justly, to love mercy, and to walk
humbly with thy God," no better division perhaps can
be adopted, than that suggested by the words. But in
general, this is the favourite method of only dry and
diffuse preachers.

3. The *scholastic* division, consisting of subject,
predicate, and copula, may be more or less related to
either of the preceding. Suppose the text is, " He
that believeth shall be saved; " and the plan of discourse is, to show first,—' What it is to believe :
secondly, what is it to be saved; and thirdly, the certainty that all who believe shall be saved ; ' the method
would accord with what is probably the prevailing taste
of the pulpit. A sermon recently published has this
text, ' The just shall live by faith.' No thought could
be more simple than the one here suggested. But the
scheme of discourse is the following ; ' I propose, first,
to show the meaning of the term just, as used in the
text. Secondly, to explain the nature of faith. And
thirdly, in what manner it is that the just may be said
to live by faith.'

Another English sermon, published 1826, on the text,
" The name of the Lord is a strong tower, the righteous
runneth into it and is safe : " has this method ;

' 1. What we are to understand by the name of the
Lord.

' 2. What by its being a strong tower.

' 3. What is the safety it affords.

' 4. Who are the persons that partake of this safety.'

But carry the same taste into a deliberative oration on
this topic for example, ' the *connexion* between *knowledge*

*and liberty among a people,*' and let the orator announce his method thus; ' 1 shall consider first, what we are to understand by knowledge ;—secondly, what by liberty; and, thirdly, how the one is connected with the other; ' and I need not say how tame and puerile this discourse would appear. Yet so strong is the tendency to 'this artificial structure, in sermonizing, that one can hardly look amiss for examples of it.

*It remains that I mention some* RULES, *by which divisions should be conducted.* And they should be,

1. *Necessary.* The subject should not only allow, but should seem to require them. It is the province of a barren invention, as I have before remarked, to give every sermon just so many heads as to correspond with the habits of the preacher, without inquiring whether the topics to be discussed are distinct or not. And where this mechanical taste prevails, it commonly happens that the requisite number of parts is made out, by forcing asunder things which really belong to the same class; or rather, by a tedious repetition of the same things, under the most insipid form of variety, a mere difference of numerical distribution.

2. *Divisions should be* WELL ARRANGED. The connexion between them should not only exist in the preacher's mind, but should be apparent to the hearers. The chief *principles* of arrangement, I shall notice briefly. When the different topics will allow it, the relation of *series* should be observed. Each preceding particular should prepare the way for the following, and lead it in, by an easy transition of thought. This principle is violated, when the first head supposes the second to be already understood, by the hearers. In most subjects of argument, the *logical* order is more or less to be observed. Thus when we reason from *causes*

to *effects*, or from *effects* to *causes*, or when things are
stated according to order of *time*, an obvious relation
exists which determines the proper arrangement.    There
are indeed some cases in which the order is nearly
*arbitrary*.    If I were discussing Christian obedience, I
might say with Tillotson, that it is *sincere*, *universal*,
and *constant*; or I might give these characteristics in a
reversed order, without injuring the entire discussion.
But if I were considering the fall and restoration of
St. Peter, the two parts of the subject cannot be indif-
ferently transposed.  It would be preposterous to describe
the *repentance* of this Apostle, before I had described
his *sin*.

On the same general principle, it would not be
proper to mingle, in a consecutive series, things which
belong to different classes.  If I were proving the divine
origin of the scriptures, and should take my first argument from miracles, my second, from the doctrines of the
Bible, and my third, from prophecy, the sources of
proof would be unexceptionable, but the arrangement
is unskilful; because the first and third topics belong to
external, and the second to internal evidences.   Nor is it
proper to confound what logicians call the *genus* and
the *species*.  If I were illustrating the dignity of man
from his faculties, it would not be proper to consider
first, his *reason*, secondly, his *will*, thirdly, his *soul*,
fourthly, his *conscience*; because the third comprehends
all the rest.

3. *Divisions should be* COMPLETE.

By this I do not mean to say, as a general rule, that
all the topics which appertain to a subject should be
introduced into a discourse on that subject; but that
when we profess to present it as a *whole*, by its several
*parts*, we should exhibit *all* those parts.    Thus, if I

were describing light, by the distribution of its rays into the principal colours, I must not enumerate red, orange, yellow, green, and then stop; but must go through the seven. If I were describing Massachusetts, by its counties, I´must not stop after naming Suffolk, Essex, Middlesex;—but must mention the whole. So when an intellectual subject is to be treated according to distinct properties or parts, the distribution should not be partial but complete.

4. *Divisions should, notwithstanding, be* FEW.

A *map* may exhibit geographical lines, mountains, rivers, cities, and a few objects of prominent importance. But attempt to make it embrace minute things, to represent private plantations and dwellings, and you frustrate its design. The eye is disgusted with this multiplicity and confusion of things. So an excessive enumeration of particulars, in a sermon, distracts the minds of the hearers. A preacher of the seventeenth century, having employed thirty divisions in explaining his text, says, ' I shall not shred the words into unnecessary parts; and then adds fifty-six more divisions to explain the subject. Another, of the same period, whose sermon had already exceeded a hundred and seventy parts, gravely apologized for omitting ' sundry useful points, pitching only on that which comprehended the marrow, and the substance.'

5. *Divisions should be* CONCISE IN TERMS. I mean that the words employed should be few; and when it is possible, the chief thought should be expressed in a *single* word. The reason of this rule is, that, in stating a head, we simply inform our hearers what is the point to be discussed; and the more simply and briefly we do this, the more easily is our division understood and remembered. Welwood, on the text, " Who maketh

thee to differ from another ? " has this tedious round of
words in his division.

' 1. The consideration of the authority of God, under
which we are all equally placed, notwithstanding the
variety in our conditions, ought to teach us an implicit
acquiescence in the duties, and in the lot assigned us.

' 2. Our obligations to cultivate the blessings we have
received, and the consequences of their perversion, are
exactly the same, whatever may be our portion of advantages ; and

' 3. The sentence which shall at last be pronounced
on our conduct at the tribunal of God, will have a
special relation to the advantages which have been
given, or have been denied us ; and to the condition in
which every individual has served God, or has sinned
against him.'

Now, if the preacher should repeat this antithetic
lumber of phrases and members a thousand times, not
one of his hearers would remember it.   But there would
have been no difficulty, had he said ; I shall prove the
duty of implicit acquiescence in the allotments of God,
first, from his *authority* over us; secondly, from the
*blessings* he confers upon us; and, thirdly, from our
*final account*.

As this principle is of elementary importance, and is
constantly violated in the pulpit, I will add, that conciseness in the form of heads, depends on such a relation
of parts, as to dispense with the greatest number of
words, by *ellipsis ;* and especially to dispense with all
ornament or explanation in the head itself.

Take as an illustration, the following plan, on the
subject of regeneration.—First, I shall consider in what
this change consists, or what is its nature.   Secondly,
show that wherever it takes place, it is produced, not

by the efficacy of means, but by the influence of the
Holy Spirit. And, thirdly, exhibit evidence, that
wherever this change is produced by the Holy Spirit, it
is followed by the fruits of holiness, or a life of obedience. See how this drapery of words is dismissed by
the aid of *ellipsis*, suspending all the heads on one
*connecting term ;* thus, in discussing regeneration, I
shall CONSIDER, 1. Its nature. 2. Its Author. And 3.
Its fruits.

Reybaz says,—' A clear division is the handle of a
vase ; in the taking hold of which, every thing it contains,
goes with it. But if it has no handle, its contents are
lost to us.' Of this clear division, we have an example
in the six particulars of Father Bernard, on the text,
'' The Lord himself shall descend from heaven with a
shout ; '' &c. ' *Quis veniat ?— Unde ?— Quo ?— Quando ?
— Quomodo ?—Ad quid ?* ' On this point I will only
add two examples, from a valuable English preacher ; [1]
so brief and clear, that a hearer might repeat them
mentally, several times, without losing more than one
sentence of the sermon. The first is on the repentance
of Judas, which is shewn to differ from true repentance
in four respects ; ' Its *origin ;—*Its *object ;—*Its *extent ;*
and its *result.*' The next is, '' On the wrath to come,''
with five heads.—' It is *divine* wrath ;— *Deserved*
wrath ;— *Unmingled* wrath ;—*Accumulated* wrath ;—
*Eternal* wrath.'

[1] Bradley.

# LECTURE XI.

HAVING stated some of the general principles which should govern the preacher in the choice and exposition of his text,—the annunciation and the division of his subject ; I am now to consider the sources and rules of argument, which fall under the head of *discussion*.

I am aware that many subjects must be introduced into the pulpit, which do not .admit of what may strictly be called reasoning. I am aware too, that in the Christian community, an opinion is cherished by many, and is countenanced by the example of some popular preachers, that reasoning is *never* appropriate to the business of the pulpit. The secular orator, it is said, speaks to men of cultivated minds, who can comprehend a train of discussion ; but to plain, unlettered men, such as the preacher addresses, every thing in the form of argument is dry and uninteresting. Certainly plain men are not logicians, but it does not follow that they are incapable of *reasoning*. Even children, in their own department of knowledge, draw conclusions from premises, as well as the philosopher in his. This tendency of the human mind, which appears in its earliest operations, ought to be cherished. Persuasion and action ought to depend on conviction, and conviction on proof. To substitute declamation for reasoning in the pulpit, is to give the preacher a loose and desultory habit of

thinking. In this way too, no stability of religious
character can be produced in *hearers*, except through
implicit faith, and blind prejudice. The preacher who
always declaims, from the supposition that his hearers
are unable to comprehend argument, gives the whole
influence of his labours, and of his own example,
against the use of their reasoning powers, in religion.
He takes the direct way to make them *bigots*, on the
one hand, or on the other *children*, liable to be " tossed
to and fro, and carried about with every wind of doctrine." Whenever such preaching prevails, for a period
long enough to produce its genuine influence, that influence is certainly unfavourable to manly discrimination, and strength in Christian attainments. The
question, then, needs not to be discussed, Whether, in
its proper place, argument should be employed in
sermons ? but, In what manner should it be employed ?

This will lead us to consider two things, the *sources*
of argument, and the *principles on which it is to be
conducted.*

My object in these remarks does not require me to
confirm or to controvert the doctrines of modern writers
on pneumatology and moral philosophy, nor to notice
them at all, in addressing those who are already conversant with these writers. My simple business is, to
inquire in what way religious truths may best be vin-
dicated and enforced by argument in the pulpit. The
laws of intellectual philosophy indeed are directly
auxiliary to this end. Even the study of geometry has
its important uses to the preacher, as it gives him discipline of thought, and precision of language. Much
of the controversy, which has distracted the church,
would have been prevented, had theologians employed
the same care in selecting and defining their terms,

which has rendered mathematical reasoning so perspicuous, and so powerful an instrument of conviction.
But is *mathematical* reasoning, as well as *moral*, appropriate to the pulpit? I answer, no. *Demonstration*,
in the exact use of the word, belongs only to the
science of abstract quantities; and it would be no more
absurd to mingle tropes with terms of geometry, than
to apply a mathematical argument to a moral truth.
Still, it is a vain triumph in which infidelity has sometimes gloried, that religion is a subject which cannot
admit of *certainty*. For in no subject of mere science
can our data be more fixed, or our conclusions more
unquestionable, than in religion. Many of our first
principles, in theology and morals, have as much clearness of intuitive evidence, as mathematical axioms ;
and we rest in our deductions with all the confidence
that attends the most perfect demonstration.

But while it is only *moral* evidence that can be
employed in preaching, this evidence arises from different
*sources*, each of which is more or less applicable, on
different occasions. The immediate end of reasoning is
to produce conviction; and this is to be effected in each
particular case, by the power of evidence that is adapted
to that case.[1]

### SOURCES OF ARGUMENT.

*The first and chief source of that evidence which is
to be employed in the pulpit, is the volume of Revelation.*
In respect to an important class of subjects, no *other*
evidence can be relied on. What we know for example,
respecting the Trinity, the incarnation and atonement of

[1] Note (13).

Christ, and justification by faith; we know *only* from
the sacred oracles. The simple and only inquiry on
such subjects is, what does the Bible teach? And just
so far as we rely on the speculations of philosophy,
where the truth lies beyond the research of reason, the
light of heaven ceases to shine on our path, and we grope
in darkness. A want of strict adherence to this obvious
principle, has been the prolific occasion of heresy and
controversy in all ages. But while on subjects of this
sort, the Bible is the sole standard of faith and of duty,
our reason is of course to be employed in ascertaining
what the Bible teaches; and also in illustrating and
applying to a particular subject, the proof which it furnishes. . This is what St. Paul meant by " reasoning out
of the Scriptures." It is so to class and exhibit our
proof, as to show distinctly that God has declared as
truth, or enjoined as duty, some particular thing.

Now this mode of reasoning, if I mistake not, as it is
too commonly found in sermons, is not sufficiently explicit and direct. In a case where the preacher does not
doubt that the ultimate appeal is exclusively to the
Bible, often a fastidious delicacy, or a perverted taste,
prevents him from giving *prominence* to the divine testimony. He thrusts forward his proof texts, perhaps in a
random and unskilful way, without proper regard to
their bearing on each other, or the end in view. Or, on
the other hand, he may assume the fine rhetorician, and
shape the declarations of the Bible into such a subser-
viency to the easy flow of his own style, that the proof is
diluted and humanized in his hands, and leaves no
strong impression on the minds of the hearers, that
" thus hath the Lord spoken." Illustrations of this
great defect might easily be given from the published
discourses of many who are called elegant or *polite*

preachers. The sermons of Edwards, on the contrary, furnish an excellent example of simple and direct reasoning from the Scriptures. His style, indeed, has many faults, and his formality in naming chapter and verse, when texts are cited, is a needless incumbrance, except in strict argument, when some difficult topic is in discussion. But though his habits of thought were those of a metaphysician, and though he never appeared as the critical commentator in the pulpit, he was eminently a *biblical* preacher. So constant was his reference to the Scriptures, that it imparted an air of sacredness to his sermons; and his hearers, like the trembling camp of Israel, at the foot of Sinai, had their eye fixed on the authority and majesty of God, and felt a deep impression of awe, as if approaching his judgment-seat.

On subjects of pure revelation, where the simple point in argument is, ' what has God said in this case?' no interest can be awakened in hearers, so strong or so salutary, as that which arises from scriptural proofs properly conducted. And when the preacher substitutes for these solid materials, the speculations of philosophy, or the embellishments of fancy, the apathy with which his sermon is commonly regarded by his audience, is but a just rebuke of his self-complacency,

There is however a large class of subjects where the proofs to be adduced in reasoning, are of a *mixed* character, partly from revelation, and partly from other sources.

If I were called to discuss a positive institution of Christianity, such as baptism or the Lord's Supper, my first business would be to open the volume of inspiration, and see what it teaches on this subject. But it might also be proper, and in some circumstances indispensable, for me to adduce collateral evidence from the Fathers, to show that the meaning which I attach to the Scriptures, is probably the true one, because it accords with the views of those whose sentiments and practice were derived immediately from the apostles. So if I were preaching on the obligations of men to worship God, or on the relative duties of parents and children, it would be proper for me to show that *reason* inculcates these duties, as well as revelation. But then, in cases of this sort, two extremes should be shunned. One is, the tendency of some men by the phraseology they adopt, so to exalt the *reasonableness* of the Bible, as to make the impression that no *implicit* faith is ever required in its declarations ; or, in other words, that the testimony of God does not of *itself* demand our assent, except as confirmed by the testimony of human reason. The other extreme appears in the habit of cautious misgiving, with which some men admit the aid of reason at all, in Christian argumentation, lest they should invalidate, while they professedly confirm the authority of the Bible. But while the declarations of this sacred book are independently and perfectly decisive where they apply, to enforce them by arguments from · reason, where these also are applicable, is to treat them with honour, not with disrespect. This holds true in practical illustration and commentary, as well as proof. For example,—I examine the character which St. Paul gives of the heathen world, in the first chapter of the Epistle to the Romans. If I undertake to show that the same character belongs to the heathen *now*, my argument must be taken from human testimony. So if I take a passage in which the doctrine of *native depravity* is asserted, concerning an individual or a community, and I undertake to show that the sacred writer *intended* also *to assert* the same doctrine, as applicable to *all men*, my argument must proceed according to the laws of biblical interpretation. But if my object is merely to show that this doctrine is *true* in reference to all men, it becomes a question of *fact*, as well as of Scripture; and may be proved, like any other point of this sort, by experience and testimony.

I have extended these remarks sufficiently to express my meaning, that the Bible is the grand store-house of argument to the preacher, and yet that he must resort to other kinds of proof.

Among these collateral sources of evidence, *that which I would rank as second to revelation, is* CONSCIOUSNESS. The distinction between this and *conscience* is, that the former respects generally the knowledge which every one has of the existence and operations of his own mind ; the latter respects only its *moral* operations. This is a kind of evidence which commands absolute assent, and that by an immediate appeal to our own bosom. In this way I know that there is a thinking existence within me, that perceives, loves, and hates. I know when I am hungry, or in pain. From this principle, acting with memory, I know that I began to exist ; and that I am the same individual as I was yesterday. I know that I deserve blame, if I have done to another what it would have been wrong in him to do towards myself; and that I am innocent, though I may have done him an injury, which proceeded from no wrong intention in me, or which it was not in my power to avoid.

Such elementary principles, from which no one can dissent, are of great value in enforcing many truths and duties of religion, especially in the removal of perplexities arising from abstruse speculations. A metaphysician may proceed with a train of reasoning which looks fair and incontrovertible, till he brings out the conclusion, that men are machines acting under a law of physical necessity, and therefore not accountable for their actions. But any plain man, while he cannot show where the fallacy lies in this reasoning, may boldly pronounce the conclusion false. It contradicts his own consciousness. He *knows* that he is *not* a machine, but a voluntary, accountable agent.

The faithful preacher, who presses truth on the conscience, will often find some fastidious objector, or some anxious sinner, resorting to refuges, which a vain philosophy has invented, to escape the charge of personal guilt. There is no way in which the pungent application of divine truth is so likely to be parried, by the self-excusing temper of the human heart, as by some objection predicated on a denial that men possess the powers of moral agency. Such objections may be met with the light of demonstration from the scriptures, and yet they are renewed with unyielding pertinacity. But let the appeal be made at once to the *consciousness* of the hearer, whether he is not a free agent, and his objections are not refuted merely, they are effectually silenced in a moment.

*A third very ample source of evidence, is that to which writers on intellectual philosophy have given the name of* COMMON SENSE.

This relates to things which do not come within the province of consciousness, but which are so plain to every reasonable mind, that they cannot be questioned. For example, propositions such as these, ' It is impossible that a thing should be and not be, at the same time.' ' Every effect must have a cause.' ' Things which I see do exist,' strike the mind with the clearness of intuition. They are accounted *self-evident*, as not admitting of proof, on the one hand, or of doubt on the other.  While it appertains to the process of reason, to draw conclusions from such premises, it is the province of *common sense* to judge of these conclusions.  Should a speculating visionary lay down axioms, from which he should fancy himself to prove, that all the present modes of travelling will become obsolete ; that men will soon navigate the interior of the earth with sails and oars, or traverse the air with wings, any man, without claiming to be a philosopher, might smile at the conclusion, and on the authority of common sense, pronounce it ridiculous.

Now to show how this sort of evidence may be applied in the pulpit, it is sufficient to show, by an example, how it has been applied.  Archbishop Tillotson, in refuting the absurd hypothesis, that the world sprung from chance, proceeds thus ; ' Will chance fit means to ends, and that in ten thousand instances, and not fail in one ? How often might a man, after he had jumbled a set of letters in a bag, fling them out upon the ground, before they would fall into an exact poem ?—yea, or so much as make a good discourse in prose ?  And may not a little book be as easily made, as this great volume of the world ?  How long might one sprinkle colours upon canvass, with a careless hand, before they would make the exact picture of a man ?  And is a man easier to be made by chance than his picture ?  How long might twenty thousand blind men, who should be sent out from the remote parts of England, wander up and down, before they would all meet upon Salisbury plain, and fall into rank and file, in the exact order of an army ?  And yet this is much more easy to be imagined, than how the innumerable blind parts of matter should rendezvous themselves into a world.  A man who sees Henry the

seventh's chapel at Westminster might with as good
reason maintain, yea, and much better, considering the
vast difference between that little structure and the huge
fabric of the world, that it was never contrived or built
by any man; but that the stones did by chance grow
into those curious figures into which we see them to have
been cut and graven; and that the materials of that
building, the stone, mortar, timber, iron, lead, and glass,
happily met together, and ranged themselves into that
delicate order in which we see them now, so closely
compacted, that it must be a very great chance that parts
them again. What would the world think of a man
that should advance such an opinion as this, and write
a book for it? If they would do him right, they
ought to look upon him as mad. But yet he might
maintain this opinion, with a little more reason than
any man can have to say, that the world was made by
chance, or that the first men grew out of the earth, as
plants do now.' [1]

Here is no process of mathematical demonstration to
refute the atheistical sentiment, that matter is eternal;
and that this world assumed its present order and beauty
without the agency of an intelligent Creator. But if such
demonstration had been adapted to the subject and the
hearers in this case, who does not feel that it would have
been far less convincing than this skilful appeal to common sense? Such an appeal is felt at once, in all its
power. Without that steady application of thought,
which abstruse reasoning demands, without any effort
indeed, even to uncultivated minds, conviction finds its
own way to the understanding, as light finds its way to the
eye. Hence this sort of evidence is peculiarly valuable

[1] Tillotson's Sermons, Vol. I. p. 31. See also Vol. II. p. 50.

to the preacher, in repelling sophistry, and in answering objections, that cannot be effectually met in any other way. Such are the cavils with which infidelity has often assailed Christian doctrines, especially when clothed in the obscure terms of scholastic theology. And such are the doubts with which anxious inquirers are sometimes distressed, under convictions of sin.

# LECTURE XII.

THERE *is a fourth source of evidence, namely, the* EVIDENCE OF FACTS, *which is more or less mingled with all the foregoing; and which includes also the evidence of experience, testimony, and authority.* It is a *general law* of both the material and intellectual worlds, that *like causes will produce like effects,* or that the future will resemble the past. This law is the sole basis of physical and of political science. Hence we know that, in all ages and countries, rivers will flow downwards, fire will burn, and poison destroy. And hence we know too, how *men* will feel and act under given circumstances. If there were no uniformity in the operations of mind, no system of government could be framed for any community; nor could social relations exist in any neighbourhood or family. The same regularity resulting from settled principles in the divine government, and in human agency, gives a fixed character to what we call Christian experience. On this ground we may expect with certainty, wherever we find unsanctified. human beings, to find them with selfish and depraved hearts; and wherever we find those who are sanctified by divine grace, to see them possess affections essentially the same as have distinguished pious men in all ages.

I need not spend time in applying these principles to the work of the preacher. He must be very unskilful not to know, that some parts of almost every subject to be discussed in the pulpit, admit of confirmation or illustration from *facts ;* and that this kind of reasoning, where it does apply, is precisely that by which men choose to be addressed, and are predisposed to be convinced. Other things being equal, he will have most power over an assembly whose mind is best stored with facts, especially scriptural facts, and who best know how to apply them with effect.

*Testimony*, as I have already said in treating of scriptural evidence, is a kind of proof that must be employed in sermons ; but it is liable to great abuse. The extent to which some have carried appeals to ecclesiastical history, on certain points of controversy, is certainly undesirable, if not totally inadmissible, in the pulpit.

In these remarks I include also the evidence of *authority*. The spirit of this age indeed is not more disposed to bow to popes and fathers, than to the mystic trifling of scolastic theology, or the categories of Aristotle.

The *abuse* of authority in reasoning is strikingly exhibited in the " *Oral Law*," or *traditions* of the Jews, which they supposed God to have delivered to Moses on Mount Sinai, though never committed to writing. By these traditions, a great many ceremonies and authoritative maxims were handed down, as of sacred obligation, among that people ; though some of them directly contradicted the written law of God, and were condemned with great severity by Christ in his sermon on the mount. Hence when the Pharisees complainingly said to Christ, " Why do thy disciples transgress the tradition of the Elders ? " he replied in the solemn rebuke, " Why do ye transgress the commandment of God by your tradition ? "

The Romish church too, as every reader of history

knows, has for ages framed to itself a set of traditions, by which the authority of the fathers is avowedly made to supersede that of the Bible.

But there is another extreme. The blindest bigotry is not more blind than the narrow and boastful prejudice that discards all respect for received opinions. This is to discard experience and testimony, and indeed all the laws of evidence, by which human opinions are governed. Say what he may of authority, no man is free from its influence, or *can* be, without renouncing his reason. It has its weight even in matters of science. Who would not presume a demonstration to be correct, if he knew that it had often passed under the scrutiny and sanction of Newton, and had been re-examined and pronounced faultless by the ablest mathematicians to this day ? Who does not feel, in any case, more reliance on the judgment of a wise man, than on that of one who is ignorant and weak ? The power over the minds of others, ascribed to the Nestor of Homer, and the Mentor of Telemachus, is a just character in poetry, solely because it accords with philosophy and experience. Precisely for the same reason, a general coincidence of sentiment, especially among wise men, if that coincidence is not explained away by the force of some obvious countervailing principle, always furnishes a high presumptive evidence that the thing believed is true.

Preserving to every one then, the right of independent judgment, that judgment still to be rational, must accord with *evidence ;* including the evidence of facts, as it appears in experience and testimony ; otherwise no faith can be reposed in history, and no step can be taken in the common affairs of life.

The practical bearing of my remarks on authority, is briefly this. If the disciples of the *Koran* should generally affirm some particular doctrine to be taught in that book, though I had never seen it, I should believe the fact without examination, unless I could see some strong reason for calling it in question.  On the same ground, a reasonable man, though he had never seen the *Bible*, would believe that it teaches a doctrine which nine tenths of those who have read it agree in affirming that it does teach.  The dissent of the other tenth would not hinder this conclusion, especially if he could explain *this dissent by the influence of some strong and obvious* prejudice.  The established laws of évidence, for example, would require such a man to believe that the Bible teaches the Unity of God, and forbids malice and murder.  And on the same evidence he must be satisfied that it teaches the *atonement of Christ*, and the kindred *doctrines of grace*.  Accordingly I have said in a former lecture, that the coincidence which we see in the confessions of faith, drawn up by evangelical churches, in different ages and countries, and professedly grounded on the Bible, would be an absolute miracle, on the supposition that these doctrines are not contained in the Bible.  Hence it has always been deemed good collateral reasoning in support of any doctrinal opinion, to show that this opinion has been entertained by the greatest and best men.

In sermons, I know this sort of reasoning is but of secondary importance; but there are occasions when it may be applied with great effect.

### RULES OF ARGUMENT.

We proceed to consider the principles, according to which, reasoning in the pulpit should be conducted.

No one will understand me to intimate, that any artificial process can confer on a man the power of carrying conviction to the minds of others. This must depend primarily on the strength of his invention; the clearness of his perceptions; the accuracy with which he combines things that are analogous, and separates things that differ; and the precision and energy with which he employs language to express his thoughts. Technical logic can no more make a reasoner than technical rhetoric can make an orator. Still, both reasoning and elocution must conform to those principles which genius has prescribed to its own operations. These principles are substantially the same in sermons as in any other department of public speaking.

As argument in sermons must depend primarily on evidence drawn from revelation, we may begin with the principles to be observed, in regard to proofs derived from the Volume of Inspiration.

First; THE UNPERVERTED MEANING OF SCRIPTURE, *must clearly support the point to be proved.*

All protestants unhesitatingly admit, that our faith is to be conformed to the Bible, and not the Bible to our faith. Yet this plain principle is often violated, even among good men, by unwarrantable liberties of straining the word of God into a sense corresponding with opinions which have been formed independent of its authority. In all cases, some allowance is to be made for innocent mistake, resulting from the imperfection of human knowledge. The heedless darings of ignorance and empiricism, in interpreting the Bible, must not be encouraged by any indulgence of our charity on the one hand, and on the other, will not be restrained by any severities of our animadversion. But beyond this, there lies a fault on men of piety, and conscience, and learning, which

ought to be, and may be corrected. Such a man is
*not warranted, carelessly and without examination, to*
adduce among his unquestionable proofs, a text of doubtful import, merely because some have classed it in the
same manner. Nor may he do this because he is aware
that his hearers will receive it as proof. Nor should he
of design, give to a doubtful passage a greater weight of
evidence on other minds, than it really has on his own.
All deliberate straining and wire-drawing of texts, to
make them fit our argument, besides being consistent
neither with honesty nor reverence for the scripture is
adapted to awaken suspicion, and to injure the cause it is
designed to promote. It is a kind of sacrilege that
involves its own punishment. The eagle in the fable,
that stole consecrated flesh from the altar, though it was
to feed her young, carried home with the flesh a coal of
fire that consumed her own nest. I need not dwell on
the endless mischiefs which the vital interests of truth
have sustained, from the unwarrantable liberties of alle-
gorizing interpreters, who make no scruple to find any
sense in a passage which suits their purpose, though it
be one never intended by the Holy Ghost. It is a
maxim worthy of being repeated here, 'The *meaning* of
the Bible is the Bible.' The foregoing remarks apply to
the reprehensible practice of throwing together in a
careless or designed amalgamation, different passages,
dissevered from their connexion, and often from their
primary signification; while the professed object is to
exhibit *proof* of something from the word of God.

Augustine says,—'Non valet—hæc ego dico, hæc tu
dicis, hæc ille dicit;—sed hæc dicit Dominus.' The
loose manner, in which the testimony of Scripture is
often introduced into sermons, may be owing in some
cases, to the very imperfect acquaintance of the preacher

with its sacred contents. This consideration led Matthew
Henry to say to young ministers—'especially, make the
Bible your study. There is no knowledge which I am
more desirous to increase in, than that. Men get wisdom
by books, but wisdom towards God is to be gotten out
of God's book; and that by *digging*. Most men do but
walk over the surface of it, and pick up here and there a
flower. Few dig into it. Read other books to help you
to understand *that* book. Fetch your prayers and sermons from thence. The volume of inspiration is a full
fountain, always overflowing, and hath always something
new.'[1]

But where there is no perversion of *sense*, the strength
of our reasoning from the Scriptures may be injured by
bad management. We may adopt the dull practice of
accumulating quotations from the word of God to fill up
the time, and supply the lack of matter. There is a
trite and heavy way of doing this, which is the opposite
extreme to that studied elegance of manner before mentioned, that strips a text of half its meaning, by the
drapery thrown around it. On a subject so plainly
revealed as to preclude all doubt, such as the holiness
of God, it may still be proper to adduce scriptural declarations for the sake of *impression ;* but it were absurd in
such a case, to cite fifty passages. On the contrary, in
proving a controverted point, though *one* clear declaration of the Bible is decisive in reality, it is not commonly so convincing, in practical effect, as a greater
number. But in cases of strict argument on a disputed
subject, a bare *citation* of texts is not sufficient, without
more or less of commentary, to show how they apply to
the case in hand. For example, in proving the entire

---

[1] Matthew Henry's Life.

and universal depravity of men, it is directly to the purpose to quote the language of St. Paul, in the third
chapter of his Epistle to the Romans. But the force
of this passage is so much increased, by looking at the
14th and 53rd Psalms, to which it refers, and at some
of the terms employed, that a few pertinent remarks on
the connexion, and on the language of the Apostle, may
give it double weight in the minds of the hearers. A
strong proof of the same doctrine of depravity is furnished
by the words of St. John, " He that loveth is born of
God." But among common hearers, not one in ten will
see the full force of this passage, as applicable to this
subject, unless besides repeating it, you show how it does
apply. I scarcely need say, however, that the explanatory remarks which I recommend, should seldom be of
the critical and philological cast ; at least they should
never depend on distinctions too nice for the apprehension
of common minds.

One more suggestion may be necessary, on the management of scriptural argument; it respects cases in which
the proof lies, not on the face of one text or more, but is
made out by comparison and induction. The duty of
*daily devotion in families* is an instance. We cannot
cite chapter and verse where this is expressly commanded
—and yet the obligation is so clearly deduced from the
general current of Scripture, as to justify this strong
declaration of Tillotson, ' The principal part of family
religion is prayer, every morning and evening, and reading some portion of scripture. And this is so necessary
to keep alive a sense of God and religion in the minds
of men, that where it is neglected, I do not see how any
family can in reason be esteemed a family of Christians,
or indeed have any religion at all.'

*A* SECOND *general rule, which applies to arguments,*

*drawn from whatever source, is, that in reasoning, we should take into account the* INFLUENCE OF PASSION AND PREJUDICE ON BELIEF. The weight of evidence in producing conviction is relative, according to the scales in which it is weighed. That may be light as a feather, in the estimation of one man, which has the power of demonstration to another. Without attempting here to analyze the reasons of a fact so wonderful, and yet so unquestionable, no man whose business it is to urge the truth on others, should forget that the affections and habits have a strong ascendency over the judgment. Solomon had his eye on this principle, when he represented the slothful man as saying—"There is a lion in the way—I shall be slain in the streets." And Shakspeare, the philosopher of poets, whose knowledge of human nature was remarkable, thus describes the partiality with which worldly favour regards the same action in different circumstances —

> ——————————— "Plate sin with *gold*,
> " And the strong lance of justice hurtless breaks;
> Arm it in *rags*, a pigmy's straw doth pierce it."

Prejudice is a complex term, by which we designate the state of a man's mind, which is unfavourable to conviction, arising from interest, habit, previous opinion, pride, or other passions. We never trust the judgment of any one in his own cause, or in that of a near friend.[1] Urge the timid man to an act of courage, or the proud man to an act of condescension, or the covetous man to an act of generosity, and his *heart* will furnish an answer to all your arguments. Or if you carry the point with him by assault, the victory is but momentary; the next day he could defy your reasoning.

[1] Quod volumus, facile credimus.

The application of these principles, to the work of the preacher, is easy. It is not enough, in any case, that his proof is good; it must be adapted to circumstances; to the time, and the state of the hearers. If they are *already settled in an opinion*, which it is his object to overthrow; especially, if that opinion is fortified by ignorance, or interest, or education, or party spirit, he must proceed with caution and wisdom. Such a case calls not for the bold onset, the language of denunciation, or severity, or even for great earnestness, particularly at the commencement. These bar the door, which would still be left open to a more discreet and gentle approach. There are the subjects on which we *know*, that our hearers are strongly prejudiced against the truth. In discussing these, there are special advantages in the *analytic* method, by which the point to be proved, is concealed at first; certain undeniable principles are made prominent; the assent to these, step by step, is rendered unavoidable; till the result we wish to establish comes out with a clearness of evidence, which cannot be questioned. These hints I know are capable only of a limited application; but for want of judgment, in adapting ourselves to circumstances, the best talents may be employed in a fruitless effort. Power, I repeat, is relative. A child may undermine a rock, which no giant could heave from its base.

# LECTURE XIII.

## RULES OF ARGUMENT.

A THIRD *rule respecting arguments is, that they be* SIMPLE, NOT COMPLICATED AND REFINED.

I refer not here to abstract terms, nor to dark construction of sentences, nor to *style* in any respect, but to *sentiment*. Systematic thinking implies a mental labour to which most men are little accustomed. We cannot expect that they will follow a train of argument, derived from such sources, and consisting of so many parts, as to demand a discriminating and close attention, for any long time. Hence the *cumulative* form of argument, when so conducted that the train of thought is complex, and so that the hearer must fail of reaching our conclusion, if he lose a single step of our process, is too refined for common understandings.

To this reluctance, and this incapacity to think intensely, must be ascribed, in some degree at least, that general feeling of dissatisfaction, excited by what is called *metaphysical* discussion in sermons. To some extent doubtless this is a *mere prejudice*, very improperly encouraged by those preachers, whose compliant practice seems to allow, that no subject befits the pulpit, which requires *thinking* from themselves or their hearers. This would set aside the most important doctrines of revelation.

In the indefinite reproaches cast on metaphysics, a

very plain distinction seems to be forgotten. In one respect or more, a truth may be incomprehensible, and yet the *proof that it is a truth* be perfectly *plain*. For example;—that God is eternal,—that he created the world,—that man acts under divine influence, and yet is free and accountable—that a sinner, to be qualified for heaven, must be renewed by the Holy Ghost, are points that I can prove at once from the Bible; and every child can understand the proof, though the subjects are in themselves deep and mysterious. So far, I am on plain ground. But if I undertake to *explain* the eternity of God, or to tell *how* matter could be created or modified by a spirit, or *how* the will of man, though free, is controlled by motives, or *how* the Holy Ghost operates in renewing the heart, my reasoning must be obscure and useless, because I attempt to go beyond the province of argument.

Now while it is clear to me, that the preacher should be conversant with the science of metaphysics, so far as to understand the powers of the human mind, and the principles of logical analysis, it is equally clear, that this kind of knowledge, as well as every other, should be under the guidance of good sense in the pulpit. He who engages in the ministry, with the weak ambition of being reputed a profound thinker, will probably acquire the habit of choosing abstruse subjects for his sermons, or of rendering plain ones abstruse. The love of paradox, that controverts first principles, and delights to puzzle, rather than instruct, is as far from the true spirit of the pulpit, as the vapouring of declamation, or the raving of fanaticism. Speculation may be called instructive preaching; but whom does it instruct? and in what? It cannot build men up in the most holy faith. It cannot interest them, till the mind is new modelled. A man of distinguished common sense said; 'I honour metaphysicians, logicians, critics,—in their places. But I dare not tell most academical, logical, frigid men, how little I account of their opinion, concerning the true method of preaching to the popular ear. They are often great men, first-rate men, in their class and sphere, but it is not their sphere to manage the world.'

It comes directly within the design of this head, to compare the *abstract* and *dialectical* kind of reasoning, with the *analogical and rhetorical*. On this subject, however, at which I have repeatedly glanced already, there is room here but for a few additional remarks.

How then do men spontaneously think and reason, on common subjects? In the abstract mode? Not at all. From the constitution of man, the language, written or spoken, by which he expresses his feelings, is primarily a sort of *painting*. It is a *representation*, of emotions, arising within himself, or suggested from the external world. Hence, every language, in its infancy, is necessarily a species of *poetry*. Not rhyme nor metre, which are only artificial and circumstantial appendages of poetry; but poetry in *essence*, that is, *imagery* and *metaphor*. To the mere philologist, as well as to the man of refined taste, it would be a subject of curious interest, should he ascertain to what extent, language is originally formed, by figures taken from objects of *sight*. But the *ear*, and the other senses, are made auxiliary to this mode of conception;—thus we say, ' Conscience will *speak* to the guilty in accents of thunder.' When we compare *rage* to a *storm*, and *benevolence* to the gentle *zephyr*, we speak a language perfectly simple and significant, and much more energetic, than when we employ mere *words*, which are totally unmeaning, except as arbitrary signs. In this manner we transfer the attributes of mind to matter, or of matter to mind;—we speak of a *broken heart*,—*a load of sorrow*, a *proud monument*. Does any one doubt the utility of employing, in the service of God, this language, which is only a mode of analogical reasoning? Let him tell why God has made men so, that they speak and feel this language, rather than any other. Let him tell why God himself speaks and reasons in this manner, in his holy word. The parable of the sower,—of the barren fig-tree,—of the wise and the foolish virgins,—to name no more examples, are beautiful and powerful specimens of analogical reasoning. The preacher then, will generally succeed best in discussion, whose arguments are arrows, pointed with truth, and sped to their mark by a lively and fervid illustration. But I cannot enlarge on the advantages of the *rhetorical*, over the *abstract* mode of reasoning.

A FOURTH *rule is, that arguments should not be* TOO MANY.

In probable reasoning it is indeed true, as Reid has said, that we must rely upon the combined force of different arguments, which lead to the same conclusion. Such evidence may be compared to a rope, made up of many slender filaments, twisted together. The rope has strength to bear the stress, though no one of the filaments would be sufficient for this purpose. But the analogy holds only to a certain extent, beyond which the parts added to argument produce weakness. The maxims of ancient criticism, ' Ne quid nimis ; ' and ' Omne supervacuum pleno de pectore manat,' are founded in good sense. A plain hearer, who listens to a rapid succession of various proofs, especially if they are novel and incongruous, is much in the condition of a rustic stranger, who is hurried through the streets of a crowded city, where a thousand objects strike his eye, not one of which leaves any distinct and permanent impression on his mind.  Cicero said, 'Arguments should be *weighed*, rather than *numbered*.'  It is certain that the preacher has misjudged, as to the number of his topics, or as to the proper treatment of them, when the sermon he delivers, is long enough for two.

A FIFTH *rule is, that the* ORDER OF ARGUMENTS SHOULD BE SUCH AS TO GIVE THEM THE GREATEST EFFECT.

The principle of arrangement, by which the rhetorical art, like the military, assigns the first rank to the beginning, and the second to the close, demands so much regard at least; as to keep us from attenuating our concluding topics, till they become feeble and tedious.   In some respects too, the order of arguments in sermons, must be influenced by the *sources* whence they are drawn.   Our strongest proof in general is taken from the inspired word ; but when this is mingled with a series of other proofs, there is a valid objection to placing it first.  I know it is common in preaching, to prove a point from Scripture and then add arguments from experience, or consciousness, or some other source.   But to my mind there is at least an apparent disrespect to the declarations of God, when we adduce these as proof of a point, and then proceed, by arguments of a different kind, to corroborate this proof, as though it were not of itself decisive.   In general, when such arguments are independent of scriptural authority, they should be arranged not after but before it.   When they are adduced to *answer objections* against the scriptural proof, or to render its meaning more clear and impressive, they must of course *follow* it in order.

There are many cases in which prejudice and wayward-

ness give only a reserved, doubting assent to proof from
the Bible. For example : If the proposition to be
proved is, ' that men are accountable for their religious
opinions,'—direct testimony from the Bible may properly take the lead in your argument; but because this
testimony is received with only a hesitating assent, by
men of lax speculations, these men should be made to
see that experience and common sense, equally with
revelation, teach the criminality of essential error in
religious opinion; since they most clearly teach, that the
*heart* is the moral man, and that *obliquity of heart* per-
verts the *understanding*.

The amount of my meaning is, that when collateral
arguments are drawn from different sources, and when
the subject is such, that proofs from the Bible will be
received with a decisive authority, undiminished by the
influence of prejudice, to arrange these proofs last in the
series, is most consistent with rhetorical order, and with
due respect for the sacred oracles.

In some cases we may hesitate between two places, in
either of which a particular topic may be introduced.
For example ; if the proposition I am discussing is, that
the *human heart is naturally destitute of holiness*, it is
pertinent to introduce among my proofs the doctrine of
*regeneration;* because the necessity of this change implies
the previous destitution of holiness. But it is equally
proper, and often more so as to practical effect, to
set this topic by for the close, to be introduced as an
*inference*.

In general, when there is any fixed principle of relation running through different topics, such as order of
*time*, or of *cause* and *effect*, that order must be observed.
Common minds follow a speaker with pleasure if he leads
them in an easy train of thought, so that they see the

connexion of things. But if he passes by fits and leaps from one point to another, these detached parts of his discourse produce nothing of that concentrated impression, which results from continuous and connected reasoning. These suggestions I need not extend, as they coincide with remarks already made on *unity*, and on *division* in sermons.

The frequent practice of opening a discussion by a set of *negative* considerations, in my opinion is not expedient, except when some disputed truth is to be guarded against mistake. In general we show sufficiently what a thing is *not*, by showing clearly what it *is*. Still the negative form of argument at the beginning of a sermon in particular subjects, is the best way of obviating difficulties. One of the most instructive preachers whom I have known, in discoursing on the text, "Vengeance is mine, I will repay, saith the Lord," made this his proposition; ' God will punish the wicked.' Instead of answering objections at the close of his discussion in the common way, he met them at the threshold, in three negative particulars, viz. ' We must not suppose that God will fail to punish the wicked, either first, on account of his *goodness;* or secondly, on account of his having *provided* an *atonement;* or thirdly, on account of his *forbearance.*' Then he proceeded to prove his proposition ' that God will punish the wicked in two ways, from what God has *said*, and from what he has *done*.'

The *antithetic* form of reasoning is attended with difficulties, as it is often carried on in *pairs* of contrasted particulars, through a sermon. This is a task which few are able to sustain. For this reason I think Bishop Taylor's method on the text, " What shall it profit a man if he shall gain the whole world and lose his own

soul ? "—where he makes a general contrast of two parts,
the value of the world on one side, and the value of the
soul on the other, is decidedly preferable to that of
Bourdaloue on the text, " Great is your reward in
heaven,"—where he breaks his contrast into parts, by
considering the reward of holiness as better than that of sin,
—because the former is *certain*, the latter is *precarious ;*
the former *great*, the latter *worthless ;* the former *eternal*,
the latter *transitory*.

In reasoning from *Authority*, when we quote the views
of another, for the confirmation of our own, it should be
in his own *words ;* and often the mention of his name,
when that is known and respected, gives additional
weight.   When the subject or length of the quotation
gives it importance, the habit of noting author and page
in the margin, may save us trouble afterwards.   And let
me say in passing, that the careless mode practised by
some good men of adopting long passages from books,
without reference or notice of any sort, if it can be recon-
ciled with integrity, is very indiscreet.   Too often for the
credit of the ministry, has this been demonstrated in
posthumous sermons committed to the press, from a
hasty partiality to their deceased authors.

*The* SIXTH *and last rule I shall mention is, that*
WE SHOULD ENDEAVOUR TO AVOID A CONTROVERSIAL
STRAIN OF REASONING.

The same Apostolic precept and example, that require
us to contend earnestly for essential truths, require us to
avoid all disputes that engender strife and mar the spirit
of godliness.   Points on which good men honestly differ
when discussed in the pulpit, as they sometimes must be,
demand special candour and gentleness.   And in general
it may be said, that a worse habit can hardly be
imagined in a preacher, than that of always creating to

himself an adversary in the pulpit, and assuming on every subject the air and spirit of a disputant.

There are *three* ways of refuting objections. The *first*, and when the case admits it, the best is to aim only at a full and clear exhibition of the truth. The *next* is to interweave objections, and answer them indirectly and without formality. The *last* is to state them in form, and refute them by distinct arguments. When this last course is adopted, it requires the following precautions.

1. State no objections that are too trivial to deserve notice. We may waste our time by refuting what needs no refutation, as well as by proving what needs no proof.

2. If objections are really weighty, never treat them as insignificant. Without evasion, without distortion, state them fairly and fully ;—give them all the weight to which they are entitled.

3. Take care that your answers be complete and decisive, so as not to leave the impression, that you have raised an adversary, whom you have not strength to withstand.

4. State no objections in which your hearers are not interested. Though weighty, and capable of complete refutation if they are such as are never likely to be known without your help, it is worse than trifling to discuss them. The physician deserves no praise for his skill in devising an antidote for poison, which his own temerity had administered. What preacher would repeat the language of obscene and profane men, with a view to condemn it? No more does Christian propriety allow us to state artful and blasphemous cavils against religion, for the same end. Even when such cavils are decent in manner, they should not be obtruded on common minds, without urgent necessity. Such minds may understand an objection, and remember it, when the force of a reply

is not seen, or is forgotten. It is from the learned labours of Christian advocates for the truth, not from their own investigations, that sceptics have

> ————' Gleaned their blunted shafts,
> And shot them at the shield of truth again.'

5. Avoid *acrimony*, as both unchristian and unwise. Meet an objector with ingenuousness and kindness. Take no advantage of verbal inadvertence; nor charge on him consequences, as intentionally admitted by him, which he disavows.

6. Seldom or never oppose sects by *name*.

# LECTURE XIV.

THE close of a regular discourse has been designated by different terms. The ancients called it *peroration*, and required that it should consist of two parts, *recapitulation* and *address to the passions*.

Suppose an argument to have been so conducted, that a brief review of its chief parts will present them in a strong and concentrated light before the hearers, this prepares them to admit an appeal to their feelings. The practicability of such a review as will answer this purpose, depends on the degree of perspicuous arrangement which has prevailed in the discourse. The admirable skill with which Cicero wrought up his materials in his defence of Milo, prepared the way for a powerful peroration. And it will not be deemed out of place for me to refer again to this great pleader, as a pattern of rhetorical method, worthy to be studied by the Christian orator who wishes his discourse to make a distinct and strong impression on the hearers. But supposing a discourse to have been loose and diffuse, without any lucid order of thought, all attempts at recapitulation must be worse than useless. In the secular oratory of Athens, where direct address to the passions was forbidden by law, recapitulation was the usual form of conclusion, in which, of course, much skill was employed to give rhetorical effect.

In sacred eloquence, the close of a discourse is sometimes called *application*, sometimes *reflections or inferences*, and sometimes, though not according to the best usage, it is called *improvement*.

Some preachers are in the habit of intermingling practical reflections with the different topics discussed throughout a sermon, instead of bringing these together at the close. There may be cases in which this is the best course. Claude, in his essay, recommends that some texts should be treated in the way of *continued application*, and gives an example in a long sermon on the passage, " Work out your own salvation," &c. His design is, to give a specimen of that preaching which is carried on in the strain of direct address. It may perhaps be considered as a *general rule*, that in proportion as a subject is treated *argumentatively*, and on the *principles of strict unity*, it demands a regular conclusion; and when a series of *independent points* are discussed, it becomes more proper for the preacher to apply each of these, as he goes on. But if this rule is just, it would seem to follow, that in proportion as the sermon has this miscellaneous character, and admits this running application, it is the less likely, in general, to produce any single and strong impression on the hearers.

As it is proper for us to derive instruction from the example of others, I shall direct your attention to some *faults* in the conclusion of sermons, as they appear both from the press and the pulpit. These, so far as they demand our present notice, may be included in the *formal* manner, the *desultory* and the dry.

The *formal* conclusion varies, with the vogue of the pulpit, at different periods. To what extent this taste formerly prevailed, may be seen from the sermons of the Puritans, and from Bishop Wilkins' Ecclesiastes, a book which was, for a considerable time, regarded as a standard work on preaching. The usual mode of concluding a sermon, was by a series of many heads, called *uses*, subdivided into minor parts. As a specimen of this manner, we may take the eleventh sermon of the pious Flavel, entitled *England's Duty*. After more than sixty heads in the body of this sermon, the application begins with a *use* of *information*, which is thrown into five *inferences*. Then comes the *use* of *exhortation*, first to *believers*, including four heads of *counsel;* then to *unbelievers*, including eight minor heads, the first of these again split into three parts, making twenty-four divisions in the conclusion. A sermon of the same preacher, on the evidences of grace, closes with a use of *information*, containing *nine inferences ;* a use of *exhortation* containing *six motives ;* a use of *direction* containing *ten rules ;* the last of these divided into eight *meditations ;* and a use of *examination* with thirteen minor heads. In the last place, the preacher says, ' It remains that I shut up all, with a use of *consolation*,' which contains five parts, making fifty-six divisions in the conclusion.

After the restoration of Charles the Second, the influence of the court being directed in every possible way to discredit puritanism, the fashion of the pulpit was changed in this as in other respects. In the English church, since the time of Jeremy Taylor and Tillotson, the conclusion of sermons has been much less formal than before. Still, the scholastic manner has been retained by many distinguished preachers of the past and the present age. A rigid formality runs through all their applications, so that whatever be the subject or occasion, the same round of particulars in the same phraseology is to be expected.

The *desultory* conclusion may arise either from *affec-*

H

*tation* or *barrenness* in the preacher.   In the former case,
the fault is commonly the opposite of that just described.
A succession of rambling, incoherent remarks, is adopted
from a false taste, which would shun at all events the
imputation of formality.   When this loose manner is
occasioned by sterility of thought, it is commonly because
the preacher, having worked up his materials, and yet
feeling it necessary to proceed, falls into a strain of
indefinite remark or exhortation.   Whether he does this,
from want of matter, or from want of method, or from
both, the attention of intelligent hearers is certainly lost,
the moment they perceive him to be merely filling up
the time with observations which have no important
relation to each other, or to the subject. Augustine, in his
precepts on preaching, says, ' When it is manifest that
the audience have understood what is said, the speaker
should close his discourse, or pass on to other topics.   As
that orator awakens interest, who removes obscurity from
what is to be made known ; so he is tedious who dilates
and repeats things that are known.'   An application
may be rich, instructive, and powerful in impression,
though very formal in its parts ; as any one may see in
the sermons of Edwards.   But thrt. vacuity of thought,
of which I am speaking, is necessarily void of interest.
Be the number or order of parts what they may, call
them inferences, reflections, or any other name, if they
are of that general cast, that might as well be attached
to another subject as to the one in hand, the character
of *barrenness* runs through the whole.   All amplification
in such a case, is the mere turning over of trite remarks,
which had constituted the body of the sermon.   So strait-
ened is this sort of preacher in his resources, that he often
makes the same thing stand as an inference, which had before
stood as his main proposition, or one of his chief heads.

The *dry* conclusion, as I shall call it for want of a better term, consists not so much in tame and hackneyed thoughts, nor in technical arrangements, as in a naked, inanimate outline of particulars, simply stated perhaps, as results from the subject discussed. These, though they may be just, and such as a warm-hearted, skilful preacher might amplify, so as to produce a vivid impression on the hearers, awaken no lively interest, because they are only *mentioned* with the same frigid brevity, as his corollaries are stated, by a mathematical lecturer.

We proceed now to consider in what consists the *excellence* of a conclusion, it being understood as prerequisite in all cases, that the subject of discourse be important, and such as admits an interesting application. To succeed in this part of his work, the preacher should,

1. AIM AT PRACTICAL EFFECT. The very institution of the Christian ministry, supposes that the great purpose of revealed religion is to promote the reformation and salvation of men. In this view, only, is all Scripture *profitable*, that " the man of God may be perfect, thoroughly furnished to every good work." All that gives value to knowledge and to correctness of belief, is their tendency to sanctify the heart and life. On this principle Christ proceeded in his preaching. On the same principle the apostles proceeded, and by this standard the worth of every sermon is to be estimated. Just so far as it is adapted to make the hearers feel the power, and cherish the spirit, and obey the precepts of the gospel, it is what a Christian sermon should be. And that sermon which does not reach the hearers as *individuals*, which is not felt to bear distinctly on their ignorance, or error, or moral defects, as *individuals*, answers no good end whatever.

2. HE 'SHOULD UNDERSTAND THE PRINCIPLES OF

THE HUMAN MIND. The aid of this knowledge in applying truth, is most important. In the moral world, as well as the physical, like causes produce like effects. We can never calculate with certainty on any end to be attained, unless we know the principles to be operated on, and the means to be applied, for the attainment of that end. But the laws of mind are as settled, as uniform, as easily applied to practical purposes, as the laws of matter. In either case, the principles most important in real life, are not such as demand skill in the abstract and profound researches of science, but such as are obvious to the eye of common sense. It was great accuracy of judgment, grounded on a thorough knowledge of history, and a careful analysis of intellectual and moral causes, operating at the time, which enabled a distinguished British statesman of the last century, to foretel, with almost prophetic exactness, the results of the French revolution.

It is according to laws which govern intellectual operations, and only according to these, that we explain the power of one mind to act upon another. Why have modern ages united in a tribute of admiration to the genius of Shakspeare? How is it that in his Julius Cæsar, every man feels the hand of the poet, searching his own bosom? How is it that in Othello, we are alternately melted to tears, thrilled with surprise, and racked with horror? One single thing accounts for this magic power of the dramatist; he had studied the human heart. He knew infallibly how to direct the movements of his hand; he knew how and when to touch any string, as he intended, and what note it would respond.

Surely the principles on which this power depends, lie equally open to the eye of the *preacher*, as of the *poet;* and if they are important to be applied, where the chief object is *amusement*, how much more so, where the *immortal interests* of men are concerned ?

Light, reflected from a mirror, resembles the truth as exhibited in the Bible. Though that mirror was not made for me in particular, yet if I stand before it with my eyes open, I see, not a general representation of every thing, but exactly my *own image*. That mirror may be covered, or placed in the dark, so as to reflect nothing. But if it speaks at all, it speaks truth. I must not look at it, if I would not see my own face ; nor, if I dislike the image, may I complain of him who made the mirror, nor of him who placed it before me ?

In applying truth to the conscience, however, there is a difference between *personality* and *individuality*. That special designation of men by name, which was practised by the prophets, and Christ, is not proper for any one possessing no more than the authority or knowledge of an uninspired teacher. Nor is it generally safe, in our preparations for the pulpit, to trust ourselves in a specific *aim at individuals ;* since the design to be effectual, must be quite apparent, and since the motive is always liable to suspicion and mistake. But the more completely truth is so exhibited, that *conscience* is compelled to do its own work, in making the application to individuals, the stronger and the better is the impression produced.

But besides this general skill in applying truth, by the agency of *conscience*, it is often useful, by a classification of hearers, to make a direct appeal to their hearts. I select one example from the Archbishop of Cambray, whose pungency and fire were so deeply impressive, especially in the close of his sermons. The address is to careless nominal Christians. " Who are *you*, profane men, who laugh when you see a renewed sinner following Jesus Christ, and stemming the torrent of all his passions? What then, you cannot endure that we should declare ourselves openly for the God who made us? With you it is a weakness to fear his eternal justice. With you it is a folly to live by faith in hope of eternal life. Who then are you that ridicule religion and the religious? Do not you believe *any* religion? Go then out of our churches;—go, live without Christ, without hope, without God in the world. Go where your impious and brutal despair would hurry you. But alas,—you are professed Christians; you have promised to renounce the world and take up the cross. You have *promised;*—you dare not deny it; you dare not renounce your salvation; you tremble when approaching death shows you the abyss opening under your feet. Miserable foolish men!—you would have us think you wise while you treat as fools those who, hoping for benefits which you pretend not to have renounced, labour to obtain them."

There is a more specific application still, in which *each* hearer is set *apart*, and feels himself to be addressed in the second person singular, as though no one else were present. I add a brief example of this from the French pulpit, rebuking the common presumption on long life. " Make the different orders of men pass before your eyes;—count them one by one, and see what proportion of the whole die before they are thirty years of age. How many die between thirty and forty! How few arrive at fifty! How very small is the number of *old* men! In a city containing a million of souls there may be *two* or *three* thousand; three hundred perhaps in one hundred thousand. Now what foolish security is it to presume, at the risk of your salvation, that *yourself* will be among these *few* exceptions? Were one to hazard his fortune on such uncertainty, he would pass for a *madman.* And thou, miserable man, dost *thou* hazard thy *soul*, thine eternal happiness, on this frivolous hope ? " These examples confirm the statement, that to make a direct and powerful application of truth, the preacher must know the human heart.

3. *The preacher should so* ARRANGE THE PARTS OF A SERMON, *that they may attend to* A SINGLE AND COMBINED EFFECT IN THE CLOSE. On this point, I have enlarged so much under the head of *unity*, that only a few additional remarks are needed here. It is not enough that we *aim* to make men feel, and that we *understand the principles of their minds*, if we fail to *adapt our discourse* to those principles. The sermon that wants *plan,* will of course want *power in the conclusion*. An important thought may lose more than half its weight by standing in a wrong *place* and *wrong connexion*. The effect of extempore address is often frustrated by the fact that a few prominent things are produced at once, and then are only dilated and repeated afterwards. With a view to a main design, steadily kept in mind, the skilful preacher will arrange his subject throughout, so that each part shall add strength to the whole.

The *convergent* method, when the subject admits it, is peculiarly adapted to this purpose. Cicero, as I have before observed, when he had a great point to carry, like a general who would break through an opposing line, considered and arranged his means with consummate skill, till at last he brought them all to bear down on that point with irresistible effect. There is something in this principle of oratory, analogous to the current of a great river. It rises in remote mountains a mere rill ; then it becomes a rivulet ; then a brook ; then, by the accession of tributary streams, it swells and widens, and

deepens in its course till it rolls on a flood of waters to
the ocean.   But imagine if you can a river *diminishing*
in force as it runs, parting off a rivulet on the right hand,
and another on the left, till the main channel is dry;
while each branch becomes less and less till it is
lost; and you have a tolerable representation of a sermon which promises well at first, but diverges into parts,
and dwindles as it goes on, till the current of thought
is exhausted in a feeble conclusion.   Not so, where the
powers of the speaker, the weight of the subject, and
the coincidence and continuity of argument and motive,
bear on an assembly in the best manner.   The sermon
grows as it proceeds, and carries on the speaker and
hearers with an increasing tide of interest to the last.
So much does the skilful preacher know the entire effect
of his discourse to depend on the *application*, that instead
of filling up this with common-place gleanings of thought,
the whole performance is adapted to the final impression
he wishes to make; and he is not ready to begin the
writing of a sermon till he has determined how it is to
close.   In the process of composing, indeed, when the
inventive powers are sharpened by exercise, he may
modify his plan.   Some topic assigned to an earlier
head, or some new thought that occurs, may advanta-
geously be set aside, that it may become more prominent
in the close.

I will add under this head, that when a sermon is
*argumentative*, whether doctrinal or practical, it may
often be closed with *inferences*.   These should always
be scriptural results from scriptural premises.   Neither
false deductions from Christian premises, nor true deductions from premises not in the Bible, deserve any better
name than a vain display of ingenuity.   But there are
several advantages in a conclusion by inferences, when

well conducted and pertinent to the subject. They exhibit the truths of religion *connectedly;* they often exhibit *disputed* truths, *unexpectedly* and *undeniably.* Where the premises would have been rejected, had the deduction been foreseen, it comes by surprise and compels assent. And what is most important, as a grand principle in preaching is, that such inferences make men *active* hearers, and not *passive,* like hortatory addresses.

4. *The success of a conclusion depends much on the* WARMTH WITH WHICH IT APPEALS TO THE HEART. ' To this part,' says Quinctilian, ' the highest powers of address should be reserved. Here, if ever, it is proper to open all the fountains of eloquence. Here, if we have succeeded in other parts, we may take possession of our hearers' minds. Having weathered the shallows any breakers we may spread full sail; and according to the chief design of a peroration, we may give free scope to magnificence in sentiment and language.'

To this part of a discourse the best institutes of oratory assign the *pathetic;* on which, however, my limits here allow only a few suggestions. My *first* remark is, that all attempts to move the passions will fail, without *simplicity* in thought and language. The precepts of books on this subject, except a few leading principles, are by far too artificial for the pulpit. The devices by which popular orators of old sought to move their hearers, would be condemned by the taste of this age, as unsuitable in any case, and especially in Christian eloquence. Nor can any *mere study of the passions* enable a man to reach them with success. There is a power in genius, combined with sensibility, to which the throbings of the heart respond, but which art cannot imitate nor explain.

A *second* remark is, that *not all kinds of emotion, nor*

*even of high emotion,* fall under the head of pathetic. Animation, vehemence, or what is often termed fire, produce strong emotion, but it is of a different sort. Grand and sublime representations awaken sentiments of awe or admiration, and perhaps overwhelm with their majesty.   But the pathetic is distinguished by its gentle insinuating, melting influence, which silently wins upon the heart, and makes it yield itself to the power that so irresistibly, and yet so delightfully controls its affections.

*A third* remark is, *the pathetic cannot be protracted.* Strong passion is necessarily short in continuance. ' Nothing,' says Quinctilian, quoting Cicero, ' nothing dries up sooner than tears.   The auditor shortly becomes weary of weeping, and relapses into tranquillity.   We must not let this work grow cold on our hands, but having wrought up the passions, leave them.'   Sometimes however, the heart may be touched for a moment, at several successive intervals ; — while at each time, its sensibilities start into action more readily, as it retains the softening influence of past emotion.   Whereas, if the same note is sounded too long at once, feeling flags, and dies away into fatigue.

*A fourth* remark is, that in all addresses to the passions, *moral painting is indispensable.*   The two chief reasons are that the senses are the primary inlet of ideas; and that *remoteness* of objects diminishes their power of impression.   Painting annihilates absence and distance, and embodies objects before the eye, as they are seen in life, or on canvass.   It thrills the heart, where mere description would leave it cold.   From this principle arises the awful interest often awakened by the delineations of scripture ; such, for example, as the transactions of the last judgment.   We see the Judge enthroned,— the retinue of angels, the books open, the heavens passing away,—the dead small and great standing before God. We forget intervening ages. The scenery is all present;—we feel ourselves encompassed with the dread realities of that occasion.

The painting to the *fancy*, which belongs to pastoral poetry, has little use in the pathetic of the pulpit. Our business is with the *heart*, which abjures amplification, and drapery, and embellishment. The most moving scene of the pulpit, the death of Christ, is often so over-drawn, with pompous decoration, as to chill the hearers .with indifference. Yet a skilful pleader will give life to the exhibition of a common murder. You see the assailant spring from his ambush; his victim calling for help. You see the blow given,—the man falling,—hear his groan,—see his gushing blood, his convulsive agonies in death. It is lamentable that the power which in poetry and romance often seizes the heart with resistless grasp, is so seldom brought to bear on the feelings of men, from the pulpit.

*A fifth remark is, that though high powers of execution in the pathetic are wanting to any preacher,* THIS IS NO REASON WHY HE SHOULD BE DULL AND COLD. The most careless hearers know too well the weight of our business, to be satisfied when we aim no strokes at the heart. The keen sting of conscience they dread, but the thrill of emotion they certainly prefer to the listlessness of indifference. The love of excitement is instinctive and universal. Suppose that you lack, what indeed few possess, the power of taking the heart by assault; yet you *must awaken feeling*, especially in the close of your discourse, or you come utterly short of the great end of preaching. A frigid temperament is no excuse in this case. Whose fault is it that his heart is cold, who speaks on a subject which fills heaven with emotion?

He has proved a great doctrine of the gospel to be true, perhaps by clear argument. What then? Shall that doctrine be left on the same footing with a mathematical axiom? Shall the hearers rest in mere assent to its truth, when its *truth* is the very thing that cuts them off from hope and heaven? Look on an assembly of immortal beings sinking down to death, under an accumulation of unpardoned guilt; think of the unspeakable love and agonies which procured for them forgiveness; anticipate your meeting with these very hearers at the judgment; and the certainty that each one of them who dies impenitent, will be an eternal outcast from God; and then, if you feel no stirrings of a mighty emotion in your own bosom, where is your compassion for dying men? Where is your love to Christ? Talk not of a piety that can offer *apology* for such a state of heart. Mourn for it rather as your *sin*.

# LECTURE XV.

STYLE OF THE PULPIT.—GENERAL REMARKS.—FAULTS OF STYLE IN SERMONS.—EXCELLENCIES.

I COME now to offer some remarks on the appropriate style of the pulpit. The opinion that the Christian preacher, when he speaks on *religion* must assume a countenance, a tone, and a style, such as are adapted to no *other* subject, has been greatly prejudicial to the interests of piety.

1. Our *first* inquiry is, how far may the preacher's style be *professional* and *peculiar*. The views which I entertain as to the peculiarity of diction, allowable in sermons, may be expressed under two general remarks.

One is, that religion must have terms, call them *technical* if you please, but terms appropriate to itself. The arts and the physical sciences require words and phrases which cannot be used in theology. For the same reason theology must have to a certain extent its own expressions, adapted to its own peculiar subjects. And Christian theology must be distinguished in this respect, from Mahometan and Pagan systems of religion. If the writers of the New Testament must have been rigidly tied down to classical usage, they could have had no words to express those thoughts which were peculiar to the gospel. Plato and Xenophon had no such thoughts; and the primary classical import of the words which they employed, could not therefore express the

meaning of St. Paul, on topics peculiar to the style he must
use in preaching the gospel. Strike out from the language
of the pulpit the words, *sin, holiness, redeemer, atonement,
regeneration, grace, covenant, justification, salvation*, and
others of similar import, and what would become of the
distinctive character of Christianity? The preacher in
this case must either not exhibit the truths of the gospel
at all, or exhibit them under all the disadvantages of an
endless and needless circumlocution. In either case, his
ministrations, whatever literary merit they might possess,
would have little tendency to instruct and save his
hearers. Before he can submit to the requisitions of a
taste so perverted, he must have forgotten the sacred
dignity of his office, as an ambassador of Christ.

My other remark is, that, with the above exception,
the general character of style in sermons, should be such
as is proper, in discussing any elevated and interesting
subject. The reasons are obvious. If we would impress
religious truth on the hearts of men, it must be done
through the medium of the understanding. We must
address them, therefore, in language to which they are
accustomed. After the example of our Saviour, we
should employ words and figures which accord with the
familiar conceptions of our hearers. By this means, too,
we may avoid any repulsive associations, which would
otherwise prevent the access of truth to the mind. If he
who speaks on religion, assumes the aspect and tones
of sadness, he makes the impression on the minds of the
irreligious, that piety is inconsistent with cheerfulness.
An effect not less favourable is produced by a correspondent peculiarity of *language*. Besides, a strong and
vivid representation of any subject cannot be made, when
the terms employed are inappropriate or indefinite.

2. We are prepared, in the next place, to glance at

those peculiarities, most common in the style of sermons, which must be accounted *faults*.

*The theological dialect*, as distinguished from what may be called classical style, results in a considerable measure, from a designed imitation of scriptural language. I say *imitation*, for unquestionably direct *quotation* from the Bible, is not only necessary in adducing proofs from this standard of religious belief and practice, but is required by good taste, for purposes of illustration and impression. Such quotations, if made with judgment, give weight and authority to a sermon. But the fault I am describing, lies in the unskilful amalgamation of sacred with common phraseology.

This sometimes arises from a *necessary familiarity with theological writers of past times*. The excellent sentiments which these often contain, expressed, perhaps, in quaint and antiquated phraseology, imperceptibly give a cast to his own diction, resembling, in its influence on other minds, the stiffness and peculiarity which would appear in his *garb*, if it were conformed to the fashion of the sixteenth century.

Having suggested these hints on the defects of pulpit style, I proceed to state some of the chief qualities which it 'ought to possess. Taking it for granted that perspicuity, strength, and a proper degree of ornament are essential attributes of all good writing, and therefore never to be neglected by the preacher, I shall consider certain properties of style, which he is under *peculiar* obligations to cultivate.

The *first* of these which I shall mention, is SIM-PLICITY.

This, as I have already observed, is required by the principles of *good taste*. But it is more to my purpose, at present, to show that it is required of the Christian

preacher, by the principles of *religion*. He is appointed
to instruct men in the way of salvation; to instruct those,
many of whom are ignorant. To instruct them in that
gospel of which it was a remarkable characteristic, at its
first publication, " that it was preached to the poor."
' In this respect our Saviour was a perfect pattern,—
accommodating his instructions to the weak and illiterate,
in distinction from the Jewish teachers, and the heathen
philosophers, who delivered their discourses only to a
few select disciples.'

The simplicity of language which a preacher should
adopt, requires him to choose such *words as are* INTEL-
LIGIBLE to his hearers. I say not that he shall adopt
the extravagant principle sometimes laid down, never to
use a word, which is not familiar to every child. This
would forbid him to preach at all, on the simplest topics,
without such a constant explanation of terms, as would
render his discourses tedious and uninteresting, to the
greater part of every assembly. But the proper rule of
conduct in this case, lies in a narrow compass.

We should take care then never to use a *hard* word,
when a *plain* one would express our meaning. The *sense*
to be expressed, is the main point, and language is only
the vehicle of communication. The affectation which
leads a man to sacrifice the object for which he speaks,
to the reputation of being an erudite or elegant speaker,
is altogether beneath the dignity of the sacred office.

Who would expect ' a teacher of babes,' to ransack
the resources of etymology, and to speak of the ' lapsed
state of man,' and the ' moral adaptation of things,'
when his proper business is to discuss the great and
simple truths of the gospel, in the plainest manner? It
is a familiar anecdote of the distinguished Prelate,
Archbishop.Tillotson, that before he delivered his ser-

mons, he sometimes read them to an illiterate old lady, of good sense, that by the aid of her remarks, he might reduce his style to the level of common capacities.

There is one more violation of simplicity in the style of sermons, which the preacher should avoid ; I mean the *display of extensive reading*. The practice of introducing scraps of quotations from classical authors, if carried beyond very moderate limits, even in literary compositions, is so repulsive to men of taste, that it is much less prevalent now than it was in some former periods. At this day, pedantry in the pulpit, is much more likely to show itself in exotic phrases, in far-fetched rhetorical figures, in citing the apothegms of illustrious men, and especially in obtruding upon plain hearers, the names and the opinions of learned writers. To seek the admiration of others by solving difficulties, which we ourselves have created, is an artifice, unworthy of any respectable man. ' It is not difficult,' says Usher, ' to make *easy* things appear *hard ;* but to render *hard* things *easy*, is the *hardest* part of a good orator and preacher.'

But when there is no *affectation* of this sort, the habits of a cultivated mind, may deceive a preacher ; and he may, imperceptibly to himself, take it for granted that his language is intelligible to his hearers, because it is so to himself. ' The extent of his knowledge,' says a competent judge on this subject, ' the quickness of his perception ; his ability to grasp a wide, and to unravel a complex subject, to appreciate the force of arguments, and to keep up his attention without fatigue, during a long and arduous investigation ; these advantages place him at a distance from uncultivated minds. But when in addition to the difficulties he must encounter from these causes, he speaks a language widely different from that of the mass of his hearers, in its copiousness, its arrangement, its images, and its very terms; he will evidently be in great danger of being generally obscure, and frequently, almost unintelligible to them. The words of Latin and of French derivation in our language, are extremely numerous; and a large proportion of them are completely naturalized, among men of education. They are so perfectly familiar to the ear of a scholar, that he has no conception before he makes the trial, how many of them are never found in the vocabulary of the lower classes. When a young man therefore, accustomed to the language of erudition, laden with academic honors, finds himself the pastor of a country congregation, what is his duty? Not indeed to adopt a barbarous and vulgar phraseology ;—but, like a missionary lately arrived in a new region, or like an inhabitant of another planet, dropped into a village, he must study the habits of mind, and the language of those among whom he is placed, before he can prosecute his ministerial *labours* with effect.' [1]

The effort required in this case, well becomes one whose honor it is, for Christ's sake, to be the servant of all. Concerning the simple rhymes, composed by the great reformer, for the sake of the vulgar, it has been well remarked ; ' For these ballads Luther may receive a greater reward, at the last day, than for whole shelves of learned folios. Vanity may make a man speak and write learnedly ; but piety only can prevail on a good scholar to simplify his speech, for the sake of the vulgar.[2]

---

[1] Note (14.)

[2] Augustine says, ' Of what value is a golden key, if it will not open what we wish ?—and what is the harm of a wooden one, if it will accomplish this purpose?—since all we seek is to obtain access to what is concealed.'

Such a preacher, though his worth may be overlooked by the undiscerning now, will one day have a name that is above every name, whether it be philosopher, poet, orator, or whatever is most revered among mankind.' [1]

The *second* quality requisite in the style of Sermons, is SERIOUSNESS.

In some departments of oratory, *ridicule* may be employed with propriety, and with great effect. In the hands of the senator or pleader, this instrument often has an invisible edge, when argument is unavailing. But the dignity of the pulpit *rejects* the aid of this weapon. I do not say that satire in sermons is *never* admissible ; but it is always dangerous, and almost always mischievous.

> ' It may correct a foible, may chastise
> The freaks of fashion, regulate the *dress* :
> But where are its sublimer trophies found ?
> What vice has it subdued ? whose heart reclaim'd
> By rigor, or whom laugh'd into reform ?
> Alas ! Leviathan is not so tam'd :
> Laugh'd at, he laughs again, and stricken hard,
> Turns to the stroke his adamantine scales,
> That fear no discipline of human hands.'

If the graver sort of irony, employed for sober purposes, can seldom be indulged in the pulpit, what shall we say of that unmeaning *levity* and *witticism* of language, which is sometimes heard in sermons? The preacher trifles in this manner, under the pretence of keeping up the attention of his hearers. But *what* attention does he desire; and for what *purpose ?* Not the attention of the theatre or the circus : but the

---

[1]. Robinson on Claude.

attention of immortal beings, to a message from God.
Let him not then degrade his office and himself, by a
preposterous levity. Surely when mingled with the
most momentous and awful subjects, there is especial
reason to say, " of laughter, it is mad, and of mirth, what
doeth it."

But seriousness in the pulpit is inconsistent, not merely
with sarcasm and witticism, but with that *affected
smartness* of expression, and that exuberance of sparkling embellishment, which betray at once a puerile taste,
and a heart unaffected with the great subjects of religion.
Bates says, ' This is like Nero's lading his gallies from
Egypt, with sand for the wrestlers, when Rome was
starving for want of corn.'

This leads me to notice a *third* excellence in the style
of sermons, which is EARNESTNESS.

Let me not be understood to recommend that false
animation which characterizes every species of artificial
eloquence. All that vain parade and pomp of elocution,
in which the speaker's effort is to exhibit himself and not
his subject, is contemptible in a lawyer; but in a minister
of the gospel, it is unpardonable. ' Shall those,' says
Fenelon, ' who ought to speak like Apostles, gather up
those flowers of rhetoric which Demosthenes, Manlius,
and Brutus trampled on? What could we think of a
preacher, who should in the most affected jingle of words
show sinners the divine judgment hanging over their
heads, and hell under their feet? There is a decency to
be observed in our language as in our clothes. A discon-
solate widow does not mourn in fringes, ribands, and
embroidery. And an Apostolical minister ought not to
preach the word of God in a pompous style, full of
affected ornaments. The Pagans would not have endured
to see even a comedy so ill acted. I love a serious

preacher who speaks for my sake, and not for his own ; who seeks my salvation, and not his own vain glory. He best deserves to be heard, who uses speech only to clothe his thoughts; and his thoughts only to promote truth and virtue. A man who has a great and active soul needs never fear the want of expressions. His most ordinary discourses will have exquisite strokes of oratory, which the florid haranguers can never imitate. He is not a slave to words, but closely pursues the truth. He knows that vehemence is, as it were, the soul of eloquence.' [1]

When a prelate inquired of Garrick, why the theatre exhibited so much more eloquence than the pulpit, the actor replied, ' We speak of fictions as if they were realities; you speak of realities as if they were fictions.' Let a stammering peasant be put to plead for his life, and he is eloquent. Let a minister of the gospel be deeply impressed with the weight of his business, and *he* will be eloquent. He will make you understand him, for he understands himself. He will make you feel, for he feels himself. The highest order of pulpit eloquence is nothing but the flame of enlightened piety, united with the flame of genius. When this glows in the bosom, it sanctifies and concentrates all the powers of the mind. It makes even the stripling warrior " valiant in fight; " and enables him to cut off the head of Goliath, with the sword wrested from his own hand.

Would you know the difference then between the pulpit declaimer and the pulpit orator? It is this—the former preaches for himself, the latter for God. One seeks the applause of his hearers, the other their salvation. One displays before them the arts of a fine speaker,

---

[1] Letter to the French Academy.

the other assails them with the lightning and thunder of
truth. One amuses the fancy; the other agitates the
conscience; forces open the eyes of the blind, and storms
the citadel of the heart.

The style of declamation may indeed be perspicuous.
But its perspicuity differs as much from that of fervid
eloquence, as the transparency of ice differs from the
glowing transparency of melted glass issuing from the
furnace.

# LECTURE XVI.

## STYLE OF THE PULPIT.—DIRECTIONS IN FORMING A STYLE.

SKILL in writing depends on genius and discipline. Without genius, industry and art can never raise a man's performance above the character of elaborate dulness. Without discipline, the best powers can never be brought to act by any uniform principles, or to any valuable end.

For the benefit of those who are still forming their intellectual habits, expecting to devote all their powers to the holy and exalted work of preaching the gospel, I shall now offer some practical suggestions as to the attainment of a good style.

*The* FIRST *of these is, always remember* THAT THE BASIS OF A GOOD STYLE IS THOUGHT.

Language is but the instrument of mind. To study it on any other principle, is to make the object to be attained subordinate to the means of its attainment. A man who would form himself as a writer, must acquire the control of his own intellectual powers. He must be capable of fixing his mind with steady attention to a single point, that he may compare and distinguish the relations of different things. 'I never thought,' says Baxter, ' that I understood any thing till I could anato-mize it, and see the parts distinctly, and the union of the

parts as they make up the whole.' This mental discipline accounts for the clearness and vigour of his style.
A writer, who has not established habits of patient exact
thinking, will use words with indeterminate meaning, and
unskilful arrangement.

But it is not enough for a writer to think clearly on
any single subject. He may understand his own meaning, and yet have but *little* meaning; he may be intelligible to others, and yet be *barren*. That his style may
be interesting, it must be rich in matter. It must exhibit
those intellectual qualities in himself, which presuppose
good inventive powers, sharpened by much reflection,
and patient acquisition of knowledge.

As a result of these principles, it must doubtless
follow, that the man who sits down to write as the mere
student of style, forgetting that language can be studied
with advantage, only as the vehicle of thought, will be
very liable to miss his aim. Some *object* he must have
in writing, distinct from the attainment of a good style,
or he will not write well. I know not that the style
of Blair was formed in the method now condemned; but
with all its good qualities, it possesses just those defects
which I should expect such a process to produce.

SECONDLY, STUDY YOUR OWN GENIUS.

As in a man's features, and other exterior qualities
of person, so in his structure of mind, and habits of thinking, and of course in his style, there is an *individuality*
of character. This appears in what he writes, with more
or less distinctness, according to his native temperament,
and the influence of circumstances, by which this temperament is strengthened or controlled or transformed.
While every writer is bound to observe the established
laws of grammar, and of rhetoric too, he is at liberty to
consult his own taste, as to the general characteristics

of the style which he shall adopt. Accordingly we find, among authors of the first rank, a considerable diversity. One is terse and sententious; another copious and flowing; another simple; another bold and metaphorical. Now, by losing sight of his own capacities and cast of mind, and attempting to be something altogether different from what his Creator intended, a man may not only fail of excellence, but make himself ridiculous. 'Plato, in his younger days, had an inclination to poetry, and made some attempts in tragedy and epic; but finding them unable to bear a comparison with the verses of Homer, he threw them into the fire, and abjured that sort of writing in which he was convinced that he must always remain an inferior.' Next to the necessity of being well acquainted with your subject and yourself, I would say,

THIRDLY,—STUDY THE BEST MODELS.

To what *extent* the ancient classic writers should be included in this direction, as addressed to theological students, and young ministers, is a question, the formal discussion of which would be inappropriate here. If sober men have good reason to be disgusted at the extravagant claims sometimes advanced in behalf of classical learning, as certainly they have, still there is another extreme. The prevailing tendency of this age doubtless is, to fix a very inadequate estimate on the ancient classics, as models of taste and eloquence. An immense field of knowledge is spread before our young men, in their training for public life; and a rapid, superficial survey of this field is expected of them, rather than the patient, elementary process of study, which is indispensable to thorough scholarship.

Classical learning is important to the preacher, because it gives him access to some of the *best examples, which*

*the world has produced, in the department of taste
and oratory.* In all the branches of general knowledge, the writings of Greece and Rome were of
course far more restricted, as to range of thought, and
richness of matter, than those of modern times. But as
models of style and eloquence, no competent judge can
doubt, that the ancient classical works still hold a
rank pre-eminent above all others. And though the
*thoughts* of their authors may be tolerably learned
from a good translation, he who would study these
great masters with a view to *style,* must read them
in their own language.

To these considerations may be added another still
of a more general character, namely, the *wide field of
improvement in theology and criticism, which is opened to
the Christian student, from familiarity with the labours
of the venerable dead.*

No wise man now will devote his life, or any large
share of it, to searching the endless tomes of antiquity,
many of which are nearly worthless. But there is another extreme. Antiquity had a few master spirits, who
gave character to their own age, and to ages following.
The influence they exerted on public opinion constitutes
the chief elements of history. What did such men as
Augustine believe?—how did they write?—how did
they preach?—are questions which deserve at least some
regard, in a liberal education for the ministry;—questions
on which every Christian scholar *must* have opinions,
either taken up at second hand, or derived from original
sources of knowledge.[1]

---

[1] In acquiring information of this sort, theological students might
perform a service at once important to themselves and the church,
by the systematic reading and translation of·select passages from the

Under the general head of *Models*, I would certainly include a few of the *best poets.* This selection should be made from those whose works are characterized by richness, and vigour, and dignity, both of thought and language. A great poet is a moral painter. He knows the sources of emotion, and all the springs of action in the human bosom. The same graphic delineation, the same glow and vivacity by which he rouses the imagination, and seizes the heart, constitute the power of eloquence. In this view, and this only, the Christian student may derive advantage from a judicious use of Shakspeare, as an anatomist of the human heart. It has been said, that ' when this poet was born, nature threw away the mould in which his mind was formed.' In respect to strong, original conception, and exact description, probably nothing of the kind has ever been written, equal to the best pieces of Shakspeare. Cowper's Task, while its object is not to exhibit a bold portraiture of the passions, often thrills the heart with touches of exquisite painting. With an ethereal delicacy and elevation of sentiment, to which Shakspeare was a stranger, it combines a more perfect command of the English language, as to copiousness and harmony of diction, than has been possessed by any of our standard writers, except Pope. The Paradise Lost, too, has passages of distinguished beauty in respect to mere diction ; while in respect to astonishing powers of imagination, it not only surpasses, but greatly surpasses every other human composition. Let any Christian student of oratory go through a patient

ancient fathers. Among these, deserve to be mentioned with special respect those illustrious cotemporaries, Jerome, Basil, Augustine, and Chrysostom, the two former distinguished for elegance, and the two latter for a fervid and powerful eloquence.

analysis of the Iliad and the Æneid, and compare these with the great poem of Milton, and he will not fail to see that the grand and majestic conceptions of the latter, were owing to the fact that his genius was trained to sublimity in the school of the sacred writers.[1]

Since the days of Milton, poems have been multiplied, possessing various, and some of them, great merits in other respects, but few of them aiming at sublimity, and none of them reaching it, with the exception of here and there a bold paragraph or a figure. To name no other, the Night Thoughts and the Course of Time, in my opinion may be read often and with much advantage, by young preachers who are forming their style.

In respect to English prose writers, who deserve to be read as models, my remarks must be brief. If I were to fix on any period as the English Augustine age, it would be that including the latter division of the seventeenth, and the former of the eighteenth century; that is, the period from Charles the Second, to George the First, inclusive;—the middle of which would be the time of Anne. To any one aiming at the cultivation of a simple, classical, English style, I should of course recommend a good degree of familiarity with the writers of that period, including Addison, Pope, Swift, Steele, and Goldsmith, to extend the list no farther.

But a remark of elementary importance to be made in

---

[1] On this subject there is as much of truth as there is of enthusiasm, in the following epigram of Dryden.

> ' Three poets, in three distant ages born,
> Greece, Italy, and England, did adorn.
> The first in loftiness of thought surpassed;
> The next in majesty;—in both, the last.
> The force of nature could no farther go;
> To make a third, she joined the former two.'

this connexion is, that essayists can be regarded only as models of style generally; but not of that style which is specially adapted to popular impression. The reasons of this distinction are obvious. The essay is a brief discussion, limited to a narrow range of thought,—written to be read,—written at leisure,—designed chiefly to amuse or instruct. The writer wants the scope, the excitement, the impelling motive, the ' *vivida vis animi*,' of him who stands up to *speak* in a public assembly with a thousand soul-inspiring eyes meeting his own. No man of common sense, if he had a real point of business to carry with such an assembly, would think of addressing them in the stately and elaborate periods of Johnson's Rambler. Nor is the style of Junius, with all its strength and pungency, adapted to the ends of public speaking. The difference between the most studied speeches of Burke, and those of Chatham, illustrates what I mean. The former scarcely received attention from the hearers; the latter kept alive in their bosoms an intense interest, while his eloquence came down upon them, peal after peal, like the electric flame and the thunderbolt. After a man has fixed the elementary character of his style, by studying the standard writers of the language, he may derive much greater advantage from the reading of good speeches, than from compositions executed in the form of essay.

As to sermons, it is a matter of course that the young preacher should make himself acquainted with those of the highest merit, especially in his own language.

I am aware that after all, the utility of models in forming a style, is altogether denied by some; but the denial is contrary to both philosophy and experience. How is it that all the useful arts are learned? Not by inspiration, nor by precepts chiefly, but by *imitation*.

How is it that we come to speak and write at all ?—by *imitation.* How did the most eloquent writers of antiquity form themselves ? Plato, though he despaired of excelling Homer in poetry, by the very attempt acquired a sweetness and majesty of style which occasioned him to be called the ' Homer of philosophers.' Demosthenes acquired his vehemence by studying Homer and Thucydides. Cicero incorporated into his manner, the strength of Demosthenes, the copiousness of Plato, and the delicacy of Isocrates.

Sir Joshua Reynolds in his Discourses before the Royal Academy, (which I will say in passing, are as worthy to be read for their sound philosophy, as for their good English,) observes : ' Invention is one of the great marks of genius; but if we consult experience, we shall find, that it is by being conversant with the inventions of others, that we learn to invent; as by reading the thoughts of others, we learn to think.' But he would caution the student against a confined and partial imitation. The formation of his own *mind* is the great object. ' He that imitates the Iliad is not imitating Homer.' ' It is not by laying up in his memory the details of great works, that a man becomes a great artist, if he stops without making himself master of the general *principles* on which these works are conducted.'

To derive advantage from models, then, they must be few ; — must have decided excellences ; and must be allowed only their proper influence, in the formation of our own taste and habits ; instead of drawing us into a servile copying of their peculiarities, especially their faults.[1]

[1] ' As the air and manner of a gentleman can be acquired only by living habitually in the best society, so skill in composition must be attained by an habitual acquaintance with classical writers. It is

*The* FOURTH *requisite which I shall mention in forming a good style, and one more important than any other,
is* THE HABIT OF WRITING.

Cicero says, ' the young orator's best master is his
pen.' It might be well supposed that educated men
who have had opportunity to be taught by their own experience, and that of others; men too who have devoted
themselves to a profession in which the pen is confessedly
a prime instrument of respectability and usefulness,
would need no lessons on this subject. But it is vain to
close our eyes against the evidence of facts. A pious
man, of good talents, may be indolent or diffident.
Writing is labour; it calls his *mind* into *effort;* it compels him, at least should compel him to *think.* He
dreads this labour. Through a false theory as to the
management of his intellectual powers, or a morbid
delicacy that holds them under restraint, especially
where exposure to observation is implied,—he thinks it
clear gain to escape exercises in writing, and to devote to
reading the time allotted to these exercises. Thus he
goes through his academical, and perhaps his professional
studies, and comes forth with a stock of knowledge more
or less complete; but with an appalling consciousnes;
that he is utterly destitute of skill to communicate hi·
knowledge to others.

The capacity of writing well is not gained by accident,

indeed necessary that we should peruse many books, which have no
merit in point of expression; but I believe it to be extremely useful
to all literary men, to counteract the effect of this miscellaneou?
reading, by maintaining a constant and familiar acquaintance with ·.
few of the most faultless models which the language affords. For
want of some standard of this sort, we often see an author's taste in
writing alter much for the worse, in the course of his life.'

*Dugald Stewart.*

nor by miracle. Like every other valuable attainment, it is the result of labour. And he who acquires the habit of yielding to his reluctance in this case, to say the least, greatly impairs his prospect of usefulness, if he does not chain himself down to obscurity for life. The man who would *become a writer*, must *write*. If his mind slumbers, if his delicacy or indolence starts back, he must apply the spur. He must be able to control his faculties, and apply them to his object, not by fits and intervals, but with a steady patience and perseverance. I would advise every man who is destined to the ministry, through his whole preparatory course, and even after it, frequently to place himself under the pressure of such an *urgent necessity* to write, as shall secure him from the danger of neglecting his pen.

The influence of *practice* on *despatch* in composition, deserves also to be mentioned. Supposing the general habit of writing with facility to be acquired, the rate at which a man may proceed, in a given case, will ordinarily be accelerated, in proportion to this facility. Much will depend, indeed, on familiarity with his subject, on the kind of subject he has in hand, on the interest it awakens in himself, and on the state of his animal and intellectual system. The operations of mind in this case, are governed by laws, which subject them to the same varieties as attend other operations, in the physical or intellectual world. As the speed of a mariner depends on wind and tide, or of a traveller on the condition of his road, and the strength of his limbs, so the rapidity of a writer is much affected by circumstances. In this respect too, there is doubtless a difference in the structure and habits of different minds.

Johnson has often been mentioned as an example of rapid writing. In one day, his biographer says, he wrote twelve octavo pages; and in another day, including part of the night, he wrote forty eight pages. And it is certain that many of his compositions, which bear the marks of great labour, were written in such haste, as not even to be read over by him, before they were printed. But it should be remembered, that Johnson had trained his mind to a peculiar discipline. His habit was to think aloud; to look through his subject, and arrange his thoughts and expressions. He made little use of his pen, till he had 'formed and polished large masses by continued meditation, and wrote his productions after they were completed.' Thus the act of writing was little more than the transferring from his memory to his paper, a composition already finished in his mind. That the *reputation* of *despatch* was not an object of ambition with Johnson, is evident from his very decided remarks on this subject; in which he says that this ambition appears in no ancient writer of any name, except Statius; and that he, as a candidate for lasting fame, chose to have it known that he employed twelve years on his Thebais.

Doubtless most men of taste have observed an important change in the general characteristics of English style, since the time of Addison. One fact may go far to account for this change. At that day readers were few, and books were in demand, almost exclusively for the use of intellectual men. Now, all the world read; and authorship, consulting the state of the market, accommodates itself to the taste of all the world. The fact that such a progress is going on in the diffusion of knowledge among all classes, is one in which every philanthropist, and especially every Christian will rejoice. But while it is reasonable to expect that a thousand-fold more books will be ushered into the world, than in

former ages, the great mass of these probably will have
but an ephemeral existence, and after their brief day,
being written only for the moment, will be forgotten.
It is probable too, that among these there will be very
few or none of those great, elementary, standard works,
which not only survive the fluctuations of caprice, and
of occasional excitements, but are held in growing estimation from age to age.  This immortality of authorship
depends not on popular suffrage, but on the judgment of
the few who read with discriminating taste, and whose
award of merit always slowly pronounced, is, when
distinctly pronounced, always irreversible.  The pitiful
sum given for the original copy-right of *Paradise Lost*,
is too familiarly known to be repeated here; and to this
day, that work has not been, and for most obvious
reasons it never can be a *popular* work, in the same sense
that many a work of modern romance is popular.  Yet,
when all these multifarious volumes, like successive
swarms of summer insects, shall have been swept away
by the breath of time, this great work of Milton will
remain an imperishable monument of its author's
genius.  So the writer of the Iliad, though held in comparatively low esteem by his cotemporaries, has been
honoured through all succeeding ages as the Father of
Poetry.                                            .

> ' Seven wealthy towns contend for Homer *dead*,
> Through which the *living* Homer begg'd his bread.'

*As an appendage to the foregoing head, I will add a*
FIFTH *and final direction;*—ALWAYS TAKE IT FOR
GRANTED THAT WHAT YOU WRITE IS CAPABLE OF
AMENDMENT.  I do not mean that whatever you write
through life, shall be corrected; but that your early

habits of exactness ought to be, and may be so formed
by proper industry, as to supersede the necessity of all
material corrections. In forming such habits, respectable men adopt different methods. One commits to
paper a rough and rapid outline of his thoughts, always
relying on his second draught for the completion of his
work. Another endeavours to make the original copy
of his thoughts as perfect as possible with the intention
of revising, but not of recomposing it, as a part of the
primary labour of his pen. The former method has
some advantages, when there is sufficient command of
time, and a call for great exactness. But my own experience would lead me to prefer the latter, as the permanent habit of one who is pressed with the multiplied
engagements of the ministry. No young man, however,
should shrink from the labour of re-writing his earlier
compositions, when he can unquestionably make them
better by the process. After an interval has elapsed,
sufficient to efface the partiality which he feels at first
towards the phraseology that he has employed to express his thoughts, he can review the composition, and
correct its faults.

Sir Joshua Reynolds, addressing young men on a
kindred subject says, ' Have no dependence on your
own genius. Nothing is denied to well directed labour ;
nothing is to be obtained without it. Impetuosity, and
impatience of regular application is the reason why many
students disappoint expectation ; and being more than
boys at sixteen, become less than men at thirty.'

Although I have already dwelt, at so much length, on
the different topics of this Lecture, I cannot close without adverting to another aspect of the subject, which
presents in a strong light, the obligation of young ministers, to aim at the attainment of skill in writing. I

refer to the intelligent cast of the age, and to the influence of the press.

It was always a truth of importance, but is more eminently so now, than in any past period since the world began, that skill in wielding the pen is *moral power*. If used aright, it invariably confers respect on its possessor. When we see a perfect clock, we know that the maker acquired skill, by studying the theoretic principles of his art, and by much practice; and that the same man who made this, can make another. So when we see a finished composition, we know at once that it was produced by some gifted mind, accustomed to writing, and able to write again. So spontaneously do men judge in this manner, that a very short piece, like Gray's Elegy, sometimes confers a literary reputation on its author, for ages.

The application of these general remarks is easy. Christian ministers should not only *acquire* the power of writing well, but should *use* this power, for the glory of God, and the good of men. The combined influence of the *pen* and the *press*, is the most astonishing moral machinery that ever was set at work in this world. It is opening a new aspect on all the affairs of men. The question is settled too, that this machinery will be kept in active operation, for good or for evil, in every civilized community. Greece and Rome in their glory had no press; and while this fact certainly contributed to the perfection of their *public speaking*, we cannot but wonder how they accomplished what they did, without the art of printing.

But the intercommunication of thought is no longer restricted to impressions to be made on popular assemblies, nor to oral addresses in any form. The influence of the press can reach every man at his fireside, and at every

hour of the day; it can carry hope to the peasants'
cottage, or thunder the note of alarm to the ear of
princes. As by the power of enchantment, it transfers
the thoughts of one mind to millions of other minds, by a
process silent and rapid, as the winds that sweep over a
continent; or like the light of day, which traverses the
nations by a succession almost instantaneous.

# LECTURE XVII.

THE preceding course of Lectures on Preaching comprises a brief view of the History of the Pulpit, with such directions as I thought proper to give, respecting the choice of texts and of subjects; the general principles to be observed in the plan and execution of a regular discourse; together with some remarks on the style of the pulpit.

But as an instructor of those who are to be instructors of others in the way of salvation, my work is by no means finished, when I have pointed out the proportions, the structure of parts, and the disposition of materials, which a skilful preacher will employ in the composition of a single discourse. There are certain *great principles of preaching*, which remain to be discussed, and which open a wide field for our contemplation. To some of these great principles, which are independent of all the local and temporary usages that human caprice may prescribe to the pulpit, in different countries and periods, I propose now to call your attention. In exhibiting those *general characteristics* which I think Christian sermons ought to possess, I shall avoid every thing of the technical and scientific manner, aiming both in sentiment and expression, to be simple, serious, and practical. Indeed, the object I have in view requires me, not so much to discuss disputed principles relative

to preaching as an art or science, as to spread before
your minds those plain, solemn views of this great work,
which may assist each of you, in his preparatory efforts,
to become "a workman that needeth not to be ashamed,
rightly dividing the word of truth."

The FIRST *characteristic of a good sermon, on which
I am about to enlarge,* IS, THAT IT SHOULD BE EVAN-
GELICAL.

To do justice to my own views on this subject, it will
be proper to state what I mean by evangelical preaching;
and then to show, that all preaching ought to possess
this character.

- 1. WHAT IS EVANGELICAL PREACHING ?    I answer,
it is the same as is sometimes called *preaching Christ,* an
expression by which the Apostles meant, not chiefly
preaching as Christ himself did, and as he commanded
ministers to preach; but especially preaching so as to
exhibit Christ in his true character, as the great object
of faith and love.  The same meaning is sometimes expressed by the phrase, ' preaching the cross,' and preaching ' Christ crucified.'

Every science is built on elementary facts, which must
go together, and must be fully exhibited to teach that
science with success.  The gospel as a complete system
of truth, has its own essential principles; and without
the clear exhibition of these, the gospel cannot be
preached, any more than geometry can be taught, while
its essential principles are denied or overlooked.  Whatever proposition in this science you undertake to prove,
you cannot proceed one step except on the admission of
the principles on which the science is built.  Just so in
preaching the gospel.  Suppose the doctrine of *atonement*
is your subject; how are you to proceed?  Of course
you must admit man to be in a state of ruin; ruin from

which he needs redemption; ruin so desperate that he could not redeem himself. If saved at all, it must be by the interposition of an all-sufficient, vicarious sacrifice. If justified at all, it must be ' freely, by the grace of God.' So it is with other subjects. The doctrines of grace must go together; you cannot consistently admit one without going the length of the whole system.

According to these views, I need not take up time in showing, that sermons in which the doctrine of atonement and other essential doctrines of the gospel are avowedly discarded, or decidedly overlooked, come altogether short of evangelical preaching. But it is to my purpose to remind you in this connexion, that even among ministers whose general views of the gospel are correct, there is much preaching which cannot be called evangelical. I would not say or imply that every sermon ought to discuss, in set form, some essential principle of Christianity; but every sermon ought to exhibit the *spirit* of Christianity, and to derive its appeals to the heart from the *motives* of Christianity. It is not enough that it inculcate what is both true and important; for this it may do, and yet deserve not the name of a Christian sermon. My meaning may be illustrated by familiar historic examples. Socrates taught the being of a God, and the doctrine of immortality, and eternal retribution. Cicero taught temperance, benevolence, truth, justice, &c. Seneca enforced the same duties by grave lessons drawn from the dialectics of the schools. Now suppose that you urge the same topics in the same manner, from the pulpit. Is it Christian preaching? By no means. The things taught are true and important; but the spirit, the motives, the tendency, are not Christian. You have delivered such a sermon as St. Paul could not have delivered, consistently with his solemn purpose not to " know any thing, but Jesus Christ and him crucified."

Do I mean then to find fault with a minister for preaching on the existence of God, the immortality of the soul, or the duties of temperance, truth, and justice? Certainly not. But I mean that he should preach these subjects, not as a heathen philosopher; preach them, not as *independent* of the Christian system, but as *parts* of that system; so that all his arguments, and motives, and exhortations shall be drawn from the authority and exhibit the spirit of the gospel. The minister who believes the divine all-sufficiency of Christ as a Saviour, and the absolute dependence of sinners on his atonement, and the efficacy of the Holy Spirit for salvation, can hardly preach a sermon on any occasion or subject without showing that he *does thus believe.* One of our venerable divines[1] has well said, ' Faithful ministers never preach mere philosophy, nor mere metaphysics, nor mere morality. If they discuss the being and perfections of God, the works and creation of providence, the powers and faculties of the human soul, or the social and relative duties, they consider all these subjects as branches of the one comprehensive system of the gospel. Hence, when they preach upon the inward exercises of the heart, they represent love, repentance, humility, submission, sobriety, &c. not as *moral virtues,* but as *Christian graces.* And when they discourse upon moral topics, they inculcate the duties of rulers and subjects, of parents and children, masters and servants, by motives drawn from the precepts and sanctions of the gospel.' [2]

II. *We are to consider the main position of this Lec-*

---

[1] Emmons.                    [2] Note (15)

*ture, namely, that* ALL PREACHING OUGHT TO BE EVANGELICAL.

Several topics that might properly be introduced under this head, will be reserved for another place. The considerations which I have now to suggest, are chiefly two :

1. That *evangelical preaching might* REASONABLY BE EXPECTED *to answer, better than any other, the great ends of preaching.* What are these ends ? The glory of God in the sanctification and salvation of sinners. How then are sinners to be sanctified and saved ? By knowing and embracing the system of truth which God has revealed in the gospel, and commanded his ministers to publish. And can it be that the system which infinite wisdom has devised, for a given purpose, is no better adapted to promote that purpose than an opposite system, or no system at all ? Will men be induced to receive and love the doctrines of grace, by the influence of that pulpit which never exhibits these doctrines ? Will they be induced to flee for refuge to the cross, by preaching which never urges upon them " Christ and him crucified ? "

Let us now glance at some of the principal points of the evangelical system, and see why these are adapted to give special interest and success to preaching.

This system shows men that with God, the *heart,* and not (as they are presumingly inclined to suppose,) the external conduct, is the standard of moral character.

It shows them that the heart of the unsanctified man is ' *very far gone from original righteousness,*' that it is his *own* heart, and he is *personally responsible to God,* for all its wrong affections ; that *eternal death* is the *just desert* of every sinner, because the law which he has broken is " holy, just, and good," and one which he is bound to obey *perfectly,* and with *all his heart.* Let us pause here for a moment. The above doctrines, if they are solemnly urged home upon the conscience, it is easy to see, must make men feel *guilty* and therefore feel *unsafe*. They *must* disturb the deadly insensibility in which careless men love to repose, and produce solicitude and alarm. But let them *be taught*, and let them *embrace* any system of lax theology which allows them to deny their own depravity; let them become persuaded that *sin* is merely ' human infirmity,' and that sinners are but the ' frail and erring children of their heavenly Father,' (for so men have often been instructed from the pulpit,) and they feel no trembling apprehension of the " fire that shall never be quenched," no deep solicitude, to " flee from the wrath to come."

But to proceed with our enumeration—The evangelical system shows men, that from the fearful curse and condemnation, which rest on every transgressor of the divine law, no one can escape, on the ground of any satisfaction which he himself is able to make. It shows them that Christ has interposed, for the rescue of lost men from this desperate condition, by the sacrifice of himself on the cross; that repentance and faith are now the indispensable and immediate duty of every sinner, to whom the gospel is known : but still, that the stubborn hostility of the carnal mind to this gospel is such, that no sinner will cordially embrace it, except through the transforming influence of the Holy Ghost.

Take the foregoing particulars, and follow them out, in reference to the principle I am illustrating, and suppose the combined influence of these truths to bear down upon the heart and conscience, in the weekly ministrations of the pulpit, and it will be most evident that the hearers of such preaching can hardly remain in total indifference to religion. The direct tendency is, to make

them solemn and anxious; to show them their dependence on a justly offended God; and to keep constantly
before the mind the great question, ' Am I in a state of
salvation, or in a state of wrath ? ' Such effects may be
reasonably expected to result from preaching, which
exhibits with power and pungency the holy strictness of
the law, and the love of a dying Saviour.

But we need not rest this argument on any abstract
*tendency* of evangelical preaching; for

2. *Another source of evidence remains, which is decisive, the evidence of* FACTS. From this it appears that
the preaching of the evangelical system, is attended with
a salutary and sanctifying efficacy, which belongs to no
other system. The question becomes one of historical
verity, on which the proof is so ample and triumphant,
as greatly to exceed the limits that can be allotted to it
in this discussion.

The ground which I take is, that God has usually
attended the faithful preaching of the gospel with a *signal
success*, through the influence of his own Spirit; and that
he has thus set upon it the unquestionable and special
stamp of his own approbation. In proof of this, the
recorded experience of the church may be adduced, in
one accumulated and overwhelming testimony. If this
cannot be established by an unbroken line of facts from
the Apostles' days, no point can ever be proved by
history.

What was it that occasioned the first great declension
from the spirit of godliness in the primitive church ? The
simple gospel, as it was preached by Christ and the
Apostles, was obscured by admixtures of human speculations, especially the theories of the Platonic philosophy. Instead of Christ crucified, the *subtilties* of the
*schools* gradually came to occupy the pulpit. Sermons

were moulded on the elaborate precepts of Grecian
oratory.  The spirit of piety was supplanted by love of
novelty, and by the vagrant dreaming of mystical theology, founded on the grossest perversion of the sacred
oracles.  What was the consequence?  When this wide
door was opened,. Pelagianism and Arianism rushed in,
like a flood, upon the church.

Now let any honest man, acquainted with history, be.
put to answer the question, who were the great moral
luminaries that beamed upon the world,  through seasons
of intervening  darkness? and he cannot fail to name
such champions of the evangelical faith, as Athanasius,
Ambrose, Augustine, Chrysostom ; afterwards, Bernard,
Huss, Jerome of Prague, Wickliffe; and the constella-
tion of illustrious reformers, in the time of Luther.  I
need scarcely add, that the state of the church in later
periods confirms the same sentiment.

# LECTURE XVIII.

## GENERAL CHARACTERISTICS OF SERMONS.

In the foregoing lecture, I endeavoured to show that
from the nature of the case, and from the actual state of
facts in the history of the church, we have no reason to
expect the blessing of God, on any preaching but that
which is distinctly *evangelical*. But other things are
requisite to constitute a good sermon, and I shall now
consider, at some length,

A SECOND, *general characteristic of a good sermon,
which is, that* IT MUST BE INSTRUCTIVE.

For the sake of method, I shall inquire,

1. WHAT THINGS ARE REQUISITE *to render a sermon
instructive.*

1. In the first place, then, I say it must have a *subject that is important ;* a subject that spreads before the
hearers some serious truth to be believed, or duty to be
done, or danger to be avoided. So obvious is this principle, that to dwell on it, or even to mention it, would
seem superfluous, were it not that many a discourse
has been preached, in which it is apparently the object
of the preacher, not so much to enlighten his hearers, as
to any one thing to be believed, or done, or avoided, as
to fill up the time allotted to a sermon. It by no means
follows that a sermon *is a good one*, because you can
state in a word, or in a short sentence, that it is on the

subject of repentance, or faith, or humility; but it certainly follows that it is *not* a good one, if neither they who hear it, nor he who delivers it, can tell concisely what is its subject. I have heretofore adverted to the common mistake of young preachers, in selecting such general subjects as ' the vanity of the world,' ' the universal desire of happiness,' &c. on which a man of genius and of experience, might indeed give to an assembly many profitable instructions, but to do which would cost him three times as much reflection, as would be requisite to preach well on some specific point of faith or practice.

The apprehension that, on a subject of the latter kind, the stock of materials for a regular discourse would be too soon exhausted, often leads him who has little skill in sermonizing, to select a subject of so much scope that he might nearly as well have no subject. .

But whether the subject be general or specific, it should be *important*. For a man who is commissioned to preach the everlasting gospel, to pass over all those topics which involve the highest interests of his hearers, and gravely to instruct them from the pulpit, on points critical, speculative, or merely curious, is ' to prostitute his noble office.' Such topics may procure a temporary reputation to himself, while he only amuses his hearers at the expense of their souls. Bishop Wilkins, who was a judicious adviser in these matters, says,—' Avoid all subjects that would *divert* the hearers, without *instructing* them. Never consult your fancy in this case, but the necessities of your flock. I would rather send away the hearers smiting on their breasts, than please the most learned audience with a fine sermon. By discussing useless questions, and things above their capacities, we too often perplex those whom we should interest. There is. a great deal of difference between their admiring the preacher, and being edified by his sermons.'

2. *A sermon to be instructive, must be* PERSPICUOUS IN METHOD AND LANGUAGE.

On the advantages and kinds of *divisions* proper in discourses from the pulpit, and the principles by which such divisions should be conducted, I have expressed my views at large in discussing the structure of sermons. I will only add in this connexion, that to give instruction, at least to common minds, without a good degree of lucid arrangement in the things taught, is quite impossible. That such arrangement should prevail in a sermon, is just as important, I must repeat, as that the hearers should understand that sermon, and remember it. For assuredly, unless they can follow the preacher step by step, in some intelligible train of thought, they will understand nothing, and of course remember nothing, to any valuable purpose ; in other words, they will gain no instruction.

That the *language* of a sermon should be intelligible, is so plainly essential to its being instructive, that no enlargement on this head is called for, except to refer you to observations which I have made on style, and to those which I shall have occasion to make on the indefinite and the direct manner in preaching. Like Paul, " I would rather speak five words in the church, with my understanding, that I might teach others also, than ten thousand words in an unknown tongue."

3. *That a sermon may be instructive,* IT MUST BE RICH IN MATTER.

Want of matter in a sermon, from whatever cause the deficiency may arise, diminishes its value to the hearers, in point of instruction. If the difficulty arises from want of native talent in the preacher, if he is destitute of

inventive power, there is no remedy. Precepts and
study may do something, but the stamp of barrenness
will be fixed on all the labours of such a mind. If it
arises not from want of intellectual *capacity*, but of intellectual *cultivation* in the preacher; in other words, if his
discourses are barren of instruction, because he has himself a scanty stock of acquired knowledge, the remedy
lies in *study*  A mind invigorated and replenished by
habits of reflection and reading, will impart its own
character to all its efforts. That the stream may be
abundant and unfailing, it must flow from a fountain
that is inexhaustible. When I speak of acquired knowledge, I mean to express the deliberate opinion, that no
man who does not, according to the direction of St. Paul,
" give himself to *reading*," can be a profitable preacher
to the same audience for any considerable time. Reliance on mere intellectual powers, to the neglect of
reading, will leave even a superior mind unfurnished with
all that store of knowledge which the progress of ages
has accumulated in books, and in books only. Besides,
the mind that has no fellowship with the world of
cotemporary minds, and of minds that have stamped
their impress on the books of past periods, such a mind,
vigorous though it may be, will lose its own elasticity.
To sustain the intellectual powers, and keep them in
readiness for action, both the *information* and the *impulse*
derived from reading are necessary : but to a mind
already well furnished, doubtless the primary advantage
of books, is their aid in rousing its own energies. Of
course, he who is called to instruct others from the
pulpit, must not merely *have been* a man of reading, he
must *read still*, while he preaches, or his sermons will be
trite and barren in thought.

I would urge every candidate for the sacred office, to

K

form, as early as possible, the habit of reading and thinking, *as a preacher*. Let all his intellectual exercises acquire this cast, and have general reference to this one grand business of his life. The painter, the sculptor, the architect, the military chief, who has professional enthusiasm, each will see in every object around him those relations to his own favourite pursuit, which are unobserved by other men. So should the preacher see with the eyes of his own profession; and when his mind goes abroad in intercourse with the external world, with men and books, it should be to bring home stores adapted for use in his business as a Christian Instructor. This will give to his sermons a richness and variety of matter, that will make them eminently useful.[1]

It may be added in passing, that such a systematical classification of a man's knowledge, especially his know-

---

[1] In respect to the point under consideration, it is of incalculable advantage to the preacher, early to adopt the habit of *classification* in his reading. Let him keep a blank-book, consisting of materials for sermons, in which he will insert, with proper heads and arrangement, the most important *subjects* on which he will have occasion to preach. I do not mean a *plan* book;—that is another affair, to be kept by itself. Under each of these subjects, let him enter some brief notice, not a transcript of passages, but a *brief notice* of what is most striking in any writer that he reads, with reference to *author*, and *page*, and *edition* too, when the book is not his own. This will never become voluminous, like the cumbrous Common Place books used for transcribing entire pages, to which practice there are insuperable objections. A quarto blank book of two hundred pages, will perhaps serve a man for life, and in a few years will become such an index of his own reading, as will enable him to avail himself, in one hour, of what he has been reading for years; and often on a given subject, will, in a few moments, put him in possession of materials for which he might otherwise search a long time, and perhaps search in vain. The *alphabetical* order for such a blank-book, is probably the best, allowing the greatest space to the most important letters.

ledge derived from books, will store his mind with *facts ;*
and give him the *power of illustration,* the want of which
will certainly make a dull preacher.

But in aiming to render sermons rich in matter, that
they may be instructive, two mistakes are to be avoided.
The first is, a *sweeping generality,* which aims to bring
the *whole system of religion into one sermon.* After
what I have already said on this point, I advert to it
here, only to remark, that discourses constructed in this
manner, instead of being rich and various in matter, are
usually distinguished for barrenness of thought. The
other mistake consists in attempting *perpetual novelty*
of matter. The former mistake commonly results from
*dulness,* the latter from *affectation.* The same sun
shines in the firmament, and the same Bible is the light
of the moral world from age to age. In regard to merely
human opinions or rules of conduct, eccentricity and
caprice are to be expected. But the prominent truths
of revealed religion, like their author, are immutable.
The same God, and Redeemer, and Sanctifier—the same
way of salvation too, are to be preached now, as were
preached by prophets and apostles. What was the example of St. Paul, as to originality and variety? Did
he deem it necessary to preach *new* doctrines in every
sermon? So far from this, he urged and reiterated the
same essential points of faith and practice, again and
again, on those whom he addressed. Just the same did
the other Apostles. Hear what Peter said to those who
had been under his instruction. " I will not be negligent
to put you always in remembrance of these things, though
ye *know* them, and be *established in the present truth."*
Nay, it was his design, not only to render these truths
familiar to his hearers, while he taught them, but so to
impress them on their minds, by frequent repetition, that

they should never be forgotten. " I will endeavour that ye may be able, after my decease, to have these things always in remembrance." So men are taught by the instructions of Providence; and so, I need not scruple to say, they have been taught, from the pulpit, by the most skilful preachers, in all ages.

But where, it may be said, on these principles, lies the room for variety and richness of matter? It lies in the endless scope for *illustration*, by which the preacher of competent powers has opportunity to present the truths of the gospel, in aspects and relations so diversified, that while the *same* truths are taught, over and over, the hearers see them in new lights, and with eager interest stretch forward in knowledge.

Is not the book of providence various, rich, beautiful, and even sublime in its instructions? Yet the sun travels the same path through the heavens, and the seasons preserve their order. Regularity and repetition, in the natural world, fix impression; so that uniformity in its laws, is the basis of knowledge. If every fact in the kingdom of nature should occur but once, and the course of events should be a succession of ab-solute *novelties*, experience could not be the ground of foresight, the lessons of providence would convey no valuable instruction to men, and the business of the world must cease. The same principles apply to the instructions of the pulpit. They need not be tame and barren of interest, because they often dwell on the same great truths of religion. On the contrary, the man who, from affectation of constant novelty, should teach his hearers the doctrine of *atonement*, for example, but once in his life, might as well never have mentioned it at all.

4. *That a sermon may be instructive,* ITS MATERIALS

SHOULD GENERALLY BE THROWN INTO THE FORM
OF DISCUSSION, IN DISTINCTION FROM THE DESUL-
TORY MANNER.

My remarks on this topic will be brief, as partly
superseded by those already made on *Argument in
Sermons*.   There is indeed a dry, technical mode of discussing subjects, which gives a logical air to a discourse,
but which wearies rather than instructs the hearers.   The
formality of propositions and corollaries, is not at all the
thing that I am recommending.   But it is incumbent on
the preacher to give his hearers substantial *reasons* for
that which he urges on them, as a matter of faith or
duty.   The Senator, or the advocate at the bar, when
he speaks, aims to establish some point by reasoning.
Why should a Christian discourse be a mere declamatory
harangue, not aiming to establish the truth of any thing,
or to make any definite impression ?   Will it be said
that, in the eloquence of the senate and the forum,
argumentation is indispensable, because men will not act
till they are enlightened and convinced ; but that, in the
sanctuary, the main object is to produce excitement and
warmth ?  Of what *value* is that warmth, which is produced by the mere vociferation of a declaimer, and
which vanishes, when the sound of his voice ceases ?
In my opinion, one of the greatest calamities that can
befal a congregation, is to be placed under the ministry of a
man who never discusses any subject in a regular manner,
nor attempts to prove any thing, from reason and scripture, but gives his hearers declamation, instead of
Christian instruction.   Such sermons, if strictly *unpremeditated*, are more likely perhaps to have occasional
flashes of vigour and vivacity, than if *precomposed*, in
*the extemporary and desultory* mode of writing.  In either
case, they will utterly fail of *instructing* the hearers.

5. *That sermons may be instructive,* THEY MUST EX-
HIBIT DIVINE TRUTH IN ITS CONNEXIONS.

Men in general spontaneously read and think very
little on religious subjects. What they know of the
gospel, they learn more from the pulpit, than from all
other sources. No one sermon can contain the whole
of Christianity; yet Christianity *is a connected, consistent whole,* which must be exhibited in parts; and no
part can be fully understood, except in its relations to
the rest. In every art or science, as I have before remarked, there are fixed principles, which are to be
learned distinctly, but which are inseparably related to
each other. A knowledge of that art or science, is a
knowledge of each part, and of its relative bearing on
other parts. One principle of geometry, detached from
the rest, signifies nothing;—the whole taken together
constitute a perfect science. The wheels of a clock,
viewed apart from the whole machinery, would apparently have no design; and any one of these wheels,
indeed, if formed by the artist without regarding its
adaptation to the rest, would be altogether useless. So
it is in the system of religious doctrines; any one of
these dissevered from its connection with the rest, may
be so distorted, that it virtually ceases to be true. It
is true in the connection in which the Bible has placed
it; but apart from that connection it is liable to be
*misunderstood,* and to have all the influence of falsehood.

To preach the gospel *instructively* then, is to preach
all its parts, especially its essential parts; and to preach
them in their symmetrical relation to one harmonious,
connected scheme of religion. This will prevent that
' inconsistency which runs through the whole course of
some men's preaching, who not only contradict in one
discourse, what they have said in another, but say and

unsay the same things, in the same discourse.' The amount of my meaning is, that no single truth of the gospel can be adequately taught from the pulpit, without being taught in its connections with the general scope of revealed religion; and the result is, that partial and superficial preaching, is not *instructive* preaching, Men may hear sermons through a whole life, which inculcate no falsehood, but on the contrary exhibit, in a detached way, one principle after another of true religion, and yet these hearers may never acquire an adequate knowledge of any one doctrine of the Bible.

The foregoing are some of the principal qualities of sermons, necessary to render them *instructive*.

# LECTURE XIX.

I shall proceed now,

II. *To look at* THE REASONS *why it ought to be a prominent object with a Christian preacher* TO RENDER HIS SERMONS INSTRUCTIVE.

1. That this *is his duty may be inferred* FROM THE CONSTITUTION OF THE HUMAN MIND. The service which God requires of men is a *reasonable* service. All the laws of his moral kingdom are adapted to the condition of intelligent, moral agents. This kingdom is a kingdom of *motives ;* and no action can possess a moral nature, except as it results from *intelligence* and *purpose* in the mind of the agent. The understanding therefore, is that leading faculty of the soul to which motives are addressed ; and through which their influence bears on the heart, and conscience, and affections. Whatever emotion or action can be produced, without any intelligent, voluntary purpose in the agent, must be as destitute of moral qualities as are the actions of a maniac, or the ebbing and flowing of the tide. But if men are so made as to be influenced by motives, and this influence can operate only through the medium of light and conviction addressed to the understanding, then the sermon that communicates no *instruction* is useless, not being adapted to the constitution of the human mind.

2. *That the Christian preacher should aim to render*

*his sermons instructive*, IS EVIDENT FROM THE NATURE
OF THE GOSPEL. What is the gospel? It is a system
of evangelical truth; a stupendous scheme of mercy, the
great design of which is to sanctify men through the
truth. The sword of the Spirit, by which only the
enmity of the human heart is slain, and the moral temper
is renovated, is the word of God. But how can divine truth
operate so as to enlighten the conscience, and sanctify
the heart, unless it is distinctly *presented to the mind*? If
evangelical belief might exist, without a knowledge of
God and the Saviour, why should the gospel be preached
at all? Most evidently when God sanctifies a human
heart, it is through the truth, and the truth so presented
to the mind as to be *perceived* and *understood*.

What is the gospel? I say farther, it is a system of
*practical* truths; in other words, a system of truths on
which is predicated a system of *duties*. The end of faith
is practice. Hence the Bible attaches importance to
each truth which it reveals, just in proportion to the influence which that truth is adapted to exert over the
heart and life. It exhibits no single doctrine as a matter
of dry speculation, without reference to its bearing on
the affections and the conduct. But it is only an *intelligent view* of truth that can exert the influence of which I
am speaking. The gospel, for example, requires me to
*repent*. Why do I need intellectual light for this?
What *is* it to repent? It is to hate my own sins, as
being the transgression of a perfect law. How then can
I repent, without a *knowledge* of my own sins, and of the
law that I have broken? The gospel enjoins *faith* in Christ
as a divine and all-sufficient Saviour. But how can I
believe in him without knowing that I *need* a Saviour,
and that he is *such* a Saviour as I need? The gospel
enjoins *prayer;* but how can I pray acceptably to a

God, of whose character and will I have no just conceptions? Ignorance may be the mother of such devotion as was offered to Diana of the Ephesians, or the unknown God of the Athenians; but the worship which the only true God will accept, is rational and spiritual. It requires that the *understanding*, as well as the affections should be employed. Short of this, whatever has the semblance of Christian devotion, is as unmeaning as the ablutions of the Hindoo, or the sacrifices at Mars Hill.

3. *That the Christian preacher should aim to render his sermons instructive, is evident from the best* EXAMPLES *of preaching.*

And here I appeal at once to the great Teacher who came from God, the perfect pattern of all other teachers. When he entered on his ministry, false religions had enveloped the world in darkness. A thousand errors had overspread even the *Jewish* church. His great object was to dissipate these errors, and to enlighten men in the knowledge of true religion. Take his sermon on the mount, for example, and it is a continued series of *instructions*, given on most important subjects. Take the whole current of his public discourses, as recorded by the evangelists, and as the basis of them all, you find the fundamental truths of the gospel inculcated. Among these I can barely mention, without enlargement, the distinct personality in unity, of the Father, Son, and Holy Ghost; his own real divinity; the doctrine of vicarious atonement, as the only ground of forgiveness; the necessity to all men, of regeneration by the Spirit of God, on account of their entire moral depravity; the necessity of repentance and faith, to salvation; the present and everlasting happiness of all true believers; and the eternal punishment of final unbelievers. As Christ committed nothing to writing himself, one of two things is unquestionable; we must rely with absolute confidence, on the men whom he inspired to preach and to write his gospel,—or we have *no gospel now*. If we do rely on these men, the proof from the Evangelists, the Acts, and the Epistles, that Christ did preach the above doctrines, stands on one and the same footing of authority; and that proof is complete. It is the evidence of testimony; the same by which we know that the Apostles themselves preached the same system of truths. That they did so, you may see in St. Peter's preaching on the day of Pentecost;—in St. Paul's at Antioch, at Athens, at Corinth; in short, throughout the whole course of their ministrations. The very end for which they were' commissioned was to "*teach* all nations," the religion of Christ. And in all subsequent ages, those who have been worthy successors of the Apostles, have been *instructive* preachers. In short, if the great end of the Christian ministry is to save sinners, by bringing them to embrace the truth, then preachers of every age, who have sought to amuse their hearers, by appeals to the fancy, or to excite them, by appeals to the passions, without *instructing* them in the great truths of the gospel, have utterly failed in their duty, as guides to souls; and are not fit to be reckoned as examples of good preaching. This leads to my next topic of remark;

4. *That the obligation of ministers to be instructive in their sermons, is evident from the best* EFFECTS *of preaching in the conversion of sinners.*

It is a fair inference from principles already established, that any system of preaching, which leaves men unacquainted with the vital truths of the gospel, leaves them without hope, and without God in the world. I shall of course be understood to speak of those who are

ignorant of the above truths to such a *degree* as is inconsistent with the exercise of Christian graces; and also
of those who have both capacity and opportunity to
receive instruction; in distinction from the case of infants
and idiots, and perhaps of individual exceptions, which
divine grace may make among the heathen. But in
respect to men of full understanding in a Christian land,
I suppose it is self-evident, that no one can be in a state
of salvation, without doing what the gospel requires; and
that no one can *do* this, without *knowing* what the gospel
requires. Ignorance of the gospel, therefore, to the extent
supposed, must be in such a case criminal and fatal.

A *human* statute-book that should professedly tolerate
in subjects a deliberate and voluntary ignorance of its
own enactments, would be stamped with absurdity. To
suppose then that *God* has given the *gospel*, with all the
requisite means for understanding it correctly, and yet
that they may be *innocent or safe* in utter *ignorance* of
the truths and duties it reveals, is to suppose that the
great Lawgiver trifles with the subjects of his moral
government, and encourages them to trample on all its
obligations. But woe to that man who, as an ambassador of Christ, proceeds on such an assumption as this!
While he fails to give his hearers evangelical instruction,
the effect of his ministrations is not to save, but to
destroy their souls. Let him look to it, how he shall
meet the reckoning that awaits him in the day of final
retribution.

But in this case as in others, the tendency of moral
causes is to be estimated from the effects which they
actually produce. On this principle let the question be,
what sort of preaching *does* God most frequently bless
to the conversion of sinners?—and the answer will be
found most conclusively in the history of the church.

# LECTURE XX.

On the general requisites to render preaching *instructive,* and the reasons why it ought to be so, I have purposely dwelt at considerable length. So fundamental, however, to the work of the Christian preacher, is the duty of communicating instruction, that the discussion on which I am next to enter, will exhibit, not so much a distinct subject, as an amplification of the foregoing, or a presentation of it under different aspects.

*I proceed then to a* THIRD *general characteristic required in a sermon, namely,* DIRECTNESS. My meaning is, that it should be *explicit,* both in doctrine and execution. It has been well said, that, ' A man who walks directly, though slowly, towards his journey's end, will reach it sooner than his neighbour, who runs into every crooked turning, or loiters to gaze at trifles, or to gather flowers by the way-side.'

I will consider what constitutes directness in preaching, and then inquire why preaching so often fails of possessing this character.

I. WHAT CONSTITUTES DIRECTNESS IN PREACH-ING ? *It consists in such an exhibition of a subject, that the hearers not only understand it,* BUT PERCEIVE IT TO BE PERTINENT AND IMPORTANT TO THEMSELVES.

If I stretch my hand towards a man at a distance, no sensation is produced in him by the movement, for I have not reached him.   But if I approach him, and lay my hand on him, he instantly perceives that he is touched.   So if I only preach *towards* a man, without reaching him, he feels nothing;   but if I bring divine truth into direct contact with his mind, he instantly feels the contact.   He is a complex being.   He has an understanding—he has a conscience—he has passions. If the sermon bears on his understanding, he feels it;   if it bears on his conscience, he feels it;   if it bears on his passions, he feels it.   Of course, if it does not touch him any where, he has no spontaneous feeling that it was meant for him.

Now, in some important respects, all men are alike. In strength and cultivation of intellect there is indeed great disparity;   but every man has a conscience, emotions, passions.   A hundred men, therefore, under the same sermon may each one feel that it is as well adapted to his own case, as though it were designed for him only. But a sermon to produce this impression, must do two things;   it must clearly present to the hearers some subject, which they see to be true and important;   and show them its adaptation to their own case.   My meaning may be illustrated by an unerring example.

*Our blessed Lord was unquestionably a direct preacher.* It was just in the way above described, that the humbling truths contained in his sermon at Nazareth, roused the prejudices of the hearers, so that they were " filled with wrath;" and that his parable of the vineyard in another case made the Jews angry, when " they perceived that he had spoken the parable against them."   How did they *know* that he meant them ?   He had not *named* them;  had not preferred any accusation against them. Yet he *did* mean them; and purposely drew such a representation, that their consciences could not fail of

making the application to their own case.   Christ knew
what was in man.   He compelled his hearers to feel that,
with the eye of omniscience, he looked directly into
every bosom, and saw what was passing there.   It was
impossible that they should not feel thus, when he
answered, as he often did, to their " inward thoughts,"
while those thoughts had not been expressed at all in
words.   Hence it was that the woman of Samaria said
to her friends, " come see a man, who told me all things
that ever I did."   Hence the men who brought to Christ
a woman, alleging against her a heavy criminal accusation, were struck dumb with confusion, by a direct appeal
to their own bosoms—" He that is without sin among
you, let him first cast a stone at her."   Silently they
, withdrew, one by one, being " convinced by their own
conscience."

Hence also, the young man who was very rich, and
who came to Christ inquiring, what shall I do, that I
may inherit eternal life, was thrown into agitation by the
simple reply, " Sell all that thou hast, and give to the
poor, and come follow me."   Nor was this a random
stroke ; for the bolt was directed with unerring aim, to
smite down the reigning idol of his heart.   Nay this
great Teacher from God sometimes assailed his hearers,
by forms of address still more explicit and direct, than
any that I have mentioned—" Wo unto you, Scribes and
Pharisees, hypocrites—Ye serpents ! ye generation of
vipers ! how can ye escape the damnation of hell."   So
he sometimes directly applied the language of consolation —" Son, be of good cheer."   " Daughter, go in
peace."

Nothing short of omniscience, or at least inspiration,
could authorize any one to use this sort of directness in
addressing men.   But still, every preacher of good

common sense, and tolerable acquaintance with human character, may, if he chooses to do so, find direct access to the hearts of his hearers. To this principle I have before adverted, when considering the *conclusion of sermons*, by showing how the agency of *conscience* is to be employed, in making the application of divine truth. It was involved too, in discussing the special interest excited by that preaching which is strictly evangelical, in distinction from that which is not. The principle implies, you will observe, that while no individual designation is made by the preacher, the exhibition of truth is so skilfully adapted to the hearer, that he feels *himself* to be as really addressed, as though he were called by name.

One more illustration of my meaning will be sufficient. Suppose yourself to be one among a crowded audience, listening to a sermon from some powerful and *direct* preacher on the *omnipresence of God*. The subject is a general one, yet its exhibition is such, that the truth comes home to each hearer, with a solemn intensity and individuality, from which there is no escape. ' God sees me,' is the one, all-absorbing thought of each mind. As the sermon proceeds, it tears away every covering, and demolishes every refuge of sin. The adulterer, who locked his door, and ' waited for the twilight, saying, no eye shall see me,' trembles, when he comes to feel that *God was there*. The thief, who said, " surely the darkness shall cover me," trembles when he comes to think of that omniscient eye, which beheld the deed of guilt; and to hear that voice which seems to echo from the judgment seat, " Can any hide himself in secret, that I shall not see him ? " The man who defrauded his neighbour by direct falsehood or skilful deception ; the hypocrite, who assumed the mask of religion, to further his purposes of iniquity; the votary of avarice, ambition or sensuality, who supposed that the lurking abominations of his heart were known only to himself; each of these as the preacher goes on to exhibit an omnipresent, heart-searching God, finds himself stripped of all disguise, and standing naked amid the all-pervading light of truth. Nay, before the sermon is finished, the summons of the last trump sounds in his ears; he is arraigned at the bar of God; the books are opened; the secrets of all hearts are revealed; the righteous are adjudged to everlasting life, and the wicked to shame and everlasting contempt.

Why is it that under a sermon, skilfully conducted, on this *general.* subject, every hearer, who has a conscience, feels the hand of the preacher, pressing heavily on *himself?* Just because the *subject* is one, not of empty speculation, but of awful and universal interest; and because the truth is so exhibited, that every one must feel its adaptation to his *own* case. This is *directness* in preaching.

The way is now prepared to inquire in the

II. *Place, what are the* CAUSES *which produce* THE INDEFINITE AND INDIRECT *sort of preaching?*

Among these causes, I would reckon the following.

1. WANT OF INTELLECTUAL PRECISION IN THE SPEAKER. When the *native structure* of a man's mind is so heavy, as to impart a character of imbecility to its movements, a correspondent indistinctness attends all his mental operations. As the sun behind a cloud, is to be seen but occasionally and obscurely, so the thoughts of this man are wanting in distinctness and vividness of impression.

Or the difficulty may lie in the *habits* of his mind, when there is no fault in its structure. If he has not

been accustomed to systematic thinking ; or if he under-
takes to discuss a particular subject, to which he has
given no time for reading and reflection, his sermon, as a
copy of his own mind, will convey no distinct instruction
to the minds of others.

Such a preacher will make no thorough discrimination
of characters.  He will deal in *general* positions, which
all perhaps will admit to be true, but which no one will
appropriate to himself.  Suppose he makes the broad
statement, *that all men are sinners,* and does this clearly.
Not one of his hearers, perhaps, disputes this ;  and yet
not one *applies it to his own character.*  The sermon
may go still further, and divide the hearers into two
general classes, saints and sinners, and yet lead no one
to make the solemn inquiry, ' To which class do I
belong ? '  A single colour of the painter indiscriminately
spread over canvass may be very proper for certain
purposes, but no one mistakes such a painting for the
likeness of a human being.  So the sermon that consists
of generalities, without any exact delineation of character, awakens no vivid interest ;  it leads no hearer to
say, ' *that means me.*'

But suppose farther, that the preacher, besides the
general classification of his hearers into saints and sinners,
goes on to show that the former will be happy and the
latter miserable ;  while he makes no intelligible discrimination between the two classes ;  will any conscience
be disturbed by that sermon ?  The grand inquiry remains,—*what is a saint?*—*what is a sinner?*  To say
that one loves God and the other does not, is a true
answer, but too general.  Among real Christians there is
great diversity of character, arising from diversity of
*doctrinal views, intellectual temperament, attainments
and habits.*  One is inclined to ultra-Calvinism, another

to the opposite extreme.   One is strong and clear in his reasoning powers, another feeble and obscure.   One has made much advance in knowledge, another little.   One is judicious, another indiscreet; one ardent, another phlegmatic; one gentle, another austere; one scrupulous, another sanguine and rash.

And there is a corresponding difference in *spiritual characteristics*.   One is a fervent, watchful Christian; another, lukewarm and negligent.   One is cheerful, another melancholy; one growing, another declining; one looks only at the state of the heart, another is strenuous for names and forms; one has too much a religion of opinion, another too much a religion of passion; one carries to extreme his conformity to the world,—another his seclusion and austerity.

Among *unconverted sinners*, too, we find great diversity.   To one the influence of instruction and example in childhood has been salutary, to another pernicious; one has been trained up in the school of Christ, another in the school of Satan; one is orthodox in belief, another sceptical; one is solemn and anxious, another a careless neglecter, or hardened despiser of religion; one is addicted to prodigality, another to parsimony; one to an ostentatious gaiety and grossness of sinful indulgence, another to sullen and solitary wickedness.

But the indefinite preaching which I condemn *amalgamates* all impenitent men, under one sweeping term *sinners*, without any adaptation of truth to the great *variety* existing among these as to age, temper, intellect, knowledge, and convictions.   It may undertake to describe the character of a sinner, and draw the picture of a demon; or on the other extreme, may represent this sinner as possessing a great preponderance of moral excellences.

Let the same preacher attempt to describe a saint, by exhibiting the separate graces of the Christian character, and here too, all is loose and declamatory. Does he speak of religious joy ?—it is ecstasy ; of contrition ?—it is melancholy ; of deadness to the world ?—it is monkish austerity ;—of submission ?—it is stoical apathy, as to temporal calamities, and as to spiritual, it is an arbitrary test of character, which puts asunder what God has joined together, holiness and heaven. Every delineation of a true Christian, which he attempts, is overdrawn. The standard of duty he confounds with the measure of actual attainment ; and thus makes sanctification, as it exists in this life, to imply perfect conformity to God. He paints a Christian ; and it is the likeness of an angel, rather than that of any imperfect son or daughter of Adam. No real saint, certainly, would presume to apply the character to himself.

Now all this confusion in sermons, may arise from want of clear, accurate habits of thinking in the preacher.

# LECTURE XXI.

2. *Indefinite preaching may arise in part from* FALSE TASTE IN THE PREACHER.

Under the foregoing head, I referred to want of logical exactness; here I refer to deficiency in rhetorical skill. The former fault lies in the *thought*, the latter in the *expression*. St. Paul says, ' And even things without life, giving sound, whether pipe or harp, except they give a *distinction* in the sounds, how shall it be known what is piped or harped? For if the *trumpet* give an *uncertain* sound, who shall prepare himself to the battle? So likewise ye, except ye utter by the tongue, words easy to be understood, how shall it be known what is spoken? for ye shall speak into the air. There are, it may be, so many kinds of voices in the world, and none of them are without signification. Therefore, if I know not the *meaning* of the voice, I shall be unto him that speaketh, a barbarian, and he that speaketh shall be a barbarian unto me."

It is by no means my intention here to consider those various qualities of style, which contribute to perspicuity; nor yet to show how strength is injured by needless accumulation of words, and complexity of structure. My object is rather to exhibit that *generality* in the choice of terms, and the formation of sentences, which is the opposite of simplicity and directness in style. This may result from a habit, unconsciously contracted by reading some writer of imposing celebrity, who has many redeeming excellences, amid great faults. Or it may arise from a designed and affected *imitation* of such a writer. The fault may be that the sentences of this writer are too *periodic*, the members being accumulated to excess, and artificially adjusted to the purpose of rotundity and cadence. Or they may be too much constructed on the principle of the *loose sentence*, in which one thought after another, is hung on by way of appendage to the principal thought, so as to form one long, obscure sentence, out of materials sufficient to constitute five or ten sentences.

But aside from rhetorical structure, there is a kind of indefinite style, which may be called a *factitious simplicity*, in which the terms employed are all intelligible, and well arranged, but so *general* as to cast an air of obscurity over the meaning. Examples of this sort abound in the published discourses of a modern divine, who, by the fascinations of his genius, his high reputation, and the drapery of peculiar diction in which he clothes his thoughts, is more likely to vitiate by his influence, the style of young preachers, than any other living model.

The same thoughts which Baxter would have expressed with unstudied brevity and directness, he expresses by a periphrastic generality. For example,— the former would say, perhaps, of two men, that 'they were intimate friends,'—the latter would say, 'they were united in the affectionateness of intimate companionship.' The former would describe the believer's conquest, by 'conformity to God;' the latter would describe it, as 'the overcoming of his passions, by the attemperament of his affections to the divine image.' The former would say, 'This is the character of all men;'

the latter, 'this is the character of the world's population.' The former would say, 'sincerity,'—the latter,
'incorruptible truthfulness;'—the former, 'he was in-
dignant,'—the latter, 'a feeling of indignancy came
over him;' the former, 'his heart was stung with remorse,'—the latter, 'with unutterable painfulness, the
feeling of remorse came over him.'

There is, it must be confessed, in the fault I am
describing, an apparent aim to depart from the customary
phraseology of the best writers ; but affectation of peculiarity is not the main difficulty. Instead of a clear,
terse, compact style, there is, in the formation of sentences, a loose *generality*, as to words and members.
Instead of a meaning specific and obvious, so expressed
that you see instantly and exactly what it is, you see
it *indistinctly*, as you see the moon through a dense mist.

Would the time permit, I might properly apply the
foregoing principles to the use of *figures* in style, the
purpose of which is often frustrated by indistinctness.
The painter would deserve little credit, who should
draw the likeness of a man, so as not to be distinguish-
able from that of an elephant. In *language*, it is a
maxim of universal application, that vivacity of impression depends on the precision and speciality of the terms
employed. Change Milton's description of Satan's
shield, which ' hung on his shoulders like the *moon*,' to
this form, 'it hung on his shoulders like a *luminous body*,'
and the figure is ruined. And the bold comparison of
the prophet, "The mountains skipped like rams, and the
little hills like lambs," would be divested entirely of its
picturesque character, if transformed into ' they moved
like animals.' A figure may be so *general* as to express
no resemblance to any thing, and therefore be much less
intensive than a plain word.

Such are the ways in which the preacher, through bad taste, may be so indefinite in phraseology, that, while his sentiments and spirit are altogether good, he may make no distinct impression on his hearers.

3. *Indefinite preaching may arise from* CONSTI-TUTIONAL DELICACY OF TEMPERAMENT IN THE PREACHER. He may be wanting in boldness to utter sentiments which he believes to be true and important.

There is, I am aware, a spurious boldness which is neither conducive to the usefulness of a Christian preacher, nor creditable in any respect to his character. There is a courage which consists in *rashness*, which pushes on at random, without regard to time, or place, or occasion; which sets at defiance the rules of discretion, and often of decorum. Sometimes it is mere *rusticity*, which falls on the most offensive manner of doing and saying things from ignorance of what is becoming. Sometimes it is an *affected fidelity* which *chooses to give offence;* and makes a merit of provoking hostility to the truth by the form of its exhibition. Sometimes it is native *asperity* or *obstinacy*, which regards all respect for the feelings of others, and all kindness of manner, as pusillanimity. A man of this description may be a very lucid and direct, and yet a very *unprofitable preacher;* for it may be easy to understand him, but hard to love him, or to love the truth, which he clothes with so repulsive an aspect.

But there is another extreme. The preacher, through an amiable delicacy of temper, may shrink from the explicit declaration of truths which he apprehends would awaken inquietude in his hearers. He is reluctant to inflict *pain* on others.

' He supposes too much in his hearers, the existence of the qualities which the Bible labors to beget. He speaks commonly in *general* terms; deals much in the

*impersonal verb*, much in the *third person*. The man
of mild temper will naturally, in addressing an audience,
take refuge in general terms, abstract truths, impersonal
verbs, third persons, and the mixture of general applause
to the mass, with the measured condemnation of individuals. Nevertheless, such mildness has no prototype
in the scriptures ; nor is it consonant to the dictates of
enlightened humanity. We do not warn the man whose
house is on fire, by the abstract assurance that ' fire is
dangerous ; ' by introducing a third person, and saying,
' *he* is in danger ; '—by adverting to those noble public
institutions, the fire insurance companies. Nor must the
delegated apostle of Christianity fail to discriminate, to
individualize, to strike home, to draw the line betwixt the
form and spirit of religion ; to show that the best church
cannot of itself sanctify those who enter it ; ' to speak,'
as old Baxter says, ' like a dying man to dying men ;
to warn, rebuke, exhort,' like one who expects to meet
his congregation next at the bar of God.' [1]

4. *Indefinite preaching may arise from the* ABSOLUTE
WANT OF PIETY, OR FROM A LOW STATE OF PIETY,
*in the preacher*. In the latter case, while his personal
religion is barely sufficient to secure his own salvation,
his preaching will do little to promote the salvation of
his hearers. The man whose governing principle is *love
to Christ*, and who solemnly believes that his hearers
must repent or perish, will speak in demonstration of the
Spirit and with power, because he *means to be understood*.

But suppose the man to be influenced by supreme love
to *himself*,—how will he preach ? Perhaps he entered
the ministry as a *mere profession*, to gain his living by it.
Will he then incur the risk of alienating his hearers, by

---

[1] Christian Observer.

L

an explicit declaration of divine truth ; No,—he does not *mean* to preach the gospel, so as to be understood.

Perhaps he is ambitious of distinction, as a man of learning and taste. Among his hearers, he numbers families, wealthy, polite, intelligent, fastidious ;—whose refined sensibilities would be shocked at the faithful portrait of their own character as sinners, and the awful retribution that awaits them hereafter. Something of Christian truth they are willing to hear from the pulpit, if it is adapted to their fancy by elegance of costume, and makes no stirring appeal to their conscience. But can the man, whose chief object is popular applause, be expected to sacrifice the favour of these worldly hearers, by preaching the gospel in a manner so direct as to be profitable to the poor and ignorant ? It is no part of his *design* to carry the truth home with power to the conscience ;—he does not *mean* to be understood.

A man who wishes to impress on other minds that which deeply interests his own, will easily find words suited to his purpose. Does the starving beggar address you with studied amplification, so as to leave you in doubt as to his object? He comes to the point at once, and asks for *bread*. Does the general in the heat of battle, when all is at stake on a single charge, seek out the recondite terms of philosophy, or the embellishments of rhetoric, in addressing his army ? No,—his language is brief and direct :—' On, comrades, on ! ' Just so the preacher, who firmly believes the message of the gospel, and solemnly feels its everlasting importance to his hearers, will deliver this message *plainly*, like a man in earnest. So did John the Baptist. He knew that his life was in danger from the sanguinary temper of Herod. But he was charged from heaven with a message of rebuke to that guilty man, and he did not scruple to

deliver it.   When John preached *generally*, Herod
' heard him gladly ; ' but when the fearless stroke was
aimed at the conscience of that licentious king, ' it is
not lawful for thee to have thy brother's wife,' he
beheaded the preacher.

Let love to *God* and *to souls*, and the solemn anticipation of meeting his hearers at the judgment, be predominant in a man's heart, and this will strip off from
his sermons all the drapery of concealment and artificial
ornament, and lead him to a plain downright searching
exhibition of divine truth, which will make his hearers'
hearts burn within them.

But let the love of *himself* be the ruling principle,
and this will probably give to his preaching some of
those forms of generality, which will frustrate all its
salutary effects.   Perhaps it will transmute what should
be a Christian sermon, into a frigid essay.   The course
of thought, with the careful avoidance of all divisions,
or obvious arrangement of any sort, flows on in the uninterrupted succession of sentences, constructed perhaps
by the nicest rules of art; but when the discourse is
ended, nothing is proved : no conviction, no light, no
excitement is given, or was meant to be given to any
mind.   Hence it is, that outrageously immoral men
often listen to such exhibitions from the pulpit, with no
inquietude ; or if any throb of conscience is felt, re-
tiring from the sanctuary, they forget what manner of
persons they are.   A general approbation of what is
right, or condemnation of what is wrong, may have
been awakened, but it is all as the parable of Nathan
to David would have been, without the application,
" Thou art the man."

Preachers, defective in piety, may use evangelical
terms, as *sin, repentance, atonement, sanctification,* and

yet preach no single doctrine of the gospel clearly. They often adopt a phraseology, so guarded and general, as not to disturb the most fastidious contemner of the gospel. Where Christ would say, " He that believeth not shall be damned,"—they speak of the ' sanctions of Christianity.' Where this divine Teacher would say, " Ye must be born again,"—they inculcate the ' importance of moral reformation.' Where Paul would say, " The carnal mind is enmity against God," they speak of ' the lapsed state of man.' Where he would inculcate " holiness,"—they descant on ' the moral fitness of things, and the beauty of virtue.'

Such sermons have no tendency to instruct the ignorant, nor to alarm the careless, nor to accomplish any one purpose of Christian preaching. The advocate who should speak to a jury, in language so indefinite, as purposely to make no distinct impression on their minds, while his client is on trial for his life, would scarcely be employed again, in any cause of magnitude. The physician, who should seem to believe that there is no such thing as dangerous disease among men; or who should barely talk of the benefits of health, to one in a burning fever ; or prescribe some palliative to a man in the consumption, and the same to a man in the dropsy, would be thought, as Baxter says, ' a sort of civil murderer.'

Why then should he who ministers to souls, trifle with his sacred charge? Why speak *obscurely*, when the truth to be uttered, is *clear as the light of heaven*, and the motives to *declare it plainly*, are *momentous as eternity ?*

# LECTURE XXII.

## GENERAL CHARACTERISTICS OF SERMONS.

THERE remains one more topic, under the general head of indefinite preaching, which it seems necessary to expand, so much as to make it the chief subject of the present lecture. I proceed then to say,

5. *That indefinite preaching may arise from* WRONG THEORY IN THE PREACHER, AS TO THE BEST MODE OF EXHIBITING DIVINE TRUTH.

This may occur, perhaps, in a given case; not because there is any obvious deficiency of taste or discrimination, or boldness, or piety, in the dispenser of the sacred oracles; but because he honestly believes, that men are less likely to be converted, under a direct and explicit declaration of Christian doctrines, than under one that is more cautious and qualified.

The principle assumed, to express it briefly, is this; that religious truth, to produce any saving effect on men, must operate according to the philosophy of the human mind; and that to exhibit this truth in such a manner that the effect to awaken opposition in the hearers, is of course to harden their hearts, and confirm them in impenitence. The assumption is, in other words, that men are predisposed to embrace the truth if it is skilfully exhibited; and that when they are excited to feelings of opposition, this must be owing to some fault in the preacher. After the remarks which I have already made on that point, no one will understand me as justifying a studied repul-

siveness of manner in the pulpit. But I regard the
theory just mentioned, though it is embraced by some
good and able preachers, as wrong in principle, and as
inconsistent both with the Bible and with facts.

Fully to show this might lead to a discussion more
extended than is consistent with my present object, which
is to suggest only those thoughts that have a direct
bearing on the point in hand.

*In the* FIRST *place, the Bible represents unsanctified
men as predisposed,* NOT TO RECEIVE AND LOVE THE
TRUTH, BUT TO HATE AND OPPOSE IT. Every such
man is an enemy to God. In proof of this I will cite
but one text as a specimen of the concurrent testimony
of the sacred oracles; " The carnal mind is enmity
against God." To say that this refers only to Jews or
to men of one age, is to trifle with the plain import of
language ; for it clearly applies to men universally of all
ages. Hence a special renovation by the Holy Spirit is
also taught in the Bible, as universally necessary to
qualify men for heaven ; because by nature they have no
holiness, and never would have any if left to themselves.

Every such man loves *himself* supremely, and is therefore opposed to the law, which requires him to love God
supremely. He loves sin, and is therefore opposed to
the law, which requires him to be holy, and threatens
him with death for every transgression. He loves tranquillity in his unbelief, and is therefore opposed to the
alarming denunciation of the Gospel, " he that believeth
not shall be damned." He is proud; and therefore is
opposed to that whole system of truth, by which " the
loftiness of men is bowed down, and the haughtiness of
men is made low, and the Lord alone is exalted."
Accordingly this system of truths, when not disguised
or explained away by preachers, has been, like the sect

of the Nazarenes, ' every where spoken against.'   And can it be, notwithstanding all this evidence as to the native temper of the human heart, that it is predisposed to love the gospel, if properly exhibited; and that all its opposition to the truth, arises from the preacher's want of skill in presenting the system of Christian doctrines, according to the laws of intellectual philosophy ?

*In the* SECOND *place, such a theory of preaching* HAS NO COUNTENANCE FROM THE PUBLIC' MINISTRY OF CHRIST.   He did not represent men as predisposed to love God, so soon as they should see his *true* character, for this true character was the very thing which they *hated.*   " Ye have both seen and hated both me and my Father."   " This is the condemnation, that light is come into the world, and men love darkness, rather than light." When hatred arises from intellectual misapprehension, light will remove it ; when it arises from the state of the heart, light will increase it.   I mean that while the heart hates the true character of God, clearer views of that character do not produce love, but more hatred. If the opposition of sinners to God were only an intellectual mistake, if it were only opposition to a *false* character of God, it could not be criminal, for every false character of God *ought* to be opposed.   But the difficulty with sinners in Isaiah's time, was not an intellectual one; " A deceived *heart* turned them aside." Just so it was in the time of Christ.   If his hearers only needed to have the truth skilfully set before them, to love it, why did they often bitterly complain under his sermons ?   Did not Christ know how to preach his own gospel ?   Was it want of acquaintance with the human heart, or of skill in adapting his instructions to the real condition of men, which led him so to exhibit the doctrine of divine sovereignty at Nazareth, that " the whole

synagogue were filled with indignation?" Suppose
that this great Teacher had conformed to the theory that
the gospel must be so preached, as not to be repulsive to
depraved hearts, the scornful and malignant opposition
that was waged against him, he would indeed have
escaped. Why? Just because he would have given
men a system of religion at once adapted to please their
pride, and to leave them without remedy and without
hope in their alienation from God. He knew that the
only way to save lost sinners, was to show them that
they were lost; and to make them feel their awful guilt
and danger. But this he could not do, without disturb-
ing the enmity of their carnal minds.

In the THIRD place, the theory that the gospel, when
properly preached, finds the unsanctified heart predisposed to embrace it, IS CONTRARY TO THE GENERAL
EVIDENCE OF FACTS.

From the ministry of its divine Founder to the present
time, the gospel has fought its way against the pride, and
prejudice, and unbelief of this same human heart, arrayed
in a thousand forms of inveterate hostility to oppose its
progress. Indeed, that this religion, in its primitive
purity, should have maintained an *existence* on earth, in
the face of so much opposition, and notwithstanding so
many motives operating on its teachers to disguise its
truths, and neutralize its character, is owing merely to
the shield of omnipotence, interposed for its protection.

To the maxim then,—*that to repel the human heart is
not the way to convert it, I reply by another maxim;—
that to appease the enmity of the heart, by accommodating
the gospel to its taste, is not the way to convert it;* but
is the direct way to frustrate the saving influence of
divine truth, and to fix men in hopeless rejection of it.
Paradoxical as it may seem to unbelief, it ought to be

no mystery to the Christian teacher, that those search‑ing, humbling truths, which inflict agony on the sinner's conscience, are the only means of his deliverance from spiritual death. So thought the great physician of souls. To those diseased with sin, he did not scruple to admi‑nister bitter medicines. And shall we imagine *ourselves* more merciful and skilful than *Christ*, while we leave untouched the deadly malady of the soul, because we choose to accommodate our prescriptions to the wishes of those who are utterly ignorant of their disease as sinners, and of the only remedy provided in the gospel?

Suppose that St. Paul, when he was going to Corinth, could have been addressed by some adept in intellectual philosophy, and told, 'it is preposterous for you to preach the doctrine of Christ crucified in that refined city. This doctrine is "to the Jews a stumbling block, and to the Greeks foolishness."' He would have said, — 'I know it, but this same doctrine is, notwithstanding, the wisdom of God, and the power of God unto salva‑tion. Your maxim of modifying the gospel, lest it should *repel* the sinful heart, would bind over the world to despair.'

Suppose you were called to devise the best method of converting *infidels* to Christianity;—would you pre‑sent it to them as it came from Christ? or as accom‑modated by a philosophical theory to their prejudices? Dr. Priestley tried this latter experiment,—fully expect‑ing that Jews and philosophical unbelievers would em‑brace what he called a *rational* Christianity. What was the result? The Jews believed, not that Christianity is true, but that Dr. Priestley was no consistent Christian. And he very candidly acknowledging the disappointment of his own hopes, said, 'I do not know that my book has converted a single unbeliever.'

Or suppose you were sent as a missionary to the heathen; would you modify the gospel, so that they might think it coincident with their own superstitions? That they might be induced to take on them the Christian name, would you amalgamate their faith with yours? This experiment, too, has been tried. The Romish missionaries in China, acting on the genuine theory of their master Loyola, carried out the plan of converting the heathen by accommodation. ' They gave up the main things in which Christians and heathens had been accustomed to differ, and allowed the Chinese every favourite species of idolatry. The consequence was, they had a great many converts such as they were; but thinking people looked upon the missionaries as more converted to heathenism, than the heathen to Christianity.[1]

I have thus imperfectly fulfilled the task which 1 assigned to myself in several preceding lectures, designed to exhibit the general characteristics of a good sermon. The first characteristic, which I stated to be indispensable in a sermon, is, that it be *evangelical.* After showing what this implies, I urged the importance of it from the twofold consideration, that no other than the evangelical system fully brought out in sermons, is *adapted* to accomplish the great *end* of preaching; and that in point of *fact,* no other ever *has accomplished* this end.

The next characteristic of a good sermon is, that it be *instructive;* namely, that it have an *important subject;* that it be *perspicuous* in method and language; that it be *rich in matter;* that it have the form of *discussion* rather than that of *declamation;* and that it exhibit divine truth in its *connexions.*

That a Christian sermon ought to be instructive,

---

[1] Fuller's Works, II. 38.

appears from the *constitution of the human mind ;*—from the *nature of the gospel ;*—from the best *examples,* and the best *effects* of preaching ;—and from the tendency of instructive preaching, and of this only, to *promote* the *unity* and *strength* of the church.

The third characteristic of a good sermon is *directness.* What this implies is illustrated from the preaching of Christ. The causes which produce the *indefinite* and *indirect* sort of preaching, are,— *Want of intellectual precision in the preacher ;—false taste in the preacher ;— constitutional delicacy of temperament in the preacher ; — and absolute want of piety, or a low state of piety.*

The topics on which I have thus expressed my thoughts at full length, I regard as of vital importance to the interests of religion.   Doubtless the real gospel may be preached so technically, or paradoxically, or controversially, or with such an air of ostentatious fidelity, as to frustrate its proper effects.   But preachers of the present day are unquestionably more in danger of erring on the side of *cautious reserve,* than of *indiscretion,* in exhibiting Christian doctrines.

# LECTURE XXIII.

## ON THE CULTIVATION OF SPIRITUAL HABITS, AND PROGRESS IN STUDY.

*[Addressed to the Students at Andover, November, 1831.]*

THE brevity with which I am compelled to treat the subject of personal religion, at this time, is not to be understood as implying that I regard its importance as secondary to that of any other subject. On the contrary, I am persuaded that whatever else you may possess or acquire, without the love of God shed abroad in your hearts by the Holy Ghost, you cannot be qualified to preach the gospel ;—nay, in the attempt to do it, you would probably become a burden on the church, and a reproach to the ministry. [1] But as my chief object lies in another direction, I cannot enlarge on the importance

---

[1] We must indeed work, like Nehemiah and his men, with the trowel in one hand and the sword in the other. We have to build and to fight at the same time, and with incessant employment. The progress of the work would be stopped by the laying down of the trowel. The enemy would gain a temporary advantage by the sheathing of the sword. Nothing therefore remains but to maintain the posture of resistance in dependance upon him who is our wise Master-builder, and the Captain of our salvation—waiting for our rest, our crown, our home.—BRIDGES.

Magnum opus omnino et arduum conamur ; sed nihil difficile amanti puto. CICERO.

The eloquent author of the Reformed Pastor, having spoken of Paul's charge to the Elders at Ephesus, says ;

of personal religion in ministers, nor even touch many interesting branches of the subject, which demand the solemn and often-repeated consideration of theological students. In this division of the Lecture, I shall remark only on one point, THE IMPORTANCE OF THE SPIRITUAL HABITS WHICH YOU FORM.

According to a settled law of our minds, habits are formed by the periodical recurrence of the same thing. Even in those habits which are called passive, regular reiteration stamps impression. No man forgets that there is a sun, or doubts his return to-morrow ; but if there were no *regularity* in the succession of day and night, no *order* in the seasons,—there could be no *experience*, and the business of the world must cease. When a man's habit of dining at a particular hour becomes fixed, it is of little absolute importance whether it is early or late ; but if that hour is *changed* continually, so as to be early one day and late another, he has *no habit;* and is liable to suffer both in comfort and health.

By the influence of custom, things laborious or irksome

---

' O brethren, write it on your study doors, or set it as your copy in capital letters still before your eyes. Could we but well learn two or three lines of it, what preachers should we be! Write all this upon your hearts, and it will do yourselves and the Church more good than twenty years' study of those lower things, which, though they get you greater applause in the world, yet separated from this, will make you but sounding brass and tinkling cymbals.' BAXTER.

' Qui cupit juxta Paulum esse διδακτικος, det operam ut prius sit Θεοδιδακτος, i. e. Divinitus edoctus.' ERASMUS.

' None but he who made the world can make a Minister of the Gospel. If a young man has capacity, culture and application may make him a scholar, a philosopher, or an orator ; but a true minister must have certain principles, motives, feelings, and aims, which no industry nor endeavours of men can either acquire or communicate. They must be given from above, or they cannot be received.'

NEWTON.

become tolerable and even pleasant; things apparently impossible become easy;—things trifling or indifferent become important.  A man of twenty may with little trouble change his room, his bed, his chair;—he breaks up no habit: but to a man of eighty the change would be a real inconvenience.

Now, to apply these illustrations.  The man who imagines that he can perform his secret devotions in the *street*, as well as in his *closet*, or as well without as with *stated times* for the purpose, is ignorant of his own mind. Intellectual and spiritual, as well as other habits, are formed on the principles of association.  In the regular recurrence of the thing to be done, there must be identity of *time*, and *place*, and *circumstances*.  He who assigns to his closet devotions a particular season, will find the return of that season bring with it the recollection of the duty; so that the omission of it at the customary time will be attended with mental uneasiness.  His avocations too will regularly become adjusted to this settled order, so as not to intrude on his hours of communion with God.  But the man who waits for *impulses*, and goes to his closet only at irregular times, has no advantage of *habit* in this duty.  He attends to it without constancy, without preparation, without enjoyment.  He has no current of spiritual feeling; other engagements thrust themselves between him and God; the day and the night pass away, without any season of retirement; he forgets to pray, because he has no *system* in the care of his own heart.  Thus perhaps he slides into estrangement from his closet for days and weeks together.

There is no point in Christian experience more settled than this, that there is an intimate connexion between *enjoyment* in closet devotions, and *their return at regular seasons*.  The best writers on the subject say so.  Devout Christians, learned and unlearned, say so. Our own experience says so.

If you would form such spiritual habits then as shall promote your progress in personal religion, draw a sacred enclosure around your hallowed seasons of retirement, to preserve them from interruption. To accomplish this, your *times* of secret devotion should be so chosen as not to interfere with *other duties:* 1 mean such duties as *stated, social devotions, exercise, voluntary associations,* and *study.* Your chief danger, probably, will be found under the last particular. For the sake of study, especially when hard pressed, you will be liable sometimes to attempt a compromise with conscience, for the neglect of your closet. The Christian merchant, mechanic, or farmer, knows that such a compromise, for the sake of mere *secular* business, would be *sinful:* but the Christian student, all whose business is sacred, may more easily fall into this temptation. Take care then that no pressure of study shall become an apology for omitting your regular devotions. Whenever you feel inclined to waver on this point, take care lest your spiritual habits be utterly supplanted. Think of Daniel, prime minister of Persia, with the affairs of one hundred and twenty provinces resting on his mind, yet finding time to go ‘ into his chamber three times a day, that he might pray and give thanks to God.’ Think of Alfred, encompassed with the cares of monarchy; of Luther, buffeted by the storms of Papal wrath ; of Thornton, encompassed with a thousand mercantile engagements, yet never allowing the hurry of business to intrude on their regular hours of devotion.

Next to *regularity* in spiritual habits, I would urge *consistency.* The most nutritious food would not preserve him in health, who should mingle with it daily, a

little portion of some deadly drug.   So the man who is
regular in his devotions, but is accustomed to violate his
conscience in other things; such as remissness in observing the sanctity of the sabbath; indulgence of colloquial
habits, that cherish levity and  frivolity of temper;
unkind and censorious remarks respecting his brethren;
or any other practice that is decidedly wrong, may have
some grace, perhaps, notwithstanding these inconsistencies, but he will not *grow* in grace.

*Vigilant and faithful self-inspection* is also indispensable.   Without this you may be a backslider, and may
have been so for months, and yet not be aware of your
condition.   Doubtless there is in our profession, from the
peculiar relations which we sustain  to those around us, a
lamentable tendency to live upon some old hope, taking
it for granted that we are Christians, without sufficient
daily evidence that it is so.   In this way probably not a
few, whose profession and business it has been to promote
the salvation of others, will fail of salvation themselves.
Constant vigilance too is necessary to theological students, in sustaining their spiritual habits, from the fact
that they have so much to do with the *theory* of religion,
and the investigation of speculative difficulties; that they
study and talk about the  Bible as a  class-book; study
for the ultimate benefit of others,  not the  direct benefit
of themselves.   Hence they are liable to rest in an
*intellectual* religion in distinction from the simple piety
of plain Christians.

Again, the success of a theological student in culti-
vating spiritual habits, depends much on the *helps to*
*devotional feeling*[1] *which he employs*.   For this end,
besides the stated reading of the Scriptures in the *common*

---

[1] Note (16.)

*version*, which will be less likely than the originals to induce philological inquiries, I would urge the daily reading more or less of the best devotional books.

I have room to glance only at one more particular ; as to the formation of spiritual habits, namely, *the motives by which you are governed*, in theological studies. Just so far as you " walk with God" in the closet, you will have an abiding sense of his presence through the day, controlling and sanctifying all your pursuits. You will feel your dependence upon God, and study with a view to his glory, and thus will make such arrangement of duties, that your time will turn to the best account. But if you *neglect* your closet, God will gradually be supplanted in your affections, by undue regard to *self*. Some form of unhallowed ambition will gain possession of your heart, will lead to undue reliance for usefulness, upon your own genius or acquisitions ; and set up as the chief object of your studies, an ultimate regard to your own reputation or interest or influence, and not to the glory of God. [1]

---

[1] 'The solidly-learned, the studious, and well-furnished man is but the unshapen mass from which the Christian minister is formed. The plastic energy—the quickening influence of the Almighty Spirit is still needed to put light, life, and motion, into the inert substance ; to mould it into his image, and to make it a " vessel of honour, meet for the Master's use." Nor must it be denied, that these studious habits, to which we have attributed considerable importance, are attended with proportionate temptations. Any enlargement of intellectual knowledge has a natural tendency to add fuel to the fire of our self-importance. The habit of study growing into a passion, may crave indulgence at the expense of conscience or propriety, by pre-occupying the time that belongs to duties of equal moment. Much, however, of apprehended danger will be repelled by the regulation of a sound judgment, and a spiritual mind, in directing these studies to the main end of the ministry. A minister should remember that himself with all his studies is consecrated to the service of the sanc-

But I must proceed to the other branch of this Lecture, namely, PROGRESS IN STUDY, on which my remarks must be more extended.

When St. Paul says to Timothy that a bishop should not be a *novice*, there is a figurative allusion in the original word, that is very significant. Literally the expression is, " not an infant." It denotes that want of knowledge or skill which we see in a new born child, that would certainly fail of success, if set to accomplish any work requiring the strength and intelligence of a man. There is a secondary sense too, that is scarcely less pertinent. It refers to a tree or plant recently set in the earth, which has not had time to become *rooted*, and is easily disturbed by the wind or any external violence. The meaning is, that a Christian minister ought not only to be mature in religious experience, but to have a sound, well-furnished understanding. Both these requisites he needs, lest being inflated with pride, he fall into the condemnation of the devil. That stability of character which can resist temptation, and qualify a man to be a guide in the church, must come from fixed religious opinions, grounded on a thorough acquaintance with divine truth. The apostle, that he might be certainly

tuary. Let every thing be done therefore with a view to one great end. Let all the rest of our knowledge be like lines drawn from the vast circumference of universal nature, pointing to that divine centre, God and religion.'—BRIDGES.

' Not to read or study at all, is to tempt God; and to do nothing but study, is to forget the ministry ; to study, only to glory in one's knowledge is a shameful vanity: to study in search of the means to flatter sinners, a deplorable prevarication; but to store one's mind with the knowledge proper to the saints by study and by prayer, and to diffuse that knowledge in solid instructions, and practical *exhortations*,—this is to be a prudent, zealous, and laborious Minister.'

QUESNEL..

understood on this subject, often exhorts Timothy to
diligence in reading, and meditation, and study of the
Scriptures, the great store-house of divine knowledge;
through which the minister might become furnished for
his work.

In remarking on this subject then, I would advance no
theories that are extravagant, none that are new—none
indeed that are not sanctioned by apostolic authority.
Let any man (if in this age of light there is any man,
who advocates the cause of clerical ignorance,) read the
epistles to Timothy and Titus, and then answer this plain
question; did a teacher of religion, who had the gift of
inspiration to understand the scriptures, and the gift of
tongues to preach—a teacher too, born amid the scenery
and customs described in the Bible, and familiar with the
language in which important parts of it were written—
did he need the aid of study to qualify him for his work?
and can a man, who has not one of all these advantages,
be qualified for the same work, *without* study?   How is
he to know what is in the Bible, till he has *studied* the
Bible? and how can he *study the Bible,* so as to have,
concerning what is peculiar in its language, local allusions
and usages, the knowledge requisite for a public teacher,
without much reading of *other* books?

Now the positions which I would take to show the
connexion between *intellectual furniture* and *success* in a
minister are these four;—a man must have *knowledge*
himself, before he can teach others;—he must have
*capacity* to learn, before he can acquire knowledge; he
must have *time* to learn; and he must have *instruction.*
The first is self-evident.  The second admits no diversity
of opinion, except as to the *degree* of native talent,
which is necessary to a minister.  Concerning this too,
all will agree thus far, that the highest powers of genius

may find ample scope in this work; and that on the other hand, decided weakness of intellect is a disqualification. *Good sense he must have;* but brilliant powers are by no means indispensable.

It is self-evident too, that he must have *time* to learn, before he can hope for success in his work. Common sense decides so, in regard to *all* acquisitions which are to be made by *study*. In the first schools of Europe, established for the two great professions, law and medicine, the period of study is *three, four,* and in some cases, *five* years, superadded to an academical education. In the same departments, three years of professional study is made a legal requisite in different parts of our own country. But is the care of men's *immortal* interests a business that demands less maturity of preparation than that of their *bodies* or *estates?* Is the interpretation of the sacred oracles, and the preaching of the everlasting gospel, so trifling an affair, that it may be safely left to any novice who chooses to undertake it? Plainly, he cannot be a successful teacher in the church of God, who has not had *time* to learn. The knowledge that he needs is to be gained, not by intuition, not by inspiration, not by any ' royal road,' but by patient long-continued study. Solomon has told him all the secret of gaining this knowledge; he must *dig* for it as for hidden treasures.[1]

---

[1] ' If knowledge is not to be despised, then it will follow that the means of obtaining it are not to be neglected, viz. study; and that this is of great use in order to a preparation for publicly instructing others. And though having the heart full of the powerful influences of the Spirit of God, may at some times enable persons to speak profitably, yea, very excellently without study, yet this will not warrant us needlessly to cast ourselves down from the pinnacle of the temple, depending upon it, that the angel of the Lord will bear

Need I add that he must have *instruction?* Not a
few young men of bright promise, who might have become champions of the truth, have been so impatient to
hasten into the ministry, that they have fatally blighted
their own prospects; and instead of attaining to distinguished success, have scarcely reached the point of
mediocrity. The minister now, whose maxim is to expect little things, and attempt little things, mistakes the
day in which he lives. What was *knowledge* in the
thirteenth century, is *ignorance* now. What was *energy*
then, is *imbecility* and *stupidity* now. As was said in
another case, it becomes not our sacred profession in this
period of intellectual progress, to remain like the ship
that is moored to its station, only to mark the rapidity
of the current that is sweeping by. Let the intelligence
of the age outstrip us and leave us behind, and religion
would sink, with its teachers into insignificance. Ignorance cannot wield this intelligence. Give to the church
a feeble ministry, and the world breaks from your hold ;
your main spring of moral influence is gone.

Would you then become burning and shining lights in
the church of God, study—indefatigable, systematic
study, is essential to the attainment of your object.

us up, and keep us from dashing our foot against a stone, when there
is another way to go down, though it be not so quick.'—EDWARDS.

' How few read enough to stock their minds ? and the mind is no
widow's cruise, which fills with knowledge as fast as we empty it.
Why should a clergyman labour less than a barrister ? since in spiritual things, as well as temporal, it is " the hand of the diligent which
maketh rich." '—BICKERSTETH.

# APPENDIX.

## I.

### ON THE DELIVERY OF SERMONS.

#### BY THE EDITOR.

ONE of the most important subjects connected with preaching, which Dr. Porter has omitted to notice in his Lectures, is that which relates to the *delivery* of sermons. The Editor is by no means insensible to the indifference which is frequently attached by preachers themselves to the manner in which they deliver their discourses from the pulpit: but when he has noticed the effect produced by the preaching of such individuals, however distinguished for their piety, their zeal, or their talents, he has generally perceived symptoms of inattention, and a want of interest in their discourses, on the part of their congregations. It is mortifying indeed to think how many excellent sermons, fraught with wisdom, and piety, with depth of argument, and beauty of style, are vainly scattered, as it were, to the winds, every Sabbath in the year, for want of that attention to their delivery from the pulpit, which alone can ensure the attention of the hearers. It is quite irrelevant to plead the doctrine of human corruption, and the alienation of the

natural heart from God, and thus to account for the
inattention of a congregation. That corruption and that
alienation remain precisely the same, whether they are
addressed in a lively, natural, energetic manner, or in a
manner exactly the reverse : but whilst in the latter
case they will generally be found inattentive and indifferent, in the former they will appear to be interested
and alive to the subject. God works by ' means,' and
generally by the means best adapted to the end. He
makes use of the talents with which he endows his ministering servants ; and if of the talent of *composing*, why not
of the equally important talent of *delivering* a discourse ?
" Faith comes by hearing, and hearing by the word of
God. But how shall they hear without a preacher,"
who studies to make himself heard, and to deliver his
message in a manner calculated at once to awaken and
rivet their attention ?

The Editor would here premise that many of the
following observations should be reduced to practice,
if possible, *before* the sacred student assumes the character and station of a preacher. It is with *delivery* as with
*composition*, there should be previous discipline and
preparation. As in the one case the style should be
already formed so as to require little or no attention from
the writer, whilst expressing his thoughts on paper, so
in the other, a happy and vigorous species of elocution,
should be attained before the preacher ascends the
pulpit, where he must become absorbed at once with
the grandeur and importance of his subject. It happens,
however, in numerous instances, that young men enter
on the work of the ministry without having had their
attention at all directed to this subject, and in consequence not only feel a considerable embarrassment in the
pulpit, but frequently fall into an unnatural, and to say

the least, an uninteresting manner of addressing their audience.

Unhappily the study of elocution is not only unprovided for in the preparatory exercises of candidates for orders, but even labours under a considerable degree of reproach which it by no means deserves. Hence it has become almost a proverb, that ' the English Clergy are the best writers of sermons, and the worst readers of them in all Christendom.' This censure is doubtless much exaggerated, as antithetical proverbs usually are : yet it is very certain that our country is not remarkable for general eloquence, and that in the Church it is less visible than either in the Senate or at the Bar. Much of the disesteem in which the cultivation of this useful talent is held, arises from a false supposition that by eloquence is meant an affected and artificial manner of speaking : or, what is worse, the mere trick of ' making the worse appear the better reason,' by the blandishments of a meretricious oratory. From such eloquence may we ever be preserved ! But the eloquence which arises from an appropriate unsophisticated mode of speaking—and which not merely tunes the organ of speech to an agreeable modulation, but allows the speaker to follow the dictates of nature in reciting energetically what he feels strongly—deserves to be assiduously cultivated.

But another current, and far more weighty objection to the cultivation of just elocution by young men intended for the sacred profession, is, that it is inconsistent with the simplicity and sincerity of their vocation as ministers of Christ. St. Paul is often quoted as an authority to decide this question : and because he abjured " the enticing words of man's wisdom," and " determined to know nothing among men but Jesus Christ, and him

M

crucified ; " it is argued, that the rules of forcible composition and just enunciation are unbecoming the study
of a Christian teacher ?   But it is very clear, that the
reprobation expressed by the apostle was levelled at that
spurious oratory which prevailed both among the Greeks
and the Romans at the time when he wrote, and has
nothing to do with a sober view of the present question.
Many of the classic rhetoricians, it is well known, taught
little else than dialectic subtilty and sophistry : too
often they instructed their pupils how to speak either for
or against a question, without any reference to truth or
moral feeling ; and were content with the triumph of
their art, independently of any valuable end to be obtained by its exertion.   It was against *such* practices
that the great apostle of the Gentiles so zealously
remonstrated.   Very different was his own style of
eloquence, " not with wisdom of words," but " in
demonstration of the Spirit and of power."   Yet who
was a greater master of *true* eloquence?   Who knew
better how to ' convince and persuade ? '   ' Who felt his
subject more deeply, or knew how to convey his conceptions more forcibly to others ? ' [1]

But whilst the Editor feels the importance of directing
the attention of the young preacher to a subject too
frequently neglected and contemned by those whom it
chiefly concerns, he almost shrinks from the delicate and
difficult task of offering suitable direction and advice.
It is in vain, however, to wish that the task had fallen
into abler hands, and that the grave *propounder* had been
at the same time, the successful *exemplar* of his rules.
He cannot pretend to construct any new system of instruction, or to enter into any elaborate discussion.   The

---

[1] Wilkes's Correlative Claims.

utmost at which he aims, is to offer a few practical
directions which occur to him as the result of his reading, his observation of other preachers, and his own
experience during a ministry of nearly twenty years
standing.

The first direction which he would suggest is of a
preliminary, but most important character, viz. *that
pains should be taken to acquire the art, and cultivate
the habit of* READING WELL.

To read in silence so as to understand the meaning of
an author, and thereby to increase our intellectual stores
is one thing ; to read aloud so as to unfold that meaning,
and communicate that knowledge to our hearers with
perspicuity and force is another. The former is an
attainment which is almost universal—the latter is possessed by comparatively few. But whilst the number
who can aspire to read remarkably well, involving as it
does a rare combination of physical and mental qualifications, will always be small, there is no room for
discouragement. Between mediocrity and perfection,
there is a wide interval, in which various degrees of
excellence may be attained by the diligent and observant
student. There are not wanting many valuable treatises
on the art, among which may be specially mentioned
those of Sheridan and Walker. But written rules alone
will not suffice : there must be added the example of a
' living voice.' Let the young student then notice and
remember the manner in which a good reader proceeds.

Let him mark the distinctness of his articulation, the
propriety of his emphasis, the correctness of his pronunciation, the ease and force with which he completes
every sentence which drops from his lips. Then, if he
possesses a tolerable ear, he will be able to enter with
intelligence and interest into the written directions of the

rhetorician. A considerable part of the task of learning to read well, will be found to consist in *unlearning* to read *ill*. Bad habits, begun probably in the nursery, increased at school, and perpetuated at the University, are like a threefold cord, not easily broken. Before, indeed, the attempt can be made, the individual must become acquainted with his own peculiar faults. Let him seek then to have them pointed out to him whilst he is young—whilst his organs of speech are pliable, and his habits have not yet assumed the character of a second nature.

With this view he should request some judicious friend to remind him from time to time of any impropriety into which he may fall when he reads before him in public or in private. ' Tell me,' he should say, ' not only when I fail to convey to you the true meaning of my author, but every instance in which I pronounce a word improperly, or lay a false emphasis. Mark also my tones and inflexions, my pauses, and pitch of voice, and fail not to apprize me in every instance of what appears unnatural, or stiff, or feeble, or affected.' His friend's compliance with such requests as these will prove, perhaps at first, a source of considerable surprize, if not of some little mortification ; for, strange as it may scem, whilst few men read well, there are still fewer who think they read ill : and none are commonly so unconscious of their imperfections as those in whom they most abound. But let him not be discouraged by the long catalogue which may be presented to him of his rhetorical delinquencies : ' to understand the disease is more than half the cure.' Let him proceed at once to the necessary task of eradicating every fault which has been pointed out to him, and of supplying every defect. By the exercise of vigilant self-inspection and persevering efforts, in compliance with the rules of some well written work on Elocution, he will, in all probability, soon acquire the ability to read comparatively well.

But let him not suppose when he has arrived at a considerable measure of excellence in the art of *reading*, that he has nothing more to acquire with a view to pulpit delivery. True, it is an important, not to say, indispensable preliminary; but it is *only* a preliminary. Reading is not preaching. A sermon may be read from the pulpit with much propriety and correctness—there may be no false quantities, nor provincial accents, nor erroneous emphasis—the tones may be agreeable, the inflexions correct, the harmony of every sentence carefully preserved—and yet after all, the sermon may not have been *preached*, it may not have conveyed for one moment the idea suggested by the term employed by our Lord and his apostles, κηρυγμα, a proclamation, a message of importance from a Sovereign to his people. The distinction is not between the delivery of *written* and *unwritten* discourses, but between the mere *reading* of a written sermon, and the *preaching* of a written sermon. An *ex-temporary* discourse may be as remote from preaching, as the tamest and most uninteresting reading of one previously composed: for if there be no life-stirring sympathy between the words and affections of the speaker, it is at best but the cold essay of a fluent tongue. The preacher is a κηρυξ—an ambassador, a herald; and he bears with him tidings in which he is most deeply and intimately concerned in common with those to whom he announces them; hence, whether his sermon be written or unwritten, he *preaches* it—he proclaims it—he publishes it abroad with corresponding life and energy. There is, in short, a *reality* in the matter to which mere reading, however excellent or even faultless, cannot attain. The preacher must convey his discourse, not from his manuscript merely, nor from the tablet of a retentive memory, but from an enlightened and approving understanding—from a heart warm with love to him from whom he receives the tidings, and to those to whom he conveys them. With this view he should make special preparation for the pulpit every time he is called upon to enter it. It is not enough that he prepare a suitable *discourse* whether written or unwritten ; he must prepare *himself* also to deliver it in a suitable manner. He should endeavour, in the first place, to make himself perfectly familiar with what he has written, by reading it over several times, and so far to fix it in his memory, as to free himself from that slavish dependence upon his manuscript, which would keep his eye continually fixed upon its pages.

In the next place he should endeavour to get his heart deeply interested in the truths which he is thus prepared to promulgate : he should ' mark, learn, and inwardly digest them,' with a view to his own spiritual edification. He should adopt, in short, the laudable practice of Philip Henry, who invariably preached every sermon to himself in private, before he ventured to preach it in public to his congregation.

It is scarcely necessary perhaps to add, in the third place, that *devout prayer* for the special blessing of God to accompany his efforts should always precede his entrance into the pulpit. The uniform experience of Christian Ministers goes to prove the truth of the testimony " benè prædicasse est benè orasse." Of many of the most eminent preachers whose lives have been handed down to posterity, it is recorded that they loved to pass at once from the closet to the pulpit—from pleading with God to pleading with immortal souls.

Thus prepared, as it respects both himself and his subject, he may humbly but confidently rely on the blessing of God, and enter the pulpit in the spirit of one commissioned from on high to " stand between the living and the dead." And there let him again lift up his heart in ejaculatory prayer during the few moments which precede the announcement of his text, that he may be freed from that " fear of man which bringeth a snare " and from that love of human praise which would marr the costliest offering which could be presented to an omniscient and heart-searching God.

In the announcement of his text, the preacher should be deliberate and distinct; and in a similar manner he should, for the most part, commence his sermon. There should be a sensible pause also between the announcement of the text and the opening of the discourse, not only for the purpose of giving time to the congregation to refer to the passage in the sacred volume, but also to avoid all appearance of precipitancy and haste. Few things indeed are more important to be guarded against at the commencement of a sermon than an agitated or hurried manner, for nothing tends more effectually to raise in the minds of the audience a suspicion that there is no depth of feeling, or of thought in the preacher—that his object is rather to get through his sermon than to enlighten their understandings or affect their hearts. He should both be, and *appear* to be, deeply impressed with the importance of his subject, and should enter upon it in a calm and becoming manner.

Much of this hurried appearance is doubtless to be attributed to a constitutional nervousness of temperament; but in most cases it may be effectually overcome by persevering efforts. Self-possession, though natural to some, may to a certain degree be attained by all. The best spiritual remedy is that suggested by Mr. Cecil, who was wont to say, 'that a realizing sense of the divine presence would annihilate a large congregation, and ennoble a small one.'

During the exordium, the pitch of his voice should be rather lower than that which is to characterize the rest of the sermon ; only let him take care to be sufficiently loud to be distinctly heard by the whole of the assembly. This is the more necessary to be observed inasmuch as the voice has a natural tendency to rise to a higher pitch as the speaker proceeds with his discourse.

And here it may be remarked, that much of the comfort, both of preacher and hearers, will depend throughout on the proper pitch and management of the voice. There are three distinct scales, or gradations of voice, which every one may notice in himself and others, —the high, the low, and the middle. The high pitch is employed when we speak, or rather shout, to a person at a considerable distance from us. The low pitch, on the contrary, is directed towards those in immediate contact with us, and approaches almost to a whisper. Between these extremes is that most agreeable and ample range of voice which may be called the middle pitch, and out of the boundaries of which the preacher should seldom, if ever, permit himself to stray. It is in fact that division or scale of voice, which is the vehicle of our ordinary conversation in the social circle, and which admits of the utmost variety, not only of tone and inflexion, but of softness and strength. ' It is erroneous to suppose that the highest pitch of voice is requisite to be well heard by a large assembly. This is confounding two things materially different, loudness, or strength of sound with the key-note of which we speak. The voice may be rendered louder with-

out altering the key ; and the speaker will always
be able to give most body—most persevering force
of sound—to that pitch of voice to which in conversation he is accustomed; whereas, if he begin on
the highest pitch of his voice, he will fatigue himself,
and speak with pain; and whenever a man speaks with
pain, he is always heard with pain by his audience.  To
the voice, therefore, may be given full strength and
swell of sound, but it should always be pitched on the
ordinary speaking key.  A greater quantity of voice
should never be uttered, than can be afforded without
pain, and without any extraordinary effort.  To be well
heard, it is useful for a speaker to direct his eyes occasionally to some of the most distant persons in the
assembly, and to consider himself as speaking to them.
We naturally and mechanically express our words with
such a degree of strength, as to be heard by one to whom
we address ourselves, provided he be within the reach of our
voice.  This will be the case in public speaking, as well
as in common conversation.  But it must be remembered
that speaking too loud is peculiarly offensive.  The ear
is wounded when the voice comes upon it in rumbling
indistinct masses : besides it appears as if assent were
demanded by mere vehemence and force of sound.  Distinctness of articulation is far more conducive to being
well heard and clearly understood, than mere loudness
of sound.  The quantity of sound requisite to fill even a
large space, is less than is generally supposed, and with
distinct articulation, a man of a weak voice will make
it extend further than the strongest voice can reach
without it.  This therefore demands peculiar attention.
Many instances occur in common life, of people, who,
though hard of hearing, prefer to be spoken to with a
moderate than a loud tone of voice.  The speaker must

give every sound which he utters its due proportion, and
make every syllable to be heard distinctly.  To succeed
in this, a rapidity of pronunciation must be avoided.  To
pronounce with a proper degree of slowness, and with
full and clear articulation, cannot be too industriously
studied, or too earnestly recommended.  Such a pronunciation gives wings and dignity to language.  It
assists the voice by the pauses and rests which it permits
it more easily to make, and enables the speaker to swell
all his sounds both with more energy and more music.
He may by this means also preserve a due command
over himself, and avoid that flutter of spirits produced by
a rapid and hurried manner which is destructive to all
due impression on the minds of the audience.' [1]

But one of the worst, and at the same time most
common faults, against which the preacher should sedu-
lously guard, is *monotony*.  A uniform sameness of tone
in the delivery of a sermon, will infallibly weaken, if not
destroy the attention of the most devout audience, and
if the attention be lost, all will be lost.  Displeasing as
eccentricity of manner doubtless is, it is by no means so
injurious to a preacher's usefulness, as that decent and
respectable, but dull and soporific monotony which
inspires indeed no disgust, but awakens at the same time
no one emotion of the mind.  Surely any kind of delivery which is not absolutely repulsive, and which keeps
up the attention of the audience, is preferable to the
most pleasing and gentle tone, which by its unvarying
uniformity lulls asleep.

It is consoling, however, to know that this cardinal
fault may in every case be corrected where vigilance and
resolution are put in exercise.  The speaker has only to

[1] Blair's Rhetoric.

ask himself the question from time to time, ' With what tone, or in what manner should I naturally utter this sentiment in *serious conversation* with a friend?' This is precisely the tone, and for the most part the manner which become also the pulpit. Nothing is more mistaken than the notion, that in the delivery of our sermons, our ordinary mode of speaking is to be abandoned, and that we are to assume some plaintive, stately, or pompous tone, which is at once unnatural to us, and uninteresting to our hearers. In extemporary preaching, there is considerably less danger of falling into this error; and hence the principal cause of its acknowledged superiority in awakening attention. But why should the written sermon be allowed to operate so unfavourably on the tone and manner of the preacher? Why should he regard his manuscript as anything more than a remembrancer, or fail to realize the thought that he is not reading an essay with which he has no concern, but conveying to his hearers, his own sentiments and feelings with as much truth and reality, and heartfelt sincerity, as can possibly be felt by the most extemporaneous preacher.

The same general direction will be found applicable to most other faults in the delivery of sermons from the pulpit, and equally serviceable in assisting the preacher to attain the manner most natural and easy to himself. For after all the rules which the Elocutionist and Rhetorician can devise, there is no one direction so material to the improvement of the speaker as this, of forming the tones and inflexions of public speaking upon those of sensible and animated conversation. Most men when engaged in speaking with others on subjects of mutual interest, will give utterance to their sentiments in the tones and cadences of natural eloquence. Let the

preacher then bear in mind that whether he is discussing
a topic of considerable interest in his own parlour in the
company of a few friends, or addressing a large assembly
from the pulpit, he still *speaks*, and should preserve the
manner and appearance of speaking, and the tones and
modulations of voice which are natural to him.   How
much of the propriety, the force, and the interest of a
discourse must depend on such modulations will appear
from this single consideration, that to almost every sentiment we utter, and every emotion we profess to feel,
nature has adapted some peculiar tone of voice ; inso-
much that he who without that corresponding tone
should tell another, that he was grieved or anxious,
or displeased, or afraid, would be so far from being
believed, that he would probably be considered as
speaking ironically.  Sympathy is one of the most
powerful principles by which persuasive discourse is made
instrumental in operating on the human mind.  The
speaker endeavours to transfuse into the minds of his
hearers his own sentiments and emotions: which he can
never be successful in doing, unless he utters them in
such a manner as to convince the audience that he feels
them.   The proper expression of tones, therefore, deserves
to be attentively considered by every one who aims with
the blessing of God to be a successful pleader with
immortal souls.

. Much also of the force of delivery will depend upon
the judicious use of *pauses*, of which there are two kinds.
The first, or ordinary pause, is that which takes place at
the close of divisions, paragraphs, sentences, or even
parts of sentences, with a view to the sense.  The other,
or extraordinary pause, is used in an arbitrary manner
before certain emphatic words depending altogether for
its success upon the taste and judgment of the speaker.

The pause to be observed at the close of a general head or division of a discourse should be of considerable length. Two important purposes will be answered by it : the attention of the hearer will be recruited by a short but complete repose; and the continuity of sound having been broken, the preacher will be able to descend with greater ease into the ordinary pitch of his voice, should he have previously risen to a higher elevation, or 'have closed the preceding division in a declamatory or pathetic strain.

On the subject of *action*, or *gesture*, little more need be said than that it should be natural and simple. The delivery of written sermons obviously admits of less action than extemporary preaching; but it is far from prohibiting it altogether. Awkwardness, affectation, and excess, are the three dangers to be shunned. The Preacher should for the most part, stand erect in the pulpit: it is at once the most natural and dignified posture, and at the same time the most conducive to the proper management of his voice and manner. He should carefully guard against the awkward habit of raising and lowering the head simultaneously with the action of the eyes in glancing at the manuscript before him. Few things tend more powerfully than this to give the delivery of a sermon the air and appearance of mere *reading*, and to divest it altogether of the character of preaching. Necessity requires that in the use of a manuscript the eyes should be withdrawn from time to time to the cushion : but in no other respect should he permit his delivery to be less natural or interesting than that of the extemporary speaker.

To the few simple rules which the Editor has thus ventured to suggest with a view to assist his younger brethren in the ministry in their laudable endeavours to obtain an unexceptionable and forcible delivery, he would add one caution. He would earnestly warn every one against giving way to the too frequent consequence of discouragement—the abandonment of all attempts at improvement. A rigid attention to rules will at first, doubtless, be irksome and unpleasant : it will distract probably the attention of the young preacher from subjects in themselves of far greater importance. But this will be only for a short time : what is at first distracting and constrained, becomes, after a little practice, natural and free. Perseverance will be found, with God's blessing, to overcome every ordinary obstacle; and good delivery will become so habitual, that instead of proving detrimental to the spirituality of the preacher, it will rather tend to promote it. He will experience fresh delight in his pulpit duties, and by observing the increased and increasing attention of his hearers, he will be stimulated with stronger desires to benefit their souls.

# II.

## ON THE PRINCIPLES, PHYSIOLOGICAL, MENTAL, AND GRAMMATICAL,—OF ORAL DELIVERY.

FROM THE CHRISTIAN OBSERVER.[1]

IF the practice of elocution had improved in proportion to the number of books which have been written upon it, it would long ago have attained no slight degree of advancement. Yet to this hour how few public speakers deliver themselves even passably well; and how rare is it to find one who, with the higher intellectual qualities of composition, combines the elocutionary aids of strength, melody, harmony, expression, and the numerous legitimate graces which constitute a pleasing and impressive address? Such being the fact, what are the causes of the deficiency ?

The first and most obvious cause is, that, among the large body of persons who are professionally called upon to speak in public, comparatively few devote themselves, as an important portion of their early training, to the diligent study of elocution. Most of the treatises which are likely to fall into the hands of a student, are rather calculated to teach the art of composition than that of speaking: they are treatises on eloquence, not elocution; rhetoric, not delivery: so that what the ancients considered the first, the second, and the third

[1] January, 1835.

requisite in eloquence, call it " pronunciation," or
" delivery," or by whatever name, is almost entirely
neglected. That it should be so neglected is astonishing,
if we consider its importance to every public speaker.
Were half the labour bestowed upon the cultivation of
solid manly elocution, which is given to attainments of
far inferior value, many a public speaker would be rendered audible, impressive, and interesting, who is at
present unable, with large mental powers and excellent
matter, to command common attention. Men of reading
are so much and so justly in the habit of bestowing their
chief solicitude upon the intrinsic value of what they
utter, that they are apt to neglect the mechanical part
of their office. They are perhaps even disgusted at
witnessing· the admiration often lavished on the most
jejune compositions delivered with agreeable fluency,
and they rather despise, than wish to attain, what they
consider only a passport to vain popularity. Yet surely
it does not become a wise man to neglect any guileless
instrument of usefulness. The musical composer does
not think it sufficient to write good music; he knows
that it requires to be skilfully performed : and the same
applies to every species of public address.

Another cause of the neglect of the art of public
speaking, at least among many students for Holy
Orders, is an idea, as intimated in the above query, that
it involves something not simple, natural, and congenial
to Christian simplicity. Now if this were the case,
the objection would, to every religious mind, be fatal
to the study. But no reason can be shewn why a
student should not pay attention to his delivery as much
as to his composition ; or why he should not avoid bad
elocution as much as bad grammar. The monitory denunciations of St. Paul against enticing words of

man's wisdom, apply to the subtle artifices or shewy ornaments of the classic sophists : they do not forbid a due attention to the proper arrangement of a discourse, and the use of solid arguments and forcible language ; and much less do they apply to the cultivation of a suitable mode of delivery, so that what is spoken may not lose any of its effect by indistinct and powerless utterance. God is the God of nature, as well as of grace ; and as he made the organs both of speech and hearing, why should they not be employed in his service ? Why are sacred things to be marred by ungainly associations ? why should not the apples of gold be framed in pictures of silver ? why should a sacred theme be played upon an instrument out of tune, when a little pains would have corrected its jarrings ?

But this leads us to another cause of the neglect of this initiatory study, which is, that public speakers are not in general aware how much may be done by judicious management to improve their delivery. They impute their deficiencies too hastily to unavoidable causes ; they have weak lungs, or imperfect organs of voice or articulation ; they cannot get over 'natural defects ; ' it is impossible for them to speak more loudly, distinctly, or forcibly : and thus, in the ignorance of despair, they never seriously make the attempt. . But has it never occurred to such persons, that some of the greatest masters of public speaking have been men who actually laboured under some physical impediment, which they were obliged with much care to strive against, till in the effort they at length surpassed others who had no such inconvenience; while, on the other hand, it frequently happens that where nature, as the phrase is, has done much, the favoured party does nothing; so that in the end the hare is outstripped by the tortoise? A speaker has, perhaps, a flowing musical voice, and organs formed for easy articulation; and such is the force of mere sweetness and richness of tone, that, notwithstanding his inflections may be inappropriate, and his whole speech painful to a well-judging mind, crowded auditories will listen to him with delight. The speakers with whom the bulk of a miscellaneous assembly are most pleased, are often persons who have what is called a natural gift, and who know no more of what they do, or how they do it, than a fish knows how it swims, or a bird how it flies. Would persons thus endowed give due attention to the mental part of the process, they would no doubt excel others in their ultimate attainments; because, of two instruments played upon with equal ability, the best will be the most agreeable. But the absence of difficulty often prevents the exertion of energy; and it is well, if, in addition to indolence, self-conceit also do not attach itself to an easily earned popularity, which the party will be inclined to attribute to something higher than mere organic fluency.

But the case of a person anxious on proper grounds to speak well, and yet labouring under natural or acquired difficulties, is very different. Speaking, in such a case, must necessarily to a considerable extent be an art. The effort to remedy a mistake, or to conquer a defect, opens new ideas to the mind: the student begins to see that oral delivery is as much under the guidance of the intellectual powers, as playing upon a musical instrument. The attention necessary to the correction of some known fault, familiarizes him to his own voice, and leads him to analyse and correct its *other* defects. Thus by practice, with a good ear and good judgment, he becomes acquainted with the various modifications of oral sound;

and learns to ascertain what it is which constitutes a
pleasing and impressive delivery, and what the contrary;
and how the one may be acquired and the other avoided.
He becomes, as it were, a skilful player on his own
voice; and though he had not a naturally good instrument to play on, he has in the end a vast advantage over
the former speaker, whose execution was perhaps as
incorrect as his instrument was agreeable. To this must
be added the important circumstance, that what appeared
at first sight physical defect, is perhaps discovered to be
merely a bad habit; the instrument, to continue the
allusion, having been blamed for what was only the
fault of the musician. It is not likely that public
speakers will devote the requisite attention to this part
of their duty, while the present popular ignorance prevails respecting the benefits of elocutionary study; nay,
while there is even a strong prejudice against it. Many
persons, of good intelligence in other matters, would
smile at the idea of any one, beyond the age of childhood, learning over again the first elementary sounds of
language, and tuning the organs of speech to new intona-
tions and articulations. The current aphorism used on
such occasions is, 'speak naturally;' but speaking
*naturally*, if we may venture to use such a paradox, is
very frequently speaking *artificially*. If a young
Northumbrian wishes to correct his *burr;* a Somerset-
shire-man, or other provincialist, his peculiar dialect;
his unlettered neighbours will advise him not to learn
new fashions, but to 'speak naturally,' as his fathers
spoke before him. Now any false tone, or tune, or
inflection, any imperfect mode of sounding or articulating
any letter, any misuse of the organs of speech, is as much
a legitimate subject of correction, as the most displeasing
provincialism. Bad speaking is not *natural*, except it

be said that every thing is natural which was learned at
an early age from an educated nurse or a youthful
companion.   It is the refuge of ignorance, to talk of any
thing being natural in conventional language: there is
nothing in the human constitution that makes it natural,
on the one side of the English Channel to speak French,
and on the other English; or for a child to hiss, or lisp,
or stammer, who might have learned to speak correctly
and melodiously, had he been better taught.   And if one
error or defect, however gross, is not necessarily to be
pronounced natural, why should an assemblage of errors
or defects be considered so ? or why should it be thought
unnatural for a young man to endeavour to correct his
habits of reading and speaking, even though the correction should extend to almost every part of the process,
so as eventually to alter his very tones and articulations ;
to bring into play those parts of the phonic apparatus
which had been imperfectly developed, and to keep down
those which had an undue or irregular action ?   There is
nothing unnatural in a painter or musician altering his
style for the better ; or in a plough-boy having his awkward limbs drilled into military gait ; and why should
not the habits of speech be similarly disciplined ?   A
speaker who is determined to be heard, and understood,
and felt, if he labour under any difficulty, such as a
harsh, or weak, or otherwise defective voice, or bad
habits of enunciation, ought in duty to apply his mind to
amend his errors and supply his defects: and if by due
attention, he should in the course of time change the
entire character of his delivery, it would not be just to
say that he spoke less naturally than before ; unless,
in unlearning his old bad habits, he had acquired
new ones, which were perhaps even more unpleasing,
from their wearing the appearance of art and study,

instead of being the result of accidental early associations.

And here we arrive at another, and perhaps the chief, reason why the art of public speaking, in its sober and legitimate application, is not more diligently studied. It is not merely that many speakers are inattentive to the subject—whether from apathy, or from a mistaken supposition that good speaking is entirely the gift of nature; but it is from the prejudice excited by the fact that of those who study public speaking few are found to succeed; and that there is usually among the pupils of the art a stiffness, a mannerism, and an affectation, which are far worse than the unstudied faults of a careless speaker. The reasons of this too common result will be further touched upon; but, in the mean time, when it is considered how many things are necessary in speaking a single sentence really well, and how completely the absence or undue preponderence of any one will mar the whole, and give to the delivery an awkward or artificial character, far worse than the ordinary defects of inattention, it must be owned, that, if the student have not good judgment and reasonable perseverance, it were almost better that he should not enter upon the pursuit. He had better ' drink deep or taste not.' The first attempt to correct a fault (not to advert to the higher attainments of elocutionary excellence) will almost necessarily cause, for a time, an awkwardness and stiffness of manner, which will tend greatly to discourage a student who has not considerable patience and mental energy; and if he never arrive beyond this point, he had better never have set out on his journey. The case is analogous in other arts. Suppose a person to have learned to play on an instrument by ear, and to have practised this for many years: it might in such a case be a question whether he

should go back to the gamut, and begin to learn to play
by note : since for a considerable period he would play
much worse by note than by ear ; but if he were a man
of intelligence and application—a man capable of forming a judicious plan, and resolutely adhering to it—he
would do well to commence anew, not heeding the remarks of those who did not understand his object and
only wondered at his apparent retrogression. It is always
humiliating to begin again, where we thought we had
made some advances ; but every man must do this who
has erected his fabric upon an unstable foundation.

If the pupils of teachers of elocution become less
effective or pleasing speakers than they would otherwise
have been, this must arise either from the rules which
they have adopted being unsound, or from their not being
well mellowed in their practice. Demosthenes probably
enunciated the letter *rho*, for a considerable time after
his attention to the subject, much worse than before he
attempted to correct his fault ; and had he listened to the
advice of ignorant auditors he would probably have been
dissuaded from continuing his efforts.[1]   Every student

---

[1] The case of Demosthenes is often cited, but we have never seen
it physiologically considered. What, for instance, was the benefit of
his running up a hill while declaiming? and also of putting pebbles
in his mouth ?

In imitation of his example, students of elocution have been very
frequently recommended to run up a hill declaiming. Thus Dr.
Bailey, in his " Art of Pronunciation and Singing," says : " To
acquire a long breath, and strengthen the lungs, there can be found
perhaps no better method than to run often up some ascent, especially in the morning, *without suffering the lungs to play quick, in the
manner called panting*." The *rationale* of this advice is to strengthen
the muscles of respiration, so that they may act forcibly; yet at the
same time to gain such vigour in the little muscle that closes the
glottis, and such command over it, as to be able to keep the wind-

who is beginning carefully to amend his reading or speaking, must be prepared for the exclamation, ' Well, if *that* is learning to speak, may I never be condemned to hear such speaking again ! ' He must feel that his object is to speak naturally, forcibly, and appropriately, without any affected tones or cadences ; and that what

chest air-tight, so that it may be capable of sustaining a strong pressure from the ribs and diaphregm, without bursting open till directed to do so at the volition of the speaker. If the valve lets out the air before sufficient muscular vigour is impressed upon the chest, there is no power of adequate vibration in the larynx for forcible vocality. To know the design of the practice is to aid the object ; for it is not convenient for every student to run up hills declaiming : but considerable accessions of theoretic and laryngeal vigour may be attained, by due exercise and habit, even in a chamber.

With regard to the pebbles, it has often been asked, what good there could be in a man's declaiming with stones in his mouth : how could that teach him to sound the letter *rho*, or in any way improve his articulation ? for if articulation depend directly upon the tongue, or other external organs, such an impediment would be more likely to get them into irregular habits, than to rescue them from them : nor, in fact, could any letter be duly sounded. We have never seen a solution of the difficulty ; but our hypothesis, that the action of the tongue and other external organs is not the direct cause of articulation, but only, or chiefly, its result, furnishes one. The pebbles prevented the speaker using his tongue as he was accustomed in the old vicious action ; he was therefore obliged to depend more directly upon the primary organs ; he thus learned to make the larynx and adjacent parts do their duty ; sound and articulation were formed and finished in the right place ; the morbid associations between the erring organs was broken ; and the tongue, when the pebbles were removed, went to its proper place.

We have dwelt much upon the distinction between the external and the primary organs of speech, because it is of great practical importance, and though obvious when explained, is not generally understood by writers on education. In a very excellent and popular book, entitled ' Hints to Parents, in the Spirit of Pestalozzi's Method,' the pupil is taught that ' *the tongue* is so flexible that it

may appear for a time awkward, is but a step towards
being natural : it is an effort to leave off what was incorrect, or feeble, or ill-judged, or ungraceful, and to
substitute something better. A young man at college,
who should determine to leave off the mouthing and
artificial intonation with which he was accustomed to

can form various tones, by the air which proceeds from the lungs ;
by it we communicate our thoughts to each other, call for help,
pray, and praise God.' Now if the child really believes what he is
here taught, that it is the tongue that forms the ' various tones,' and
tries to act upon his information, his speech must be strangely
unnatural. We have expressed our doubts whether the tongue
makes even the *articulations*; but that it makes the *tones*, which
every physiologist, without a shadow of dispute, imputes to the
larynx, is as erroneous as if it were said that the elbows or knees
made them. So far from bringing in the tongue upon every occasion,
we would rather say, Forget that you have a tongue ; speak rightly,
and your tongue will fall rightly, without any artificial placing. An
infant learns to speak by ear, by means of laryngeal action, which is
of necessity connected with a certain opening and shutting of the
jaws, and other claspings and positions of the various secondary
organs, the lips and other parts falling rightly for the purpose ; and
this the infant would do even if it were blind, and had never seen a
person's lips move; but it would not do so if, though it saw, it were
deaf, and therefore could not hear the sound ; which is a clear proof
that the rules about placing the lips and tongue are erroneous, and
only lead to irregular and displeasing habits. There is no direction
which, if we were teachers of elocution, we should more strongly urge,
than that of depending as little as possible upon the external organs—
for rather, we might say, indicators—of speech ; and of stimulating the
primary organs to their duty. There is scarcely any common defect
of the external apparatus which may not be rendered unimportant,
if the primary organs act as becomes them. For example: A person
lisps, and we lay the fault perhaps on his incisor teeth; but many
persons, with teeth worse disposed, do not lisp, and this person
could in all probability overcome the defect, by not allowing, if we
may so say, the glottis to lisp. We may illustrate the matter thus :—
A person who has a front tooth removed often begins to lisp, though

spout a public-school declamation, would probably at first find his utterance, when not thus stilted, miserably tame ; and practice and good judgment would be required to throw his energies into a right channel. A few partial faults may be easily eradicated ; but to unlearn a whole tissue of wrong habits of early life, requires a taste, a feeling, an ear, and a perseverance, which few persons possess.

We shall not attempt to detail the various causes why public speakers so often acquire unpleasing modes of address ; but one of them is the following :—Ordinary speaking is a sort of miniature, in which blemishes and defects, though they may be numerous, are too minute

not five minutes before he spoke distinctly; but after a few days the defect often goes off, and he speaks perhaps nearly as well as ever : and why ? not because there is not the same cause of lisping as there was immediately after the oral mutilation, but because the 'primary organs have learned to give the right sound, and to send the tongue to the right place under the new arrangements, to which arrangements the tongue accommodates itself. The defect of the teeth, though the *inciting* cause of the lisp, was not therefore of necessity an insuperable cause. A person who has a well formed mouth, and does not lisp, may lisp in imitation, by catching the sound by ear, without seeing the lisper's face. The lisp was not in this case caused by the irregular structure of the mouth ; though, if it had been allowed to become habitual, it would in general be so accounted for. Persons who jumble and clutter their words, sometimes seem to be taking great pains to speak plainly and articulately, and yet fail of their object ; while others, who never seem, we might almost say, to make any use of their tongue at all, speak distinctly. The chief difference (for allowance must of course, after all, be made for differences of organic *structure*, both of the external and internal organs) is owing to the greater or less correctness of glottal action. What is called mincing pronunciation, or, in popular phrase, speaking *mimine pimine*, is caused by directing affected attention to the tongue and lips, instead of speaking from the larynx.

N

to be noticed ; but the same picture, when magnified to
the proportions of public speaking, becomes more conspicuous, and each part occupies a large share of observation.  Many a person will pronounce a sentence with
tolerable correctness in ordinary conversation, who, if
called upon to repeat it in a slow and deliberate manner,
will betray a variety of faults, which before were scarcely
discernible.  This happens still more frequently in *reading* than in speaking; and most of all in addressing a
large auditory.  For this reason, among others, the
clergy, generally speaking, are far from being the best
public speakers.  Their manner, whether cheerful or
grave, slow or rapid, inflected or monotonous, or however differing in other respects, is often *unnatural*.  To
read or speak to a large auditory, especially in a church,
and on a sacred subject, in a manner really *natural*, is a
difficult attainment.  Every thing conspires to prevent,
in many cases, even the attempt.  But supposing the
attempt made, the first error would probably be an appearance of *familiarity ;* but this is *not* natural ; for
nothing is, or ought to be, less natural than familiarity in
such a place, and on such an occasion.  To avoid familiarity therefore, pompousness, or declamation, or artificial
intonation, is perhaps resorted to : besides which, the
time is set too fast or too slow ; the inflections are either
almost monotonous, or are varied to a rant ; in short, the
whole is any thing but *natural*.

Indeed, the very circumstance of wishing to speak
with force, or with pathos, or even with loudness, so
as to be heard by a considerable assembly, is almost
sure both to magnify habitual faults, and to create
new ones.  To recur to a former allusion : there are few
men whose ordinary speaking is sufficiently correct to
bear being magnified to the size necessary for a public

address : [1] besides which, in general the magnifying process is accompanied by another, which, to keep up the
metaphor, may be compared to the unequal operation
of certain optical glasses, which not only *enlarge* but
*distort* the image. If, for example, a person is somewhat too nasal, or buccinal, or pectoral, or guttural, or
dental, or sibilant, in his ordinary speech (and there are
few speakers who have *no* such faults), the defect will
be far more visible in public speaking, where he exerts
himself with more energy. Again, different persons
employ, in different proportions, different parts of the
organs of voice and articulation—for almost every man
has some parts of his organs of speech better formed or
developed than the others, and on which, therefore, he
learns principally to depend ; or he has been accustomed,
by morbid habit, to admit this undue preponderance ;—
when, therefore, he exerts himself in public speaking,
the favoured part will naturally take more than its due
share of the extra burden. This will destroy the whole

---

[1] The first lesson of a teacher of elocution, is to direct the student
to pronounce deliberately and forcibly all the elementary sounds of
the language (which are more numerous than the letters of the
alphabet) ; and in most cases it is found that he cannot do this with
precision ; that he cannot either give the correct sound, or sustain it
for a prolonged time. He cannot, as it were, *sol fa* his speech. The
unintelligible sounds known by the name of 'London cries' are an
exemplification of the difficulty which an uneducated person finds in
speaking loudly and slowly what he can speak well enough in conversation. If the itinerant tried to give the right articulation, he could
not : he speaks by rote, but he cannot analyse the several elements.
The same remark applies in its degree to not a few public speakers.
A vowel passes off glibly in current speech ; but a public speaker must
learn to dwell upon, and prolong and swell it, without whining, or
ranting, or drawling. If he cannot rehearse the single elements,
*a, e, i, o, u,* &c. in this manner separately, as an exercise, how can he
duly fill them out in solemn speech ?

symmetry of speech.   The question is immediately asked,
' Why does not that man speak in public as he does in
private ?'   The just answer might be, ' He did not know
how to do so.'   A correct volition is not sufficient;  knowledge and practice are necessary to render most persons
able to speak in public as they do in private.   To say
nothing of timidity, anxiety, and various other affections
of mind, which might disturb the balance, a speaker,
even when he has most self-possession, when he is really
affected with his subject, and has every thing in his
favour, may still find it difficult to be *natural* when
placed in a situation so artificial as that described.

We may illustrate this by a recurrence to what we
have before remarked of the character of speech.   The
speaking apparatus is to the full as much a *stringed*, or
rather a vibratory, as a *wind* instrument.   The bones and
muscles of the head, the chest, and all the upper part
of the body, vibrate in unison with the sound issued from
the larynx ;  and it is on some of these vibrations, even
more than on the primary sound, that the force and
energy of speaking consist.   In ordinary conversation, the
wind and the stringed part of the apparatus generally do
their duty pretty well together ;  but no sooner does a
person unskilled in speaking become either nervous or
animated, than the several agents are in danger of losing
their due proportion.   Suppose a person unaccustomed
to public speaking endeavouring to be heard by a larger
auditory than he knows how to command, what will be
the natural consequence ?   He will generally begin to
exert the wind part of the instrument in greater proportion than the stringed.   There will also probably be
many other faults, of which the *want of due articulation*
will be one of the chief ;  but we confine ourselves to one
part of the case.   The windpipe is forced to give out

louder sounds than usual, while the vibratory part of the apparatus is not sufficiently affected. Hence the voice becomes shrill, and in other respects unpleasing; in much the same manner as a flute, into which we blow too forcibly, gives a sharp and displeasing tone. Yet, not-withstanding this quantity of *noise*, for want of due vibration there is no *force or fulness;* whereas, had *the wind instrument* given a less quantity of sound, yet with strong vibration, the voice would have been *felt* even at a distance where it was scarcely audible.

A clergyman has greater difficulties to contend with than a barrister. A legal advocate usually addresses but a few individuals, and these at no great distance. His subjects also are of ordinary occurrence; and every thing *unnatural* would be injurious to his cause. He therefore must appear as if really *talking*, only with more than usual pathos and energy. The voice thus assumes nearly its regular conversational pitch; indeed, it would be difficult to speak under such circumstances in any other, except where the speaker has occasion to *declaim*, which does not come into the present consider-ation. A counsellor could not address a judge in the pitch and tones employed by many clergymen in large churches: he must literally *talk:* he may be swift or slow, forcible or feeble, pathetic or facetious, but he must *talk.* This keeps him within due bounds. What-ever may be his zeal for his client, his professional eagerness, or the stimulus of opposition, his voice must be conversational.

But a clergyman is usually placed under very different circumstances. Ordinarily, he reads, instead of speaks, which of itself is one deviation from nature. Then again his auditory is at a distance, and perhaps not always alive to the subject; and there is nothing in the shape of reply or contradiction to keep alive the feeling of *reality*. There is therefore danger of becoming, on the one hand, careless and monotonous, or, on the other, declamatory. Determined to be *heard*, he pours forth an undue volume of voice, without sufficient *articulation* and vibration. This may lead to a habit of being clamorous without being forcible; a habit the opposite of that of being energetic without being noisy. A speaker who thus unfairly uses his wind instrument is in danger of losing his voice, as has been the lot of many clergymen of great zeal. But a speaker who depends more on the stringed part of his instrument, and makes himself heard and felt by vibration rather than by noise, seldom injures either his voice or constitution by public speaking. If a young man, on first taking Holy Orders, resolutely determined, till the habit became familiar, to be distinctly heard in a large auditory, without making more *noise* than he finds easy to his own organs of speech and to his neighbours' ears, he would naturally be led to vibrate his sounds, in the manner which is observable in the impressive parts of the elocution of a good speaker. In really powerful yet easy speaking, scarcely a muscle of the face is in a state of tension; the mouth assumes an intelligent placidity, which indicates that every fibre and cartilage vibrates freely with every sound that issues from the wind-pipe, thus augmenting its fulness, variety, and impressiveness of intonation.[1]

[1] The common direction to young clergymen, to look at the most distant part of their auditory, and to address them, tends, if not rightly understood, to strain the voice. In speaking to a person at a distance, we naturally raise our pitch; and we could not long speak thus without raving and hoarseness. What a public speaker should desire to attain, is due loudness, not shrillness; not a high pitch of voice, but force in his natural pitch. If a young clergyman would learn to be heard by the most distant person in his audience without

We would not be understood to mean that all the elementary discipline which we have described is needful for every person when first he begins to speak in public. Some men have a voice so powerful, that even their ordinary sounds are sufficient to fill a large building; and others have had correct principles mellowed into practice in their childhood, without their knowledge. Mr. Pitt was a powerful public speaker at the age of twenty years; but it was because, in addition to great native powers, he had been early instructed by his illustrious parent; so that he had little or nothing to unlearn. This, however, is not often the case; for it does not often happen that a Pitt has a Chatham for the tutor of his infancy and childhood. Mr. Pitt had only to *magnify* his ordinary conversation to render it fit for public speaking: the elements were correct.

But perhaps one of the greatest impediments to the cultivation of the art of speaking, is the vague use of the terms employed by those who teach it. After all that has been said and written, the majority of professed students of elocution know nothing of the various accidents that affect speech. If, indeed, two such palpably distinct things as *quantity* and *accent* are often confounded, it cannot be expected that the other terms necessary to convey information on the subject of speaking should be found generally to excite in the hearer correct ideas. Scarcely two writers mean the same thing by the same word, when they write respecting the affections of speech. Sheridan literally did not know the

straining his voice, he should pitch it at its conversational height, and try to speak with sufficient loudness and force in that key, but avoid being betrayed into a higher note. The organs of speech will gradually strengthen themselves in the proper key; and the speech will thus be audible without being unnatural.

distinction between accent and quantity.   Even Mr.
Walker did not consider the physiology of accent; and
consequently confounds it with a particular kind of
force, or loudness; whereas a syllable may be accented
and yet neither be loud nor forcible.   An analysis of the
affections of speech is of great importance to students
of elocution, as without it they cannot have clear ideas
of their art, and are constantly liable to be misled with
contradictory assertions, and with the confused use of the
same term for different ideas, and of different terms for
the same idea.   The heads of such an analysis would
comprise, among others, the following accidents of
speech :—Every syllable is                      .

1. Higher     or     Lower.
2. Louder     or     Softer.
3. Longer     or     Shorter.
4. Accented   or     Unaccented.
5. Rising,    Falling,   or   Circumflex.

A brief definition of these affections we reserve for
another occasion; and we hope not to overload the diges-
tion of those readers who have no particular taste for
such inquiries.   Our younger readers, especially academical students, will, we trust, find the disquisition practically useful, by turning their attention to the subject.

--------

To the foregoing observations, the following may not
improperly be added.   They are taken from a paper in
the Christian Observer, for March, 1835.

\*     \*     \*     \*     \*      ' Permit me to recal to
your own recollection, and to that of your readers, a
paper in your volume for 1821, under the signature of
' Pastor,' (which was reprinted and circulated among
some of the young men in Cambridge, by our venerable
friend Mr. Simeon, without any secret being made of the

authorship of the paper,) containing some valuable suggestions, in his own striking manner, which will bear repetition in your columns, especially as some of your present readers may not have the volume for 1821 before them.  Your venerable correspondent appears to have concurred by anticipation with yourself, in considering the usual habits of clerical enunciation as an ' unnatural and artificial' mode of speaking; and also in what you have said of the impropriety of the oft-repeated recommendation to regulate the voice by looking at a distant auditor, which is almost sure to cause an' undue exaltation of ' pitch ; '—instead of determining to keep the pitch at its natural conversational height, but giving to the voice, by effort and practice due loudness, vibration and intensity, and also by clearly articulating every element.   I have heard Mr. Simeon himself ' thrill an audience' as you express it, in a voice scarcely audible : while many injudicious speakers bellow inarticulate volumes of sound, to the serious distress of their own chest and windpipe, and the tympana of the ears of their auditors, but with little access either to the understanding or the heart.

Mr. Simeon's directions are as follow :—

' Diaconus.  Is there any thing against which you would particularly guard me in delivering my sermons ?

' Pastor.  Yes : guard against speaking in an unnatural and artificial voice.

' D.  I am glad you have mentioned this : for I perceive that almost every minister in the pulpit, speaks in a voice which he never uses on any other occasion :  and I am well assured, that it is that which makes sermons in general so uninteresting.   Can you tell me how I may manage to find, as it were, my natural voice ?

' P.  Yes : before you read your 'sermon at home,

speak some sentence in a whisper to your chair, or writing desk, if you please, as to a living object; and then suppose this imaginary auditor to recede from you to the distance of five yards, ten yards, twenty yards, and strengthen your voice progressively in proportion to the distance : and then again, suppose him to approach you gradually, in the manner in which he had receded, and let the force of your voice proportionably abate, till on account of his proximity, you find a whisper will suffice. Do this; and if your whisper at the beginning and end be a natural whisper, you may be sure that you have kept your natural voice. If you speak to two thousand people, you should not rise to a different key, but still preserve your customary pitch. The only difference you are to make, is from the piano to the forte of the same note. You know that on a violincello, you may sound scarcely to be heard : or, that you may strike it with such force, that it shall twang again. So it is with your voice : it is by the strength, and not by the elevation of it that you are heard. You will remember that a whole discourse is to be delivered : and if you get into an unnatural key, you will both injure yourself, and weary your audience.

'D. And is this the plan you would recommend for reading the prayers ?

'P. No : I have an easier and better plan for that. Never *read* the prayers, but *pray* them. Utter them precisely as you would if you were addressing the Almighty, in the same language in your secret chamber : only of course you must strengthen your voice as in the former case.'

I have quoted the above directions the rather, because coming from the pen of such a man as Mr. Simeon, they may be listened to by some young clerical readers and academical students, who either by mistake, or through indolence, despise study and pains-taking in this and other matters, under the notion of following the example of St. Paul. That eminent Apostle of Christ discarded vain, sophistical pleadings : but he did not, we may presume, forego any proprieties of enunciation which he had acquired in his academical studies.     *     *     *

*     *     * The cause of God, though ultimately dependant on nothing human, yet consecrates and adorns every faculty and gift. Our heavenly Father disdains not the services of any of our members, and certainly not that of the best member that we have.

# III.

## ON THE OUTLINE OR SYNOPSIS OF A SERMON.

BY THE EDITOR.

THERE are three distinct kinds of outlines of sermons to be noticed, each appropriate to the end specially designed. The first is a rough draft of the elements of a written discourse, comprising the principal ideas which the writer intends to expound, with an arrangement sufficiently exact to serve as his land-mark or guide-post in the composition of his sermon.

The second is a shorter, but more finished outline of what has been previously prepared, and intended to be used in the pulpit in the form of notes, having all the leading ideas compressed into as narrow a space as possible, and the various references to scripture distinctly marked.

The third species differs from both the preceding, being still more full and complete, and designed, like Mr. Simeon's Homileticæ, for the benefit, not of the writer himself, but of others.

Of the first of the above species of synopses, the following example may perhaps suffice.

Suppose the text selected to be 2 Cor. iv. 7, " We have this treasure in earthen vessels, that the excellency of the power may be of God, and not of us." Having sought the assistance of God's Holy Spirit in humble and earnest prayer, the preacher will proceed to meditate on the words of the Apostle with patient and laborious thought, taking care to consult the original Greek, and to peruse attentively the context. When he comes at length to arrange his ideas on paper, he will express them perhaps in something like the following order, and in some such brief terms as these :

2 COR. iv. 7.

If we were intrusted with the charge of some valuable treasure, we should naturally inquire into the extent of our power of safe keeping—and if we discovered that we possessed no advantages either of strength, or wisdom, or fortitude—we should feel at a loss to discover the reason of our having been selected to be its depositories.

A similar train of thought seems to have been pursued by the Apostle in the context. Overwhelmed with a sense of the value of the Gospel dispensation, he inquires the reason, &c. and finds it intended to promote *the divine glory*.

We may consider, *The treasure here spoken of—the Repositories in which it is laid up—and the end designed by thus depositing it.*

## I. THE TREASURE HERE SPOKEN OF.

Having adverted in the preceding part of the chapter to the manner in which he had preached the Gospel, and to its awful rejection by multitudes, the Apostle adds, in the words of the text, "But we have *this treasure* in earthen vessels." The gospel is justly called a *treasure.* St. Paul counted all things but loss, &c. Such was the treasure hid in the field. It conveys glad tidings—par-

don to the condemned malefactor—release from slavery—
"a faithful saying," &c.  It reveals to us the knowledge
of  Christ—his  advents—his  sufferings—his  exaltation.
It points out to his various *offices*, &c.

### II. The Repositories in which it is laid up—
In " earthen vessels."

Vessels are employed both for *security* and *conveyance*.
Christ's ministers are so employed.  They are intrusted,
   (1) *With the preservation of the truth.*

The Apostles were specially careful to guard the
Church against errors.  The Epistles abound with warnings and exhortations to that effect.

Nor were they faithful only as individuals,—they
selected others to assist, and ultimately to succeed them ;
such as Timothy and Titus.  These they charged to hold
fast, &c.

   (2) *With its conveyance.*

St. Paul "a chosen vessel *to bear the name of Christ,
&c.*" Acts ix. 15.  How zealous should the ministers
of Christ be !  In season—out of season, &c.

But notwithstanding the inestimable value of the
treasure, the Repositories are mean and worthless—
they are " *earthen* vessels"—they are frail—feeble—
imperfect.  The Apostles themselves plain and humble
men.  Hear how St. Paul speaks of himself and his
inspired brethren, 1 Cor. i. 27—29. and iv. 9, 13.

We might naturally have supposed that God would
have chosen for the Repositories of this treasure some
of the *angels*—or at least men of profound learning and
science,—gifted with all the splendour of genius, and
with all the fascinations of oratory.  But it was otherwise determined· ·which leads us to consider,

III. The end designed by thus depositing it. "That the excellency of the power may be of God, and not of us."

God's glory would not have been equally manifested, had more powerful agents been employed.

The "excellency of the power" was signally manifested in the propagation of the gospel. See Acts i. 47, and xix. 20; 1 Cor. i. 23—25. Its prevalence and effects still visible in the hearts and lives of millions. "If I be lifted up," &c. No preacher more successful than St. Paul—and more ready to ascribe all the glory to God. See 1 Cor. ii. 1—5.

In conclusion,

Inquire, Have you individually experienced the true efficacy of the Gospel on your hearts,—your tempers,—your sentiments,—your conduct? Have you received it not as the word of man? &c. The vision of dry bones in Ezekiel.

Though the faithful minister is not answerable for *results*, he must feel his awful responsibility as one that should be faithful, &c. "Who is sufficient for these things?" Intercede for us. Collect for Ember week. Remember that your minister's spiritual prosperity is virtually your own. Brethren, pray for us!

The preceding is a sketch of one of the Editor's printed sermons,[1] and which he here republishes with a view to give the young student some notion of the manner in which such a brief outline may be filled up. The outline and the full sermon should of course be closely compared throughout the several divisions.

[1] Published by Hatchard, and Seeley, in one vol. 8vo.

### THE SERMON.

2 CORINTHIANS iv. 7.—" *We have this treasure in earthen vessels, that the excellency of the power may be of God, and not of us.*"

Were any of you, my brethren, intrusted with the care of some invaluable deposit, you would naturally turn your thoughts, in the first instance, to the immensity of its worth. You would then as naturally inquire into the powers of safe keeping which you possessed,—how far you were endowed with those moral and physical advantages, which might enable you at once to preserve it from all spoliation, and to distribute it in the manner and after the measure prescribed by the donor. And further, if, upon instituting such an inquiry, you discovered that you were peculiarly defective in all these advantages,—that instead of being strong, you were feeble in the extreme, and instead of being wise and skilful, were quite the reverse, you would naturally feel surprised, and inquire, in the third place, what could possibly have induced the proprietor to intrust such a treasure to your custody?

Now this is precisely the train of thought which appears to have suggested itself to the apostle's mind, when he wrote the words of the text. He had been speaking of the ministry of the word, " the light of the knowledge of the glory of God," as reflected from the face of the incarnate Saivour. He was overwhelmed with a sense of the value of this treasure, and stood in amazement at the thought that it had been committed to the charge of men of like passions and infirmities with others. This led him to inquire into the reason of so remarkable a circumstance; when he arrived at the conclusion, that God intended it *for the promotion of his own glory.* " We *have this treasure in earthen vessels, that the excellency of the power may be of God, and not of us."*

Our attention may, with God's blessing, be profitably directed to these several particulars. Let us consider, then,

I. THE TREASURE HERE SPOKEN OF.

This, as I have already observed, is the *ministration of the gospel.* The apostle commences the chapter with an immediate reference to it. " Therefore," says he, '' seeing we have this ministry, as we have received mercy, we faint not." He then speaks of the simple and faithful manner in which he and his fellow labourers endeavoured to fulfil it, viz. by " renouncing the hidden things of dishonesty; " and, instead of " handling the word of God deceitfully, commending themselves to every man's conscience in the sight of God, by the manifestation of the truth." Then follows this explanation of the awful fact, that by multitudes this glorious gospel was rejected. " But if our gospel be hid, it is hid to them that are lost. In whom the god of this world hath blinded the minds of them that believe not, lest the light of the glorious gospel of Christ, who is the image of God, should shine unto them. For we preach," he adds, " not ourselves, but Christ Jesus the Lord ; and ourselves your servants for Jesus' sake. For God, who commanded the light to shine out of darkness, hath shined in our hearts, to give the light of the knowledge of the glory of God in the face of Jesus Christ." And then follow the words we are considering ; " But we have *this treasure* in earthen vessels." And is not the gospel, I would ask, justly termed a " treasure ?" Is there any thing, how valuable soever, which can be properly compared with it? If " the god of this world " hath not blinded our eyes also, we shall esteem it beyond all price ; " yea, doubtless," we shall, with the apostle,

" count all things but loss for the excellency of the knowledge of Christ Jesus our Lord." He " suffered the loss of all things, and counted them but dung, that he might win Christ; that he might know him, and be found in him." And so also shall we. " To them that believe, Christ is precious," and consequently the gospel which reveals him. Such was the " treasure," of which the parable speaks, " hid in a field." The individual who had the felicity to discover it, " went and sold all that he had, and bought it."

Consider what the gospel is, my brethren, and then judge of its value. It is a message of mercy to a lost world; it is the " ministry of reconciliation " to a guilty and rebellious race. What greater treasure could you present to a condemned malefactor, waiting in awful suspense the execution of his sentence, than an authoritative reprieve, and a full remission of his punishment? In vain would you proffer him the wealth of an universe; to him it would be a thing of nought. But bring him the document which suspends his execution, and unlocks his fetters, and sets him free, and you bring him a treasure indeed. Such is the gospel message of free pardon and full salvation to a sinner awakened to a sense of his guilt and danger. He feels himself to be in the situation of a criminal under the sentence of a three-fold death. He cries out, in the bitterness of his grief, and in the anxiety of his soul, " What shall I do to be saved?" And oh! what value must he attach to the apostolic reply, when once he has faith to receive it, " Believe in the Lord Jesus Christ, and thou shalt be saved." Then does he account it not only a " faithful saying," but an infinitely precious saying, and one " worthy of all acceptation, that Jesus Christ came into the world to save sinners."

The leading blessing conferred by the gospel is the *knowledge of Christ.* To know him, together with the Father, is declared to be everlasting life. The gospel reveals him to us, both in his divine and human nature, as the everlasting Son of the everlasting Father; as the Word incarnate; as "Immanuel, God with us;" as coming down from above, assuming our nature, living, suffering, dying for us men, and for our salvation; as rising again from the dead, ascending up into heaven, and sitting at the right hand of the Father, where he rules the world and the church, making intercession for us, and whence he will "come the second time without sin unto salvation." It declares to us the efficacy of his atoning sufferings, and the power of his resurrection. It assures us that by believing in him, we shall be "justified from all things;" and not only "justified," but "saved;" for that "he ever liveth to make intercession for us." It reveals to us, also, the means of our salvation, through the communicated influences of the Spirit which Christ bestows upon his disciples; and urges us to follow the "steps of his most holy life." It presents the Saviour to us, in short, in all his offices, as our "Prophet, Priest, and King;" and declares him to be at once "our wisdom, our righteousness, our sanctification, and our redemption." These are some of the chief particulars of the "excellency of the knowledge of Christ Jesus our Lord" —these unite to form "the treasury" of the Christian church, the value of which, neither human nor angelic tongues can adequately describe.

II. Having thus considered the "treasure" itself, I would direct your attention, secondly, to THE REPOSITORIES IN WHICH IT IS LAID UP. "We have this treasure in *earthen vessels.*" The expression is peculiarly significant. "A vessel" is used for the two-fold purpose of *security* and *conveyance* ; which well accord with the two great ends for which the ministry is ordained.

1. To the Christian priesthood is intrusted, in the first place, the *preservation of the faith.* When our blessed Lord had completed his personal ministry, he constituted his apostles the first repositories of his truth. He not only wished them to retain the knowledge they had acquired, but promised to give them his Holy Spirit, to bring all things to their remembrance which they had heard of him, to enlighten their minds, and to guide them into all truth. They were required, by their office, to guard the church against the reception of error, and to preserve the gospel of their Redeemer from all spoliation or injury. Accordingly we find, as well from the brief notices recorded in the Acts, as from the general tenor of their epistolary writings, that they were solicitous to fulfil these important duties. We find them, on one occasion, assembled together to consult on a question of difficulty, which had distracted the minds of some Gentile converts. Imploring the promised guidance of the Holy Spirit, they deliberated on the subject ; and having come to an unanimous decision, they recorded it for the future guidance of the church. St. Peter, St. James, St. Jude,—in fact *all* the apostles whose writings are still extant,— display a watchful anxiety to preserve whole and undefiled, "the truth as it is in Jesus." Nor was the amiable John, " the disciple whom Jesus loved," less distinguished than his brethren in the exercise of this care. It was the grief of his old age to witness the progress of error in the Christian church ; and earnestly did he beseech his converts to be upon their guard : " Beloved," says he, " believe not every spirit, but try the spirits whether they are of God : because many

false prophets are gone out into the world." But to the apostle Paul we should look more especially for examples of this nature. Of the fourteen epistles which he wrote, scarcely one can be mentioned in which he displays not a watchful solicitude to drive away error. In some instances, he not only denounces erroneous doctrines, but puts his converts on their guard against the individuals who were attempting to propagate them. "If any man," he observes, in his epistle to the Galatians, "preach any other gospel unto you than that ye have received, let him be accursed." To the Thessalonians he writes, "Now we command you, brethren, in the name of our Lord Jesus Christ, that ye withdraw yourselves from every brother that walketh disorderly, *and not after the tradition which he received of us.*" Having mentioned the opposition of Alexander, the coppersmith, to the truth, he enjoins Timothy to be watchful, and to withdraw from his society; "of whom be thou ware, also, for he hath greatly withstood our words." In a similar manner he alludes to Hymeneus and Philetus, "whose word did eat as a canker; who concerning the truth had erred, saying that the resurrection was past already; and overthrew the faith of some.

But the apostles were careful not only to preserve individually the trust reposed in them, but to secure its integrity and safe keeping in after generations. For this purpose, as well as for the general propagation of the faith, (to which I shall soon have occasion to allude,) they selected from among their converts faithful and upright men, whom they solemnly set apart for the sacred ministry. These were termed, for the most part, "elders;" though it is evident that there were, at that time, several descriptions of ministers. "For," as St.

Paul observes, " unto every one of us is given grace according to the measure of the gift of Christ...... And he gave some, apostles; and some, prophets; and, some, evangelists; and some, pastors and teachers; for the perfecting of the saints, for the work of the ministry, for the edifying of the body of Christ." [1] It is quite clear, also, that the apostles not only ordained ministers themselves, but gave authority to others to do the same. Thus Timothy, who, in the early part of his ministry, appears to have fulfilled the office of an " evangelist," was subsequently empowered to appoint elders, and to rule with some special authority in the church. St. Paul, in his first epistle to Timothy, enters at some length into the qualifications which he was to look for in those whom he might ordain, whether as deacons or elders; and charges him to " lay hands suddenly on no man." To Titus, also, he gave similar instructions, reminding him that the purpose for which he had left him in Crete, was " to set in order the things that were wanting, and to *ordain elders in every city.*"

It was after this manner then, my brethren, that the Christian priesthood became repositories of the " treasure " spoken of in the text; and we have the fullest evidence for believing, that in the transmission of such ministerial authority down to the generation which now exists, the chain of succession remains unbroken. It is still our office, as it was that of the primitive elders, to guard the sacred deposit with which we are intrusted, from the hands both of the spoiler and the defiler. It is ours to watch against all intermixture of error, and all withdrawment of truth. On the one hand we have the lover of science falsely so called, who is too rational to

---

[1] Ephes. iv. 7, 11, 12.

receive " the whole truth ; " and on the other hand,
we have the superstitious devotee, who is not sufficiently
rational to receive " nothing but the truth." But
whilst it is the duty of every one to " buy the truth, and
sell it not; " to " prove all things, and to hold fast that
which is good; " it is more especially incumbent upon
the *ministers* of the sanctuary to " contend earnestly for
the faith once delivered to the saints,"—" in meekness
instructing those that oppose themselves, if God perad-
venture will give them repentance to the acknowledging
of the truth." Still is it the character of a true pastor,
that he takes heed both unto himself and his doctrine,
" holding fast the faithful word as he has been taught,
that he may be able, by sound doctrine, both to exhort
and to convince the gainsayers." Still is it his bounden
duty to hold fast the form of sound words which has
been delivered to him, and so to preach the gospel of the
kingdom, as to be able to take his people to record, that
he has not " shunned to declare unto them all the counsel
of God."

2. And this leads me to the consideration of the
second purpose for which vessels are usually designed,
namely, that of *conveyance*. In this sense we meet
with a striking instance of the use of this figure, with
reference to the apostle Paul. " He is a *chosen vessel*
unto me," said the Lord to Ananias, " *to bear my name*
before the Gentiles, and kings, and the children of
Israel." The treasure of Christianity is not like earthly
possessions, which " perish with the using." On the
contrary, it is " inexhaustible," as well as " undefiled."
Let the Christian instructor impart what he may, it is
only like the overflowings of a perennial spring, whose
capacious basin, whence they descend to fertilize the
valley, remains ever full. He is not himself the poorer

for all the gifts which he bestows. *His* are " the barrel
of meal, and the cruse of oil," which shall never fail
whilst there is one individual on the earth who " hungers
and thirsts after righteousness."

How ready, then, should every Christian minister be,
to convey the knowledge of salvation to all within his
reach ; to preach the word with all boldness, and with
all fidelity, " in season and out of season ! "   As, in the
instructive parable of our Lord, the slothful servant was
condemned for hiding his master's talent in a napkin, so
is *he* to be reproved, who, careful only to preserve his
own creed unimpaired, feels no anxiety, and makes no
effort, to extend to others the savour of the knowledge
of Christ.

But whilst we acknowledge that such unworthy
repositories of Christian truth deserve reprehension, let
us not forget that the ministers of the sanctuary are,
" at their best estate," but " earthen vessels."   The
epithet is well suited to express their meanness, and their
frailty.   The apostles themselves, even the most eminent
amongst them, were men of like feelings and infirmities
with others.   Though sanctified by the Spirit of God,
they were not impeccable ; though endowed with miraculous powers, they were equally exposed with others to
weariness and fatigue, to hunger and thirst, to cold and
nakedness.   They were, for the most part, mean in
their extraction, and mean in their external appearance.
With the exception of St. Paul, they were plain, unlearned men, without riches, without honours, without
worldly influence.   The pencil of the artist and the
fancy of the poet have, it is true, encircled their heads
with a halo of glory ; but, in reality, they had " neither
form nor comeliness," that mankind should " desire "
them.   " 1 think," says St. Paul, " that God hath set

forth us, the apostles, last, as it were appointed to death:
for we are made a spectacle unto the world, and to
angels and to men. We are fools for Christ's sake, . . .
weak and despised. Even unto this present hour we
both hunger, and thirst, and are naked, and are buffeted,
and have no certain dwelling-place. . . . We are made
as the filth of the earth, and are the offscouring of all
things." And though the outward condition of the
Christian priesthood has improved since the establish-
ment of Christianity on the ruins of Judaism and Paganism, yet is it still seen, that the most useful of God's
ministering servants are frequently the most destitute of
worldly comforts, and the most despised by the great ones
of the earth. Under the names of the most evangelical,
holy, and laborious preachers of the truth, in every age
of the church, might the aphorism of the apostle be
aptly inscribed,—" poor, yet making many rich." They
were distinguished, perhaps, neither for eloquence nor
learning; and yet their extraordinary success in turning
many to righteousness, and in building up believers in
their most holy faith, proves incontestibly that they were
chosen vessels of the Lord.

In making choice of such repositories of gospel blessings, the Almighty has shown us that his thoughts are
not as our thoughts, nor his ways as our ways. We
should naturally have expected, that instead of putting
such a treasure in frail earthen vessels, defiled with sin,
and marked with imperfection, he would have selected
for his purpose, some of the most honourable and mighty
among the celestial hosts, some of those principalities and
powers in heavenly places, of which we read, even the
cherubim and seraphim, and the angels who excel in
might. Or had he condescended to employ human
agents, we should naturally have expected that he would

o

raise up some men of extraordinary genius, gifted with
an eloquence which nothing could resist, and enriched
with every mental and corporeal endowment. We
should have expected, in short, that they should be so
qualified, by outward advantages and inward graces, as
that they might confidently traverse the globe with their
treasure, scattering their gifts without let or hindrance,
and bringing every individual to an instant conviction
that they were the messengers of the Most High God.
But he has been pleased, as we have seen, to determine
otherwise, and to make choice of ordinary men, and, for
the most part, of an humble rank in life, and distinguished by no secular advantages, to be the most successful ministers of his word. Nor are we left to conjecture
*why* he has so determined. " We have this treasure
in earthen vessels, *that the excellency of the power may
be of God, and not of us.*"

III. This is the third and last particular, which now
requires our attention. The self-existent Jehovah, even
the God over all, designs in this, as in all his arrangements, TO MANIFEST HIS OWN GLORY. Had he employed any of the instruments already mentioned,
then the achievements of Christianity would have been
referred, not to the power of his gospel, accompanied by
the influences of his Spirit, but to the learning, the
eloquence, the skill, the worldly influence of those distinguished individuals. Acting, therefore, upon that
one uniform and essential principle, that he " will not
give" his " honour to another," he has selected such
instruments as cannot possibly be regarded as the unaided
accomplishers of the mighty effects which result from
their ministry. Thus, to use the language of the apostle,
" he hath chosen the foolish things of the world to
confound the wise ; and the weak things of the world to

confound the things that are mighty; *that no flesh should glory in his presence,*—that, according as it is written, *He that glorieth let him glory in the Lord.*"

That the preaching of the gospel is attended with "excellency of power," there can be no question. It was so in the days of the apostles, as exhibited in the *propagation of Christianity.* Though the gospel was diametrically at variance with the notions which generally prevailed, whether in Palestine or Greece; though it was violently opposed by all the influence, authority, and learning of mankind; though it called upon its converts to deny themselves, and take up their cross, and follow an exalted but once crucified Jesus through present disgrace, hardships, bonds and privations; though it promised nothing, either of glory or of ease, but what was future and unseen; yet did it march onward and prevail, in spite of all opposition. Though " to the Jews the preaching of the cross was a stumbling-block, and to the Greeks foolishness," yet to multitudes who were pricked in their hearts, and enabled " to believe," it proved " the *power* of God unto salvation."

Its blessed effects, when accompanied by the influence of the Holy Spirit, are still exhibited in the renewal and sanctification of men's hearts and lives. Is it not evident to every one who is at all conversant with the state of religion in this country, and in our own particular church, that in every instance in which the doctrines of the gospel, in opposition to the mere theory of morals, are plainly, zealously, and affectionately pressed, that God is glorified by the conversion of many evil livers, the humbling of many a proud heart, and the consoling of many a sorrowful heart? Cannot the faithful minister of religion still testify with the apostle Paul, after a similar experience, " I am not ashamed of the gospel of

Christ: for it is the power of God unto salvation to
every one that believeth?" Yes! we see that when
Christ is "lifted up," he still "draweth all men unto
him." It is not the preacher's eloquence that renews
the heart, and engenders faith, and kindles love, and
excites joy. These are no other than "fruits of the
Spirit."

What preacher more successful than the great apostle
of the Gentiles? And yet this is the testimony recorded
by his own pen; "And I, brethren, when I came unto
you, came not with excellency of speech or of wisdom,
declaring unto you the testimony of God. For I determined not to know any thing among you, save Jesus
Christ, and him crucified. And I was with you in
weakness, and in fear, and in much trembling. And my
speech and my preaching was not with enticing words
of man's wisdom, but *in demonstration of the Spirit, and
of power : that your faith should not stand in the wisdom of men, but in the power of God.*"

Seeing then, my brethren, that such are the blessed
effects of a preached gospel, when rightly received, permit me to ask, in conclusion, whether *you* have experienced them? This "excellency of power" invariably
accompanies a proper reception of the truth. Inquire
therefore, I beseech you, whether you have "received
it, not as the word of man, but as it is in truth, the word
of God, which effectually worketh in them that believe?"
If the preaching of the gospel has served merely to
modify some of your notions about religion, to correct a
few prejudices, and throw a little glimmering of light into
your understanding, leaving your heart at the same time
unrenewed, and your affections still fixed supremely on
things below, no "excellency of power" has been displayed in you. No; before this power can be said to

have exerted itself in the salvation of your souls, we must see something of that shaking of " the dry bones," of which the prophet speaks in his instructive vision. Yea, more than a "shaking" must take place; they must even " come together ; the sinews and the flesh also must come upon them, and the skin must cover them above." Nor will even this suffice. Another most important circumstance must be realized, before " the excellency " of God's power in the ministry of his word can be fully exhibited. The " breath of heaven" must come into them; and then shall they live, and stand up upon their feet. Would to God that this glorious and mighty result may be experienced by every one here present as yet dead in trespasses and sins. " Come from the four winds, O breath, and breathe upon these slain, and they shall live."

It is cheering to the Christian minister to know, that though he is responsible to God for a faithful and laborious prosecution of his high calling, he is not answerable for its *results*. If it were otherwise, who could dare to assume the dread, the tremendous office ? Even as it is, we are compelled to exclaim, with the apostle, " Who is sufficient for these things ? " So inestimably valuable is the treasure,—so frail, and mean, and worthless the earthen vessels in which it is deposited,—that we are sometimes tempted to despond. But we are reminded by the same apostle, that " our sufficiency is of God ; " that the grace " of our Redeemer is sufficient for us; and that as our day is, so our strength shall be." We thus remind you, my brethren, as well as ourselves, of our weakness and infirmities, in order to stir you up to the exercise of that too much neglected duty, intercessory prayer. I beseech you to remember, in your petitions, the ministers of religion. Pray, in the language of our liturgy, that the giver of all good gifts, "who of his divine Providence has appointed divers orders in his church, may give his grace unto all who are called to any office and administration in the same; and so replenish them with the truth of his doctrine, and endue them with innocency of life, that they may faithfully serve before him, to the glory of his great name, and the benefit of his holy church." And more especially let me intreat your prayers in behalf of him who now addresses you. The vessel which is appointed to convey to you the rich treasure of the gospel is, indeed, an "earthen vessel." Pray that, notwithstanding all its frailty and imperfection, it may yet prove effectual, through the grace and strength of the Redeemer, to accomplish the two great ends of the ministerial office. It is at once your interest, your privilege, and your duty, to pray for your minister. His prosperity is yours also. The more unalloyed and entire he is enabled to preserve the "treasure" committed to his care, and the more fitted he becomes to convey it to others, the more will your own advantages as a people be increased. Let him, then, under the consciousness of many wants and failings, conclude his discourse with a request, which he feels confident will not be denied him; " BRETHREN, PRAY FOR US ! "

The second species of outline, consisting of notes, condensed in a form best adapted for the use of an *extemporary* preacher, requires also to be illustrated by examples. The two following specimens occur in the Memoirs of the late Rev. T. Robinson, M. A. Vicar of St. Mary's, Leicester, the author of " Scripture Characters," &c. and one of the most popular as well as judicious preachers of his time.

## 1 JOHN iv. 17.

*" As he is, so are we in this world."*

What are Christians?—Important question! Redeemed by Christ—Rejoicing in him—But their *character* as well as *state* is changed—they are *followers* or *imitators* of Him—Who can adopt these words ?—Examine

I. We are not so by nature. Rom. viii. 7. Eph. ii. 1—3. Titus iii. 3.

II. We are made so *by grace.* Philosophy and reason do not effect this change. Rom. viii. 29. Gal. iii. 27. 2 Peter i. 4. Eph. iv. 24. Fruits of the Spirit.

III. We must *appear* to be so. 1 Peter ii. 21. 1 John ii. 6.
1. In *zeal for God*—public and private devotions.
2. In *abstraction from the world*—not of it—and hated by it.
3. In *holy tempers*—meekness, and love. Matt. xi. 29. Eph. v. 2. Phil. ii. 5. bearing—forgiving—kind. Psalm cix. Rom. xv. 3. 1 Peter ii. 23.

IV. By *what means* we must become so.
    1. *The Scriptures*—study him there.
    2. *Contemplation.* Heb. xii.
    3. *Faith.* John vi. 2 Cor. iii. 18.
    4. *Prayer for the Spirit.* Psalm li. 13.

Apply
    1. To Christians—your likeness is defective here, will be complete hereafter. Phil. iii. 21. Col. iii. iv. 1 John iii. 2.
    2. To *sinners.* Whom do you resemble—with whom can you dwell?

### COLOSS. i. 19.

" *It pleased the Father that in him should all fulness dwell.*"

My business is to speak of Christ—
But O ! how unfit—O Lord assist !
This is the apostle's subject—most glorious—

I. The fulness of Christ as head of all things—
This is—
    (1.) The fulness of *Deity—Shechinah—*Christ's body is the temple—Godhead resides in it—
    It was *manifested* in Him—
    The scriptures *assert* that it was in Him—
    His works and offices *imply* that it was in Him—
    He *sustains,* and *supports* all things.
    O worship—adore—serve Him !
    (2.) The fulness of *all spiritual blessings*—The view here is not to his own character, but to his office as Mediator.
    He is the fountain head—grand depository—
    Having purchased grace he bestows it—

Righteousness for justification.

Wisdom, as light from the sun. Col. ii. 3.

Strength for duties and trials. 2 Cor. iii. 5.
Eph. iv. 7—16. 2 Cor. xii. 9.

Comfort. John xiv. 27; xvi. 33; xv. 11.
Psalm xvi. 11.

These graces he possesses *without measure*—enough,
For *all* the wants of believers.

For *all* believers however numerous.

By faith you must receive—

II. The good pleasure of the Father—a blessed union,
    1. The Father hath *appropriated* this way.
    2. The Father considers it as most glorious to himself.
    3. The Father requires the acquiescence and submission of sinners.

Improve by advising
    1. To cease from man—who is vanity.
    From yourselves.
    From others—who will disappoint you.
    2. To study the glory of Christ—
    3. Not to object to their own emptiness—
    4. To communicate to others—thus resembling Christ—
    In spiritual things.
    In temporal.
    5. To be satisfied if Christ be yours.
    But let nothing less, nothing else, satisfy you.
    1 Cor. iii. 21.

To the two preceding specimens, the Editor subjoins a synopsis of a discourse on 2 Cor. iv. 16, the original of which he possesses in Mr. Robinson's own hand writing.

## 2 Cor. iv. 16.

We are anxious for the welfare of friends. This not wrong—but our attention too confined.

We look to the body—forget the soul. -
Bodily health of great value—that of the soul greater.
Is yours what you understand? Examine.
Text describes, a prosperous state of soul in bodily weakness. 3 John 2.
Consider,

I. The renovation of the soul.
Beginning of life—why necessary.
Not mere amendment of life, or reformation.
Faculties restored to their proper use.
(1.) Understanding. (2.) Will. (3.) Affections.
Inquire as to the reality of religion.

II. The gradual progress of the work.
Life is at first in a weak state—maintained—carried on—DAY BY DAY. Babes—children—fathers.
Little increasings—purified as metals—grow as *grass, corn, trees*. Spreads as leaven —rises as a building.
All Christians need *daily provision*.
They differ—from others—from themselves.
All mourn defects—liable to fall—do actually depart—&c. not perfect.

Should pray: for their increase and revival. Phil.
i. 9. Psalms.
Should seek after. Phil. iii. 12—14. 2 Pet. iii. 18.
Lament sloth—earthliness—&c.

III. Its obstructions. Various.
Outward troubles are a TEST, but necessarily
hindrances.
Body perishes—doomed to die—infirmities—pains—
sickness—age.
Will these prevent? No—grace triumphs.
These may forward the work. Better than prosperity.
Drive to God—humble—endear Christ and heaven.
Glorious sights exhibited on sick beds.
But many are hindered by—remaining corruptions.
occasional temptations.
sad relapses,
Apply,
(1.) Take care by what marks you judge.
Trust not in a mere profession.
in great confidence or joy.
Be not discouraged—though unfitted by disorder.
though sorely tempted.
(2.) Admire the work of God—carried on—his grace,
his strength—preserving life against so much
opposition, a spark of fire in the ocean.
Pray—and trust—and give thanks.
(3.) What a sad contrast in the sinner.
More careless—confirmed—obdurate—mischievous—fitted for destruction.
Mourn and weep. O fear !
Your outward man must perish.
Then where must you dwell.

The preceding sketches were evidently designed by the preacher, to refresh his memory in the pulpit, should occasion require, and to keep himself within the prescribed limits of his subject. The notes themselves indicate no particular talent nor skill: the ability consisted in employing them as he did, in a distinguished and masterly manner, retaining a listening throng, hanging upon his lips, awed, penetrated, delighted, and instructed by his manly unaffected eloquence. ' Who ever heard him,' asks his still more eloquent panegyrist,[1] ' without feeling a persuasion that it was the man of God who addressed him ; or without being struck with the perspicuity of his statement, the solidity of his thoughts, and the rich unction of his spirit? It was the harp of David, which, struck with his powerful hand, sent forth more than mortal sounds, and produced an impression far more deep and permanent than the thunder of Demosthenes, or the splendid conflagrations of Cicero. The hearers of Mr. Robinson were too much occupied by the subject he presented to their attention, to waste a thought on the speaker : this occupied a second place in the order of their reflections; but when it did occur, it assumed the character, not of superficial admiration, but of profound attachment. Their feelings towards him were not those of persons gratified, but benefitted, and they listened to his instructions, not as a source of amusement, but as a spring of living water. There never was a settled pastor, probably, who had formed a juster conception of the true end of preaching, who pursued it more steadily, or attained it to a greater extent. He preached immortal truth with a most extraordinary

[1] The late Rev. Robert Hall.

simplicity, perspicuity, and energy, in a style adapted
to all capacities, equally removed from vulgarity and
affected refinement; and the tribute paid to his exertions, consisted not in loud applauses ; it was of a higher
order ; it consisted of penitential sighs, holy resolutions
of a determination of the whole soul for God, and such
impressions on the spirits of men as will form the line
of separation betwixt the happy and the miserable to all
eternity.'

From the Memoirs[1] of this distinguished preacher,
it appears that during the first seven years of his ministry, he composed all his sermons before preaching, and
delivered them without alteration or addition from the
manuscripts he had prepared. After that period he
preached from short notes, such as have been given in
the two preceding specimens. These contained the main
divisions of his subject, and a sketch of all the leading
ideas which he meant to introduce, together with his
formal references to Scripture. The impression produced
by his written, and by his extemporary sermons, is said
to have been much the same; only it was remarked that
he was slower and more deliberate in the delivery of
these than of the former.

---

[1] See ' Some account' of his Life, &c. by the late Rev. E. T.
Vaughan, M. A.

The *third* species of analysis, to which allusion has
been made, yet remains to be considered. It differs
from the two preceding species by being still more
ample and complete, and designed by the writer, not for
his own use, but for that of others.

It is not perhaps generally understood that the venerable author of the Horæ Homileticæ penned those
valuable compositions *after* having preached the substance of them from the pulpit. The analysis, which in
every instance he previously prepared, and took with
him into the pulpit, was much shorter, and more compressed. It consisted in fact, of short notes, resembling
the specimens already given from the pen of Mr.
Robinson.

The Editor trusts that his revered friend will pardon
the liberty he takes in illustrating this observation by
presenting to the younger clergy, to whom he has shewn
himself preeminently a benefactor, one or two specimens
of his pulpit notes, selected out of about half-a-dozen,
which he kindly left with him as memorials of his highly
valued visit at Liverpool some years ago. They were
sketched, it must be remembered, for the occasion, with
no view whatever to meet the public eye, or indeed any
eye, but his own; yet, it is remarkable what order and
method, what correctness and precision they evince, and
how much important matter is compressed within so
small a space.

The first specimen which I shall produce is from
Isaiah xxvii. 12, 13, containing the matter and sub-
stance of what he gives us in No. 500 of his Horæ
Homileticæ. It will prove an interesting occupation to

the student, who may possess that valuable work, to compare the one with the other in their several parts.

## ISAIAH xxvii. 12, 13.

A mistaken notion that God will convert the Jews by miracle, and not by means.

The text refutes that, and encourages the use of means.——Consider,

I. The mercy reserved for the Jewish people,
II. The way in which it shall be vouchsafed to them.

And I. The mercy reserved for the Jewish people. They shall " be gathered and worship," &c.

(1.) Literally.

Many doubt this—but it seems certain. Deut. xxx. 1—5. Zech. viii. 3—9, 23.

(2.) Spiritually.

The Christian church is Mount Zion.

To it shall they be gathered.

This is foretold. Ezek. xxxiv. 11—16, 23, 24. Hosea iii. 5 ; especially Rom. ii. 12, 15, 19, 20, 24.

Regarding this as certain, we may proceed to consider,

II. The way in which this mercy shall be vouchsafed to them.——This we will trace

(1.) In its commencement.

The extent of territory before promised, Gen. xv. 18.

But driven thence, they are compared to an olive tree stripped. Isaiah xvii. 4—6.

God, however, will send his servants to "seek" and "beat off" or "*shake* off."

The success of this will not be great: "one by one."

But to them it will be a joyful event.

  Isa. xxiv. 13, 14.

  Jer. iii. 14, "one of a city."

They only a remnant, Isa. x. 22.

Yet as the first-fruits of harvest.

(2.) In its progress.

The great trumpet will be blown.

These used for convincing—in the wilderness regulating their journeys, Numb. x. 2; proclaiming jubilee, Lev. xxv.

The gospel is this trumpet.

Then will that be fulfilled, Isa. xi. 11, 12, 15, 16.

Multitudes will accompany them, Isa. xix. 23—25.

A matter of joy, Jer. xxxi. 6—14.

Thus shall all Israel be saved, Rom. xi. 26, 27.

Infer,

1. How groundless is the objection which so many raise against the efforts that are making for the conversion of the Jews, that they are useless! Many malignantly ask, "What have you done?"

Ans. "Not sow and reap in one day."

  Heathen missions (Greenland) not at once.

  But it is erroneous to think they will be converted by miracle. There will be indeed a resurrection, Ezek. xxxvii. But the commencement as *gleanings*. Christ and his apostles converted few— yet this no reason for relaxing. We have as many as could reasonably be expected.

  If they be few, should we not still seek them? e. g. a house on fire.

See the description, " outcasts " — " ready to
perish."

They are the " lost sheep of," &c.

One sheep should be sought.

Not the Father's will that *one* perish. Matt.
xviii. 12—14.

But this cannot be done—if not to seek, and beat
them off.——Can there be a convocation if none
blow the trumpet? We want instruments and
missionaries.

2. What we all need in order to our own salvation.

We are as in bad a state as the Jews.

" All we like sheep have gone astray."

We are but a remnant, or *gleanings* —" little flock "
—few in the narrow way.

I would " beat you off from the tree."

————— sound the trumpet.

————— be thankful to gather "one by one,"
"two or three on the topmost—four or five on
outmost," &c.

All that is necessary for Jews, is necessary for
you also.

The second specimen which I shall present, consists
of still shorter notes upon 2 Cor. iii. 15, 16 ; and may
be compared with No. 985 of the Horæ Homileticæ.

2 COR. iii. 15, 16.

I. The present blindness of the Jews.

II. The manifestations that await them.

First. The present, &c.

Moses is read—yet they see not.

(1) The scope and intent of the Mosaic dispensation.

This is complicated. The *moral* law is a republication of, &c.

The *ceremonial* law – a shadowing forth—— grace.

These they mistake. The *judicial* law a national covenant.

The *moral*—not seeing its spirituality, but as a letter.

The *ceremonial*—viewing it as a real atonement, instead of a typical exhibition.

The *judicial*—as the whole—by which to obtain . acceptance.

(2) The true meaning of their prophecies.

There is a chain—but they saw it imperfectly.

Even the Apostles at one time thought of a temporal Messiah.

The present Jews have a still deeper veil—denying much which their ancestors saw.

They had no idea of the whole as we see it.
$\left\{\begin{array}{l}\text{incarnate.}\\\text{living.}\\\text{dying.}\\\text{rising.}\\\text{reigning.}\end{array}\right.$

Secondly. The manifestations that await them.

Moses went in before the Lord. Exod. xxxiv. 34.

So they, when they turn to *him*, shall see, and not to the RABBIES.

(1) The truth and certainty.

The types and prophecies mark with such fulness 10,000 particulars—a *seal*—an *impression*.

(2) The mysteriousness and sublimity.

    In these they will see the *true* temple, altar, sacrifice, priest, prophet, king.    ·

(3) The fulness and excellency.

    A complete atonement—not a mere remembrance.

    A full pardon—and satisfactory to conscience.

    Sanctification—purged from dead works to serve, &c.

    The law made nothing perfect.

    They will have a different view from a heathen.  Sun-dial — machine — EDUCATION.

Infer,

1. What we should desire for ourselves.

    We have a veil too.   *Our views like those of the Jews.*

    We should pray for the removal of it.  " God open the eyes of our understanding!"

    We should go to the Lord—learn of him, and be taught by him.

2. What we should desire in behalf of the Jews.

    The veil on the Scriptures is taken away in Christ; and we should desire to remove the veil from their hearts————endeavour to do it.

    N. B. The Scriptures have been committed to us for that end. Rom. ii. 24, 25.

    Their blindness imputable to *us*.  *A lighthouse.*

    Let us NOW endeavour—and unite for that end.

    *They* enlightened *us*—let *us* enlighten *them*.

In referring the young preacher to the valuable assistance which such works as the Thesaurus Theologicus of
Beveridge,· and the Skeletons of Sermons, and Horæ
Homileticæ of Mr. Simeon, are calculated to afford, the
Editor ventures to suggest the importance of making a
*proper use* of them. They were intended to *aid* the
minister in his preparation for the pulpit, but by no
means to supersede his own exertions. ' The preacher,'
observes Mr. Simeon, ' should first make himself master
of the Skeleton before him, and then write in *his own
language*, and according to his own conceptions, his
views of the subject; and he will find that ' verba
provisam rem not invita sequentur.' Mr. Bridges, in
his valuable work on the Christian Ministry, speaking
on the same subject, observes, that ' a thoughtful mind
will find ample and profitable employment in clothing
the Skeletons, and exhibiting them fitted with solid
matter, in the form of symmetry and strength. ' As an
illustration,' he adds, ' Henry Martyn's Sermon on Psalm
ix. 17. is the filling up of Mr. Simeon's Skeleton on that
text. It was worked out (as we accidentally learn from
his life) under circumstances of peculiar disadvantage
and mental agitation. But the life that is infused
throughout, the variety of its enlargements, the accuracy
of the proportions of its several parts, the skill with
which the breaks are completed, and the warm and
strong colouring given to the whole—all combine to give
it the power and effect of an original and talented
composition.' [1]

With a view to render this peculiarly happy illustration the more complete, the Editor here subjoins for the
inspection and comparison of the Student both the

[1] See his Life, p. 130—132.

Skeleton and the Sermon. The former which may be found in Mr. Simeon's Helps to Composition, Vol. IV. Skeleton, 357, is as follows.

### THE DANGER OF FORGETTING GOD.

Psalm ix. 17. " The wicked shall be turned into hell, and all the nations that forget God."

[The most eminent saints are represented in Scripture as weeping over an ungodly world.——Nor would this exercise of compassion be so rare, if we duly considered how great occasion there is for it.——The words before us are a plain and unequivocal declaration from God himself respecting the doom which awaits every impenitent sinner.——May God impress our minds with a solemn awe, while we shew—]

I. Who they are whom God esteems wicked.

[If we consult the opinions of men, we shall find that they differ widely from each other in their ideas of moral guilt, and that they include more or less in their definition of wickedness according to their own peculiar habits of life; every one being careful so to draw the line that he himself may not be comprehended within it. But God does not consult our wishes, or accommodate his word to our partial regards : he denominates all them wicked, who "forget" him. Doubtless there are degrees of guilt; but all those are wicked in his sight who are forgetful of—]

1. His laws.

[These ought to be written on our hearts, and to be the invariable rule of our conduct. It should be our constant inquiry, What is duty? what does God command? But if this be no part of our concern, if our inquiry be continually, ' What will please myself—what will advance my interests—what will suit the taste of those

around me ; ' are we not wicked? Do we not in all such
instances rebel against God, and become, as it were, a
God unto ourselves? Yet who amongst us has not been
guilty in these respects?]

2. His mercies.

[Every day and hour of our lives we have been laden
with mercies by a kind and bountiful benefactor—and
should they not have excited correspondent emotions of
gratitude in our hearts? Yea, should they not have
filled our mouths with praises and thanksgivings? But
what shall we say to that greatest of all mercies, the gift
of God's dear Son to die for us? Has not *that* deserved
our devoutest acknowledgments? What then if we have
passed days and years without any affectionate remembrance of God? What if we have even abused the
bounties of his Providence, and poured contempt upon
the riches of his grace? What if we have " trodden
under foot the Son of' God, and done despite to the
Spirit of grace ?" Are we not wicked? Do we account
such ingratitude a venal offence, when exercised by a
dependent towards ourselves?]

3. His presence.

[God is every where present, and every object around
us has this inscription upon it, "Thou God seest me."
Now it is our duty and privilege to walk with God as
his friends, and to set him before us all the day long.
But, suppose we have been unmindful of his presence,
and have indulged without remorse those thoughts, which
we could not have endured to carry into effect in the
presence of a fellow-creature; suppose we have been
careless and unconcerned even when we' were assembled
in God's house of prayer; suppose that instead of having
him in all our thoughts, we have lived " without him in
the world," are we not wicked? Is it necessary to have

added murder and adultery to such crimes as these in
order to constitute us wicked? Does God judge thus,
when he declares that they who are thus without God,
are at the same time "without hope?"[1]]

While we rectify our notions respecting the persons
that are wicked, let us inquire—

II. What is to be their final doom.

[The word "hell" sometimes imports no more than the
grave; but here it must mean somewhat far more awful;
because the righteous go into the grave as well as the
most abandoned.]

Hell is a place of inconceivable misery.

[Men in general do not wish to hear this place so much
as mentioned, much less described as the portion of the
wicked; but it is better far to hear of it, than to dwell
in it; and it is by hearing of it that we must be persuaded to avoid it.[2] Our Lord represents it as a place
originally formed for the reception of the fallen angels;
and very frequently labours to deter men from sin by the
consideration of its terrors.[3] And who that reflects
upon that "lake of fire and brimstone," where the wicked
"dwell with everlasting burnings," and "weep, and
wail, and gnash their teeth," without so much as the
smallest hope of deliverance from it, and where "the
smoke of their torment ascendeth up for ever and ever;"
who that considers what it must be to have the devils for
our companions, and to have the vials of God's wrath
poured out upon us, without intermission and without
end; who that considers these things, must not tremble
at the thought of taking up his abode in that place.——]

Yet must that be the portion of all that forget God.

[*Now* scoffers make light of eternal torments, and

---

[1] Eph. ii. 12.    [2] 2 Cor. v. xi.
[3] Luke xii. 5.  Mark ix. 43—48.

puff at the denunciations of God's wrath; but ere long they will wish that "the rocks might fall upon them, and the hills cover them" from his impending judgments. But, however reluctant they be to obey the Divine mandate, they must "depart;" they will be "turned" into hell with irresistible violence, and with fiery indignation. Their numbers will not at all secure them against the threatened vengeance; though there be whole "nations," they will not be able to withstand the arm of God; nor will they excite commiseration in his heart: neither will their misery be the less because of the multitudes who partake of it; for, instead of alleviating one another's sorrows with tender sympathy, they will accuse one another with the bitterest invectives. The power and veracity of God are pledged to execute this judgment; and sooner shall heaven and earth be annihilated, than one jot or tittle of his word shall fail. ——]

INFER.

1. How awful is the insensibility in which the world are living!

[Men seem as careless and indifferent about their eternal interests, as if they had nothing to apprehend; or as if God had promised that the wicked should be received into heaven. But can they set aside the declaration that is now before us? Or do they suppose it is intended merely to alarm us; and that it shall never be executed upon us? "Is God then a man that he should lie, or a son of man, that he should repent?" O that they would awake from their infatuation, and flee from the wrath to come. ——]

2. How just will be the condemnation of sinners in the last day!

[Many think it a hard thing that so heavy a judgment

should be denounced merely for forgetting God. But is this so small an offence as they imagine? Is it not rather exceedingly heinous? Does it not imply the basest ingratitude, the most daring rebellion? Yea, a great degree even of atheism itself? And shall not God visit for these things, and be avenged on such transgressors as these? Shall they be at liberty to abase God's mercies, and God not be at liberty to suspend the communication of his blessings? Shall they despise and trample on God's laws, and God not be at liberty to assert their authority? Shall they say to God, "Depart from us, we desire not the knowledge of thy ways;" and shall God be accused of injustice if he say to them, "Depart, ye shall never have one glimpse of my presence any more?" But if they *will dare* to open their mouths against him now, the time is shortly coming, when they will stand self-convicted, and self-condemned. ——]

3. How marvellous are the patience and the mercy of God!

[God has seen the whole race of man departing from him, and blotting out, as much as they could, the remembrance of him from the earth. His authority, his love, his mercy, are, as it were, by common consent banished from the conversation and from the very thoughts of men. Yet, instead of burning with indignation against us, and " turning us all quick into hell," he bears with us, he invites us to mercy, he says, " Deliver them from going down into the pit, for I have found a ransom." [1] O that we might be duly sensible of his mercy! O that we might flee for refuge to the hope set before us! If once we be cast into hell, we

[1] Job xxxiii. 24.

P

shall never obtain one drop of water to cool our tongues : " but " this is the accepted time ; " the Lord grant that we may find it also " the day of salvation ! "

The Sermon of Henry Martyn, corresponding with the above, is as follows.

## Psalm ix. 17.

" The wicked shall be turned into hell, and all the people that forget God."

Men and brethren, if religion were only a cunningly-devised fable, if that hell, of which you read in the Bible, were only an invention of crafty deceivers, you might. despise their threatenings, and go on in sin. Moreover, if it were only the drunkard, the murderer, the adulterer, the sabbath-breaker, or the common swearer, that was to find his portion in hell, then the sober and moral among you might please themselves with the hope of escape. But if the Almighty has himself thundered out of heaven, and made known to all men, not only that he hath prepared a place of torment for the wicked, but that all who *forget God* shall be turned into it, it behoveth every one of us to hear, believe, and tremble.

Brethren, let the words of our text convince you that the word of God speaks plainly. Certain vain and ignorant persons are shocked at the coarseness of this subject, but you now hear God speaking for himself. This then is the threatening of Jehovah, which his justice and truth engage him to execute, that *the wicked shall be turned into hell, and all the nations that forget God.*

At the very recital of these words, some of you must

be convinced that they are in danger : their consciences must testify, that, if they die as they are now living, they must perish. But by far the greater number are saying to themselves, ' Whatever others may be, I have no reason to believe myself to be wicked, or that I forget God.' Now, my brethren, you that speak after this manner, may *perhaps* be right, but it is *possible* you may be *wrong*. If you are right, you need not fear to inquire into your reasons for thinking so : if you are wrong, it will be but a poor exchange to obtain a false peace for a little while in this world, at the expense of awakening from delusion in the next. It is therefore far wiser to ascertain the point. Let us then for this purpose, first inquire, who are the persons described in the text : and, in the second place, declare their final doom.

I. We shall inquire, who are *the persons described in the text*.

We apprehend that *the wicked*, and *all the nations that forget God*, are the same persons. In the sight of God, all are wicked who forget him : yet, in compliance with the usual sense put upon these words, let us suppose two sorts of persons spoken of—the wicked, those who are openly immoral ; and the other, those who are more decent in their conduct.

1. The *wicked* or immoral are those whose sins carry the sentence of their condemnation along with them. To call these sins into a particular review, were unnecessary. Deeply marked with the character of hell, they proclaim to every beholder to what place they are tending. Let it suffice to adduce certain passages of Scripture, in which God has summed up these workers of iniquity, in one complete catalogue, and assigned one doom to them all. " Know ye not, that the unrighteous shall not inherit

the kingdom of God? Be not deceived; neither fornicators, nor idolators, nor adulterers, nor thieves, nor covetous, nor drunkards, nor revilers, nor extortioners, shall inherit the kingdom of God." 1 Cor. vi. 9, 10. " Now the works of the flesh are manifest, which are these : adultery, fornication, uncleanness, lasciviousness, idolatry, drunkenness, and such like : of the which I tell you before, as I have also told you in time past, that they which do such things shall not inherit the kingdom of God." Gal. v. 19, 21. Would there were none such in the present assembly!

2. Leaving these texts to their consideration, we proceed to inquire who they are that *forget God*.

God hath commanded us to remember him in *all* our ways. Not to do this is to forget him. ' What then,' you ask, ' is it possible for any man to be always thinking of God? Is there not a time for all things? Is it not sufficient that we think of him at proper seasons : such as on the Sabbath, or at morning or evening prayer?' No, brethren; it is not sufficient. God says, " My son, give me thy heart," Prov. xxiii. 26.— thine affections : love me, and you will think of me. The good man may through infirmity, lose sight of God : but he always accounts it a loss, and longs to regain it : but it is a sign of *wickedness*, if we forget God wilfully and deliberately in any part of our conduct. God requires *All* the heart, and *All* the life to be devoted to his service. And, indeed, there is as much reason why we should remember him in *all* our ways, as in *any one* of them ; if it were lawful to forget him, that is, to have no regard to his authority in one particular, it would be lawful also to forget him in another: thus the rule of right would be left to every man's own choice, and God would be no longer the governor of the world.

It is therefore, trifling with scripture to urge that you do not forget God, merely from this circumstance, that you sometimes think of him ; for you may now certainly perceive, if God be wilfully excluded from any one of your thoughts, you are so far wicked. But we need not strain this point to prove your guilt. It is easy to show, concerning a great part of you, that he is scarcely in any of your thoughts; you forget his laws—you forget his mercies—you forget his presence.

(1.) There are some who forget God, as a lawgiver, to such a degree, that they never inquire what laws he has given ; nay, disobey those laws which they know.

Ask yourselves, whether you are not living in the daily habit of seeking your *own* pleasure—whether it be not your daily question, not ' What is the will of God?' but ' What is *my* will ?'—not ' What does God command me to do?' but ' What do I think fit to do? what will gratify the flesh, or secure most pleasure to myself? what will promote my honour, or advance my interests in the world?' Are not these the considerations that tacitly suggest themselves ; and these the principles that move us to action? We do not ask whether you run the road of dissipation, and are known in the circles of fashion ; perhaps many of you have not the means of following your own humour, and the bent of your own inclination, except in a few instances. Do you not find, that, whenever you have the means of enjoyment, you immediately set about inquiring how you may gratify yourself to the utmost? When you have now and then leisure, do you send up a petition to God, that he would direct you to pass your time to his glory and the good of your soul? or do you not rather waste your hours in idle conversation, and employ them according to your own humour? But is not this neglect of inquiring about his will, a forgetfulness of God your Maker? What must be said of that servant, who would not take the trouble so much as to know his master's will? Indeed, "A son honoureth his father, and a servant his master: if then, I be a father, where is mine honour? and if I be a master, where is my fear? saith the Lord of Hosts unto you." Mal. i. 6.

Further, Consider whether you do not through forgetfulness of God, disobey those laws which you know to be his. You call yourselves Christians: there is probably therefore, not one here who does not know that "God has commanded all men, every where to repent;" to "be born again;" to "renounce the world and its vanities;" to "crucify the flesh, with its affections and lusts;" to be "poor in spirit;" to "mourn for sin;" to "hunger and thirst after righteousness;" to be "pure in heart;" to be constant and "earnest in prayer;" to be "laying up treasures in heaven;" to "enter in at the strait gate," and to walk along the narrow way that leadeth unto life—and in fine to be "looking for the day of God, in all holy conversation and godliness;" and yet are you not conscious that you do not put one of these into practice, but that you live in the habitual neglect of some or all these duties, every one of which you know God has commanded?

(2.) You forget God in another particular, namely, by forgetting his mercies.

On this head let me ask you, whether you acknowledge his mercies—whether you bow your knees in fervent and affectionate thanksgiving, for having been blessed with health, for having been fed by his bounty; for mercies personal, social? Do you confess that every thing which you receive at the hand of God is mere mercy? If he were to afflict you with disease and strip

you of all your comforts, would he give you no more
than you deserve? If he were to condemn you to
everlasting misery, would he be just? Do you believe
that you deserve it? ' No,' you say, ' What have
I done to deserve it?' You think God would be
unmerciful if he were to destroy you!

And above all, my brethren, what think ye of Christ,
who is, according to Scripture, God's unspeakable gift?
Do you shew that you bear due regard to God's mercy
in sending Christ, by believing in him, coming to him,
casting yourself upon him as a lost and ruined sinner?
Have you ever devoted yourself to him—becoming his
disciple, esteeming his reproach, and saying, in short,
with a true heart, " Henceforth I will not live unto
myself," 2 Cor. v. 15. Ask yourselves whether you
ever thought of Christ, with real pleasure and genuine
satisfaction of heart. When you speak of him, or of
God's mercy in giving him, as you sometimes do in the
public prayers, is it not rather a forced or thoughtless
acknowledgment, to the grateful tribute of a broken
heart? Christ has said, " He that loveth father or
mother more than me, is not worthy of me; and he that
loveth son or daughter more than me, is not worthy of
me; and he that taketh not up his cross and followeth
after me, is not worthy of me." Matt. x. 37, 38. Do
you thus love and obey him, counting all things but
dung and dross to win him, and forsaking all to follow
him? Alas! my friends, you know it is no such thing;
and what is worse, you do not even desire that it should
be so. You start at the thought of unceasing self-
denial! You would think yourselves miserable in a life
of godliness! You seek your happiness, not from God
but the world. You could in your opinion be as happy
as you are, if there were no God—no Saviour. I may

say to you as our Lord to the Jews. " Ye have not the love of God in you." John v. 42.

Thus you slight and neglect the rich mercies of God, either by not counting the cost, or by determining not to pay it : thus proving that altogether you undervalue the blessing to be bought !

(3.) Let us proceed to remark, in the third place, that you forget God by forgetting his Presence.

It is God's presence which made and upholds the universe, and which directs every event of our lives. It is this, therefore, that makes the frame of nature sacred, and hallows the varying turns of providence. We do not ask whether you admire the marks of his creating finger, and trace his footsteps as they are seen when he goes to and fro over the earth. Let us come nearer home. God's eye pierces into our hearts. " All things are naked and opened unto the eyes of him with whom we have to do !" Heb. iv. 13. " He knoweth our thoughts afar off." Psalm cxxxix. 2.

Do you thus remember his awful presence ? Are you anxious that your hearts should be a pure and living temple to his praise. Do you love to walk with God ; to cry to him with holy confidence, " Search me, O God, and know my heart : try me, and know my thoughts : and see if there be any wicked way in me ? " Psalm cxxxix. 23, 24.

On the contrary, do not you know that if you were to profess to have any such secret communion with God, you would " lie to the Holy Ghost," and would almost expect the fate of Ananias ? Do you not know that you securely indulge the lustful thought, and secret vanity, and covetous desire of gain, and bitterness of revenge and anger ; and freely give the reins to those appetites, which the eye of man cannot scrutinize ? God sees them, and sees them with anger; but you are not concerned. What you would be ashamed and shocked for man to know, that you commit before God without fear and without remorse! You say, in excuse, that you are not aware of God's presence; that you forget that his eye is fixed upon you; but by so saying, you confess what we aimed at proving, namely, that you forget his presence.

Thus, then, we have described a character, not difficult to be drawn. Let not such persons expect that they shall dwell with God: forgetting his laws, they cannot join in the blessed obedience of angels: forgetting his mercies, they could not sing praises to the Lamb: forgetting his presence, they shall be banished from his presence for ever!

But it is not a negative suffering only which they are to undergo; for we know him that hath said "Vengeance is mine; I will repay, saith the Lord." Rom. xii. 19. They have paid me contempt; I will repay them vengeance.

II. Hear, therefore, their FINAL DOOM. "The wicked shall be turned into hell, and all the nations that forget God!"

Men, in general, do not wish to hear this place so much as mentioned, much less described as the portion of the wicked: but it is better to hear of it than to dwell in it; and it is by hearing of it that we must be stirred up to escape it. It is degrading to human nature, that we must draw an argument from such a source—that we must dip our shafts in the lake that burneth with fire. It is painful and humiliating to reflect that beings, capable of being constrained by love, should require to be driven by an iron scourge! Hell is often described by our Lord Jesus Christ. He was too compassionate

and serious to excite groundless terrors.   As he said to
his disciples,  " In my Father's house are many mansions;  if it were not so,  I would have told you." John
xiv. 2 :  so we may say of hell :  there, then, are many
mansions, if it were not so he would have told us.   Hell
is often described by him as a place in which both body
and  soul  are  tormented  for  ever.   To one  of these
descriptions we will refer you.

In the ninth chapter of St. Mark's gospel, the eternity
of torment is six times described !   The fire and the
worm are such images of the causes of suffering as are
addressed to the senses.   Christ describes hell as a place
of inconceivable torment and everlasting misery.   He
describes it by saying, their fire is not quenched.   Fire,
a dreadful element, is a scorching thing, and enters deep
into the senses :  yet hell is represented to be " a lake of
fire and brimstone." Rev. xix. 20.   But if there were
any period set to their sufferings—if after millions of
years, they were to be reduced to nothing, they might
bear it :  but this is their misery, that it is for ever !
Think how tedious is the motion of time when you are
in pain—how you wish the hours away !   What must
it be to suffer such pain as will make every moment
appear an age ? and yet there must be an eternity of
those ages !   Our Lord also compares it to the gnawing
of a worm, which preys on the vitals :  by which is
signified that anguish of spirit and remorse of conscience,
which they must for ever feel, and keen disappointment
at having lost for ever past opportunities: " their worm
dieth not."   They have fallen into the hands of the
living God :  therefore, so long as he liveth, that is, for
ever, so long must they be subject to the execution of
his wrath !   These things are within the apprehension of
all—it is a very plain thing of which we speak.   Who-

ever do go to a place of torment, continue there for ever!

This place will be the portion of them that forget God. Here, foolish and ignorant men scoff at eternal torments: they say within themselves of sin—' is it not a little thing? will a merciful God, who knows our weakness, punish so dreadfully what we can scarcely help doing?' But what says God? " Thou thoughtest that I was altogether such an one as thyself." Ps. l. 21. Because thou didst smile at sin, thou thoughtest I should do so too. Because I forgave the sins of my penitent people, thou thoughtest I should forgive thine without repentance. They will find that God was in earnest when he warned them " to flee from the wrath to come." Matt. iii. 7. He said to them on earth, " If ye live after the flesh, ye shall die." Rom. viii. 13. they did live after the flesh: hoping, no doubt, that God would not be true to his word. But do not they find, now that they feel the pains of hell get hold upon them, now that they have actually died and are in hell, that God is faithful? Though we believe not, but deny him, yet he cannot deny himself. Believe it, brethren, " God is not a man, that he should lie: neither the son of man, that he should repent. Hath he said, and shall he not do it? or hath he spoken, and shall he not make it good? Numb. xxiii. 19.

Some are so weak as to suppose that the numbers who must perish, if all this be true, will secure them against the threatened vengeance; or at least move the commiseration of the judge. But we read in the text, that though they be whole nations, they cannot withstand his almighty arm: however numerous, or however strong, he can in a moment hurl the mightiest criminals into endless ruin: thus he speaks by his prophet, " Hell hath

enlarged herself, and opened her mouth without measure :
and their glory and their multitude, and their pomp,
and he that rejoiceth shall descend into it." Is. v. 14.
" and as the fire devoureth the stubble, and the flame
consumeth the chaff, so their root shall be as rottenness,
and their blossom shall go up as dust: because they
have cast away the law of the Lord of hosts, and
despised the word of the Holy One of Israel." Is. v.
24.   And hath not this dreadful threatening been fulfilled? hath not our Lord told us of a rich man, who, in
hell lifted up his eyes being in torment? it was not said
that he was sent thither for being a drunkard, or a forni-
cator, or an extortioner : but he had forgotten God.
That narrative, I mean of Dives and Lazarus, exhibits
realities.   Is there such a place as hell?   Does any one
descend into it, and find himself actually there ?   The
rich man did !   Let it then be established as an awful
truth, that they who wilfully neglect to obey any of
God's laws which they know, or who live without Christ,
that is, ignorant of him—do not follow him in the regeneration, or who indulge the secret sins of the heart;
thus disregarding the divine presence, are those that
forget God, and shall be turned into hell.

Now pause a while, and reflect !   Some of you, perhaps by this time, instead of making a wise resolve, have
begun to wonder that so heavy a judgment should be
denounced merely against forgetfulness.

But look at the affairs of common life, and be taught
by them.   Do not neglect, and want of attention, and
not looking about us to see what we have to do—do not
any of these bring upon us consequences, as ruinous to
our worldly business as any *active* misbehaviour?   It is
an event of every day, that a man by mere laziness and
inattention to his business, does as certainly bring him-

self and family to poverty, and end his days in a gaol, as if he were in wanton mischief, to set fire to his own house. So it is also with the affairs of the soul : neglect of that—forgetfulness of God, who only can save it, will work his ruin as surely as a long and daring course of profligate wickedness.

When any one has been recollecting the proper proofs of a future state of rewards and punishments, nothing, methinks, can give him so sensible an apprehension of punishment, or such a representation of it to the mind, as observing, that, after the many disregarded checks, admonitions, and warnings, which people meet with in the ways of vice, folly, and extravagance—warnings from their very nature, from the examples of others, from the lesser inconveniences which they bring upon themselves, from the instructions of wise and good men ; after these have been long despised, scorned, ridiculed ; after the chief bad consequences (temporal consequences) of their follies have been delayed for a great while, at length they break in irresistibly like an armed force : repentance is too late to relieve, and can serve only to aggravate their distress : the case has become desperate ; and poverty and sickness, remorse and anguish, infamy and death, the effects of their own doings, overwhelm them beyond possibility of remedy or escape. This is an account of what is, in fact, the general constitution of nature.

But is the forgetfulness of God so light a matter ? Think what ingratitude, rebellion and atheism there is at the bottom of it ! Sirs, you have " a carnal mind which is enmity against God." Rom. viii. 7. Do not suppose that you have but to make a slight effort, and you will cease to forget him : it is your nature to forget him : it is your nature to hate him : so that nothing less than an entire change of heart and nature, will ever deliver you from this state of enmity. Our nature is not subject to the law of God, neither indeed can be. They that are "in the flesh, cannot please God." Rom. viii. 7, 8. From this state, let the fearful menace in the text, persuade you to arise! Need we remind you again of the dreadfulness of hell, of the certainty that it shall overtake the impenitent sinner? Enough has been said; and can any of you be still so hardened, and such enemies to your souls, as still to cleave to sin? Will you still venture to continue any more in the hazard of falling into the hands of God? Alas! "Who among us shall dwell with the devouring fire? Who among us shall dwell with everlasting burnings?" Isaiah xxxiii. 14. "Can thine heart endure, or can thine hands be strong, in the days that I shall deal with thee? I the Lord have spoken it, and will do it!" Ezekiel xxii. 14.

Observe that men have dealt with sinners; ministers have dealt with them; at last God will take them in hand, and deal with them! Though not so daring as to defy God, yet, brethren, in all probability you put off repentance. Will you securely walk a little longer along the brinks of the burning furnace of the Almighty's fury? "As the Lord liveth, and as thy soul liveth, there is but a step between thee and death!" 1 Samuel xx. 3. When you lie down you know not but you may be in it before the morning, and when you rise, you know not but God may say, "Thou fool! this night thy soul shall be required of thee!" When once the word is given to cut you down, the business is over. You are cut off from your lying refuges and beloved sins, from the world, from your friends, from the light, from happiness, from hope for ever. Be wise, then, my friends, and reasonable; give neither sleep to your eyes, nor slumber to your eye-lids, till you have resolved on your knees before God, to forget him no more. Go home and pray. Do not dare to fly, as it were, in the face of your Maker, by seeking your pleasure on his holy day ; but if you are alarmed at this subject, as well you may be, go and pray to God that you may forget him no more. It is high time to awake out of sleep. It is high time to have done with hesitation ; time does not wait for you; nor will God wait till you are pleased to turn. He hath bent his bow and made it ready; halt no more between two opinions : hasten, tarry not in all the plain, but flee from the wrath to come. Pray for grace, without which you can do nothing. Pray for the knowledge of Christ, and of your own danger and help-lessness, without which you cannot know what it is to find refuge in him. It is not our design to terrify, without pointing out the means of safety. Let us then observe, that if it should have pleased God to awaken any of you to a sense of your danger, you should beware of betaking yourselves to a refuge of lies.

But, through the mercy of God, many among us have found repentance unto life, have fled for refuge to the hope set before them, have seen their danger and fled to Christ. Think with yourselves what it is now to have escaped destruction ; what it will be to hear at the last day our acquittal, when it shall be said to others, " Depart from me, ye cursed, into everlasting fire." Let the sense of the mercy of God gild all the paths of life. On the other hand, since it is they who forget God that are to bear the weight of his wrath, let us beware, brethren, how we forget him, through concern about this world, or through unbelief, or through sloth. Let us be punctual in all our engagements with him. With earnest at-tention and holy awe ought we to hear his voice, cherish the sense of his presence, and perform the duties of his worship.   No covenant relation or Gospel grace can render him less holy, less jealous, or less majestic. "Wherefore let us have grace whereby we may serve God acceptably, with reverence and godly fear; for our God is a consuming fire."

## IV.

A LETTER FROM THE LATE REV. ROBERT HALL, M.A.
OF LEICESTER, TO THE EDITOR, WHEN A STUDENT
AT CAMBRIDGE.

So highly are the writings of the late Robert Hall esteemed by all classes of readers, that the Editor has occasionally been led to regret having so long withheld from them the following valuable remarks. He ought perhaps to have furnished the Publisher of his works with a copy at the time when his correspondence was in a state of preparation for the press. He makes, however, the best reparation in his power by introducing it into the present work, to which it is in all respects most appropriate.

*Leicester, Feb.* 17, 1814.

DEAR SIR,

I am happy to hear, as in the instance before me, that God is inclining by his Spirit so many young Students to devote themselves to the ministry from the purest and most evangelical motives. With such views and dispositions you may be assured of your receiving a competent measure of that sacred unction that teacheth all things. But as you have condescended to ask my advice respecting the best mode of preparing yourself for the sacred work of the ministry, I can only lament my incompetence for the task you have assigned me. In

the mean time I have no doubt you will take in good
part the few suggestions which I shall present you,
without suspecting me of a disposition to dictate or
dogmatize.

With respect to your first inquiry, I have no doubt
that the extemporaneous mode of preaching is the best;
by which I am far from intending the neglect of previous
study, but the practice of delivering sermons with little
or no immediate use of notes. That it possesses a superior power of keeping up attention, and exciting an impression, can scarcely be doubted; and all that can be
said on the other side is, that it is unfavourable to accuracy. But why should sermons be more elaborately
exact in point of composition, than the speeches in
Parliament, or at the Bar—or the force and pathos
naturally attendant on the extemporary mode of speaking
be excluded only from the inculcation of divine truth;
that truth which we are enjoined by the highest example
and authority not to attempt to combine with excellency
of speech, or of wisdom?

The matter appears to me to be this. The general
decay of piety amongst the regular clergy in the reign of
the two Charles's, almost extinguished pulpit eloquence.
And when true religion began to be held in dis-esteem,
nothing remained to be cultivated but a scrupulous and
timid correctness; when the Preacher, instead of attempting 'dominari in concionibus,' was chiefly solicitous to avoid ridicule, satisfied with the negative praise
of not giving offence. This is surely a very confined
limit for the ambition of a Christian Minister: but
whoever would greatly surpass it, and accomplish to
any considerable extent the true objects of preaching,
must, after deeply meditating his subject, and making a
tolerably copious analysis, trust the clothing of his ideas

to the feeling of the moment. I would not, however, urge a young preacher to attempt all this at once; but rather *never* to read *entirely*—to write the whole or a good part of his sermon for a while—then to trust himself gradually more to his extemporaneous powers.

With respect to the course of study to be pursued, and the proper books to be read by a young man who is preparing for sacred orders, I am ashamed to attempt to give my opinion, conscious as I am of being so deficient myself in the knowledge, which, if not absolutely requisite, is yet highly conducive to the profitable discharge of the Christian Ministry.

I suppose the most necessary study of all is the acquiring an intimate acquaintance with both Testaments in their original languages, never losing sight of the Septuagint, which is the best interpreter of the Hebrew words, as well as of the Hellenistic dialect, which pervades the New Testament. This, I presume, should form a part, and a considerable one, of the daily study of a young divine.

Next, Ecclesiastical History will demand his attention, which, without neglecting some modern historians, will be best learned out of Eusebius; and, if he wishes to pursue the history of the church beyond the fourth century, from Socrates and Sozomen. The compilation of Eusebius is invaluable, and the History of Socrates very entertaining, and full of melancholy instruction.

For Jewish Antiquities, I know nothing better than Beausobre and L'Enfant's Introduction to the Prussian Testament; though the subject is handled more fully by Jennings, in two volumes, octavo.

Of Commentators, I am not very competent to speak, having not conversed with them very widely. Grotius is perhaps the most profound and enlightened—particu-

larly on the Gospels. His legal views of religion, however, almost always confounding sanctification and justification, require to be strictly guarded against. Matthew
Henry, as a practical and devotional Commentator,
exceeds all praise, and suggests most matter for sermonizing of any. [1]

[1] The Editor will stand excused with every one who is conversant
with the Family Expositor of the late Thomas Scott, if he ventures
strongly to recommend to the Student and the Preacher the comments of that judicious and laborious writer. ‘ It is difficult,’ says a
very competent authority, the present Bishop of Calcutta,[1] ‘ to form
a just estimate of a work which cost its author the labour of thirty-
three years. Its capital excellence consists in its following more
closely, than, perhaps any other, the fair and adequate meaning
of every part of Scripture, without regard to the niceties of human
systems. It is a *scriptural* comment. Its originality is likewise a
strong recommendation of it. Every part of it is thought out by the
author for himself, not borrowed from others. It is not a compilation ; it is an original work, in which you have the deliberate judgment of a masculine and independent mind on all the parts of Holy
Scripture. Every student will understand the value of such a production. Further, it is the comment of our age, furnishing the last
interpretations which history throws on prophecy, giving the substance of the remarks which sound criticism has accumulated from
the different branches of sacred literature, obviating the chief objections which modern annotators have advanced against the doctrines
of the Gospel, and adapting the instructions of Scripture to the particular circumstances of the times in which we live.......The time is
not distant, when, the passing controversies of the day having been
forgotten, this prodigious work will be almost universally confessed
in the Protestant churches, to be one of the most sound and instructive comments of our own or any other age.’ ‘ To almost every part
of this panegyric’ observes his reviewer, ‘ we heartily subscribe.
Perhaps however, we should demur to the acknowledgment that, even
in this work the defects of Mr. Scott’s style do not materially detract
from the value of the work, especially as a work for family reading.
Even here there is a considerable want of that perspicuity—of these

[1] See his two sermons on the death of the Rev. T. Scott.

As to general theologians, I much prefer Howe to any whom it has been my lot to meet with. He was at once a man of stupendous genius, and of great unction; though his style is harsh and repulsive. I should recommend a

dense and terse expressions—of those pithy practical counsels—of these tender and pathetic remonstrances—of these cheerful and varied addresses, which abound so much in the Commentary of Matthew Henry. This, however, is to be remembered, in comparing the two writers, that for one offence against *taste* in Mr. Scott, it would be easy to find a hundred in his predecessor; and that the modern commentator is as much distinguished by forbearance and propriety in the exposition of scripture, as the ancient expositor by the strained and imaginative interpretation so common in the days in which he lived. Matthew Henry appears to us to surpass Mr. Scott and every other writer in his Exposition of the Gospels: Mr. Scott to have considerably the superiority in his Commentary on the Epistles. And as a textuary, Mr. Scott is, we think, without a rival. We fully anticipate the increasing celebrity of his Commentary; and, with it the extension of sound and scriptural views of religion. Without pronouncing any opinion on his sentiments as to some disputed and most difficult points, we entertain the deepest reverence of his judgment on all the principles of that 'common Christianity' recognized in the confessions of the Protestant churches. And when we consider the circumstances to which Mr. Wilson so justly refers, namely the 'originality' of his exposition, or, in other words, how much he drew from himself, and how little from others, and contrast the fulness and explicitness of his judgments upon many dark and perplexing passages of scripture, with the leanness and ambiguity of certain modern interpretations avowedly casting far and near for authorities, and living to the utmost possible extent upon "borrowed light," we cannot but consider the work as an astonishing evidence of the powers of honest energy in well doing. It reminds us more of 'those days in which,' as our old and revered monarch George III. was heard to say, 'there were *giants* in theology,' than of these puny and dwarfish days in which writers give us indeed a 'meadow of margin,' but a 'rivulet of text:' and in which the prettiness of the book is transcended only by the barrenness of the matter.'

young man who is entering on the ministry to make himself intimately acquainted with our older writers, Barrow, Tillotson, Hooker, Milton, Chillingworth, Pearson, &c.—of whom, in comparison with later writers, I should be disposed to say, with very few exceptions, " No one, having tasted old wine, straightway desireth new ; for he saith the old is better."

Thus I have attempted very briefly to comply with your request: and with my sincere prayers and wishes that you may be enabled to " approve yourself to God a workman that needeth not to be ashamed,"

I remain, with sincere esteem,

Your's most respectfully,

ROBERT HALL.

# NOTES.

---

(¹) Page 3. 'When a young minister sets out, he should sit down and ask himself, how he may best qualify himself for his office?'

'How does a physician qualify himself? It is not enough that he offers to feel the pulse. He must read, and inquire, and observe, and make experiments, and correct himself again and again. He must lay in a stock of medical knowledge before he begins to feel the pulse.

'The minister is a physician of a far higher order. He has a vast field before him. He has to study an infinite variety of constitutions. He is to furnish himself with the knowledge of the whole system of remedies. He is to be a man of skill and expedient. If one thing fail, he must know how to apply another. Many intricate and perplexed cases will come before him: it will be disgraceful to him not to be prepared for such. His patients will put many questions to him: it will be disgraceful to him not to be prepared to answer them. He is a merchant embarking in extensive concerns. A little ready money in the pocket will not answer the demands that will be made upon him. Some of us seem to think it will, but they are grossly deceived. There must be a well-furnished account at the banker's.'
—Cecil.

(²) Page 4. The Editor takes leave to remind the reader, that this advice is given to the *Student* rather than to the *Preacher*—to the novice who is endeavouring to form or improve his style, and not to the parochial minister, amidst the daily and hourly calls of pastoral duty. A curious instance of laborious trifling is seen in the life and correspondence of a late divine, distinguished indeed for his literary attainments, but lamentably defective in his views of divine truth. The writer of his Memoir informs us that one of his Sermons which he preached and subsequently published in behalf of a popular charity, cost him months of incessant labour, and had been the subject of a year's voluminous correspondence with a literary friend. Of another of his sermons we are told that " he transcribed the exordium at least *thirty times*, before he was satisfied *with the effect*: it being his object to make this discourse a model for himself, and a *specimen of the capabilities of the English language for rhythmical composition*." ' We shall not be suspected,' observes a judicious Reviewer of the recent life and correspondence to which I allude, ' of wishing to recommend to a young clergyman, or to any clergyman, to put forth his first crude thoughts in his first unstudied words; for no time and effort that can be called reasonable are too great for the service of the Christian pulpit; but thirty transcriptions by a middle aged clergyman of an exordium for the sake of ' effect ; ' and we must presume a good year's labour to make the discourse ' a specimen of the capabilities of the English language for rhythmical composition ; ' argues a weakness and a vanity, that his biographer did not well to expose to the world, unless by way of salutary warning. Life, especially the life of a Christian pastor, is too precious to be spent in such trifling. His flock would have been much more likely to be benefited by an ample supply of simple practical expository discourses about the plain matters of the gospel, than by the most rhythmical composition that ever divine or poet fabricated.'

That Dr. Porter himself would cordially assent to these observations, the subsequent pages of his work sufficiently evince. His object in the present instance is to encourage the young minister, and more especially the candidate for holy orders to spare no pains in endeavouring to improve his compositions by carefully correcting and revising them from time to time.

(3) Page 7. This admission on the part of a critic such as Dr. Porter, will not be lost upon the attentive reader. How important soever correctness, precision, and good taste undoubtedly are, they should never be permitted to stand in the way of far more important objects. It is pleasing to meet with testimonies corroborative of this remark from men distinguished for the excellence of those attainments which too frequently serve to prejudice the mind against the *simplicity* of preaching. 'Let zeal and industry,' observes Bishop Sumner, 'be directed by piety, and a minister will not fail to command attention, though he may not be eloquent —and will be useful though he may be plain. Were his subject indeed one of common interest or importance, the graces of oratory or the splendours of composition might be requisite. But death and judgment, heaven and hell, are topics in which all have so intimate a concern, that the subject supplies what is wanting in the manner. Let the congregation be once persuaded that they have a personal interest in the discourse, and they will listen to it with the earnestness which personal interest never fails to inspire, and which in this case nothing else can com-

Q

mand. Critical power to judge of the composition they
have not ; but reason they have which will tell them
whether the voice of the preacher is re-echoed by the
words of Scripture ; and conscience they have, which
will apply his appeal to their hearts more powerfully
than the best turned period. It is only where they hear
little of the Bible, and the means of salvation that the
people have fastidious ears.

' In fact, elaborate composition is so far from being
necessary to the success of public discourses, that in
many situations a person of delicate and refined taste
will be obliged to maintain a severe conflict between his
duty and his habits, before he can become useful to
others from the pulpit. He must descend from the high
and lofty tone of language to which he is accustomed, to
walk in the humble terms of Scripture ; he must limit
his rounded periods to the extent of vulgar comprehension ;
he must abound in interrogations, and addresses which
the rules of composition condemn in writing, though the
rules of nature sanction them in speaking : in short he
must put off all sense of personal importance, and assume
the character of his office ; he must forget himself and
remember only his situation as the messenger of Christ,
and his business of converting sinners from the error of
their way.' [1]

(⁴) Page 23. Whilst the Editor admits the justice
of this remark, he would remind the reader that these
' forms of Arian and Socinian error ' were assumed not by
the members of the established church, but by the des-
cendants of those who dissented from her discipline.

(⁵) Page 26. As young ministers cannot reasonably

[1] Bishop Sumner's Apostolical Preaching.

be supposed to have read very extensively the writings
of the early Fathers, and may therefore be unduly
influenced by the disparaging remarks of Dr. Porter,
the Editor thinks it may not be without its use to present them with the following observations from the pen
of a distinguished scholar and prelate of the Irish
Church. " It will not be disputed,' says Bishop Jebb,
' that the ancient writers of the Christian church have
suffered no small injury from excessive praise, and that
the implicit veneration of former ages has too naturally
been followed by an equally indiscriminate depreciation.
It is certain, that if the Fathers were to be estimated
solely by their literary merits, and compared not with
their own contemporaries, but with the classical standards
of Greece and Rome, the issue of such a trial could be
no other than unfavourable. But because it is extravagant to place Lactantius above Cicero, or to prefer Saint
Basil to Demosthenes, does it therefore follow, that
every degree of respect and estimation which has been
adjudged to these reputed luminaries, is alike unfounded,
and untenable? Let the ' imposing effect produced upon
the minds of their admirers by the sanctity of their subjects' be ever so gross, or ever so delusive, an appeal
may still be made to other judges, whose decision cannot be impeached on any ground, either of prejudice or
of incompetency.'

" A more remarkable testimony could scarcely be
adduced than the following from the pen of the celebrated Daille, the professed assailant of the ancient
Fathers. ' Expunge if you choose, the name of Augustine from his most excellent works, ' De.Civitate Dei,'
and ' De Doctrinâ Christianâ;' yet each work, though
I were ignorant of the author's name, if I but read, will
admirably teach me many things most worthy to be

known. And so it is with all the rest. In the first
place, these monuments of the Fathers contain most
numerous and weighty exhortations to sanctity of morals,
and accurate observance of Christian discipline. They
abound also with striking arguments, by which the
universally acknowledged fundamentals of the Christian
faith are most luminously illustrated and confirmed : and
with very many precious documents of most extreme
utility, as well for the general interpretation of the
Scriptures, as for the special elucidation of those mysteries contained in the sacred word. Their very authority,
too, may be highly serviceable to us in proving the
truth of Christianity. For is it not a wondrous fact,
that so many men of such mental energy, of such happy
genius, born at different times, and in different places
during the space of fifteen hundred years, various in their
temperaments, their studies, and sometimes their opinions,
should have so uniformly, and as it were, with one heart
and with one soul, conspired and concurred in all the
fundamentals of Christianity; and so unlike in other
particulars, should have adored one and the same Christ,
co-exhorted to the same sanctification, hoped for the
same immortality, received the same Gospels, and, in
those Gospels, all admired the same great and sublime
mysteries? Internal evidence, I admit in itself estab-
lishes the truth of Christianity; the exquisite wisdom
of the entire system, and a certain unexampled beauty,
which affords intuitive and instant proof that it is heavenly and divine, these are abundantly sufficient to preclude the necessity of any other argument more certain
or more clear. Yet it is by no means to be despised,
that this astonishing consent of the Fathers respecting
the truth of the Gospel, affords us no slight corroborative evidence. For it is abhorrent from all colour of

truth, that so many men of transcendent genius (which their works attest,) and endowed with most acute and perspicacious minds could have so absurdly blundered, as to stake all their substance and all their fortunes on the faith of Christianity; as to encounter boldly every danger for its sake; as, with alacrity and joy, to pour forth their very life-blood in its cause, unless it really possessed some divine power to affect and animate the minds of men.'

" These, be it observed, are the expressions of one who strenuously laboured to reduce the authority of the Fathers to the lowest possible level. His concessions are, therefore, extorted tributes to irresistible truth; and consequently, they carry as great weight, as could, in any instance be ascribed to human sentiments.

" But in order to decide the merits of the Christian Fathers, no well instructed member of the Church of England, need have recourse to the Gallican church, or to any church whatever but his own. It is to a Christian Bishop and Father, that we are indebted for the substance of our invaluable Liturgy: it was to the Christian Fathers that the great divines of our most learned, and not least pious days, (those " giants in the land," as they were called by our good old king) resorted, when desirous, either to corroborate their faith, or to nourish their devotion. And till a race of theologians arise, who shall eclipse the Hookers and the Hammonds, the Pearsons and the Medes, the Barrows and the Taylors, the Beveridges and the Bulls, no man need be ashamed to kindle his torch at the same pure and unextinguishable flame which communicated light to the footsteps, and warmth to the hearts of this illustrious company. Dr. Barrow in particular, was a profound and sober mathematician, little to be suspected of unreasonable flights

of fancy. Yet, mathematician as he was, he committed
an extravagance which will, perhaps, first astound, and
then scandalize certain of his panegyrists. He stands
convicted of no common delinquency. He called in
local emotion, to the aid of personal enthusiasm. He
studied every page and paragraph of the ' florid and
effeminate Chrysostom,' in Chrysostom's own archiepis-
copal city of Constantinople. Yet some there are who
will forgive him this wrong : some who will forgive the
still greater extravagance of his later years : for the
Fathers were the cherished companions of his maturity,
no less than the chosen instructors of his youth : and the
result is manifest in every page of those volumes which
will render the name of Barrow coeval with the English
language."

(6)' Page 27.—-The advantages and disadvantages of
extempore preaching are more fairly and judiciously
stated in the following passage from the very useful
' Remarks' of Mr. Raikes on ' Clerical Education,'
than in any other work with which the Editor is
acquainted. ' One thing seems certain, that though the
power of preaching extempore may probably, and in
some degree, be gained by all, it is acquired with much
greater facility by some men than by others ; and that
if there is one talent which more than another deserves
to be considered as a gift it is this. Learning will not
produce it : knowledge, imagination, reasoning powers,
warmth of feeling, piety, and all the qualities which
seem essential to ministerial usefulness, may be possessed
in a very considerable degree, and still if they are not
compounded in a manner which it is not for man to specify
or describe, they may fail in producing this result, and
impede, rather than facilitate the power which is wished

for. To some men it seems to come with a sort of spontaneous ease which we are unable to account for. In the case of others not inferior to them in any quality which may seem essential to the faculty, it is laboured for, and laboured for in vain. The thoughts rise too rapidly, or too slowly : the feelings are too weak to give force to the delivery, or so strong that they obstruct it ; the imagination is too fertile or barren ; and the mind which can reason powerfully and conclusively in the retirement of the closet, loses all self-possession in public through the weakness of a nervous temperament, or the diffidence of extreme humility. In a case like this, it would be unjust to impose one only method for all, where the state of none was the same ; or to lay down one system to which every intellect, and every character should be formed. That each system has its advantage, the most zealous advocates of either, are found to concede. And since it seems impossible that all should adopt one plan with equal facility, or practice it with equal success, it seems best to advise, that each taking the line to which the peculiar frame of his mind directs him, should labour to excel in the manner which is most natural to him, without aiming at any laborious eminence in that for which he feels no bias.

' Each however, should bear in mind the failing to which his peculiar method is most exposed, and be on his guard against it. The preacher who writes his sermons must remember, that compositions prepared in the study are apt to come out in the language of the study, too learned, too refined, too elevated for common hearers ; and he should labour to obtain clearness of statement and sim-plicity of language. Those sermons also which are written in retirement, are naturally apt to be deficient in animation ; they become essays rather than addresses,

and as such are too often systematic, cold, and unim-
passioned. This evil must be met by awakening, even
in the closet, the feelings of one who stands as the minister of God, and who sees the eternal interests of his
hearers at stake; it must be met by a spirit of Christian
love, excited by prayer and meditation. The danger
which still remains of coldness, must be avoided by
warmth and fervour in delivery; nor can we doubt, that
by God's blessing on exertions such as these, all the
peculiar evils of written compositions might be obviated,
and as large a measure of usefulness be obtained as it is
possible to hope for.

'Nor must the extempore preacher forget that his style
is still more exposed to danger, though the voice of
public feeling may speak strongly in its favour. That
facility of utterance which probably decides his choice
as to the line of preaching he adopts, too often leads him
to forget the necessity of previous study and preparation
for the pulpit. The apparent success of his ministry
seems a convincing proof of the power which accompanies it. The crowds which are attracted, are considered as seals which it would be incredulity to doubt;
and while fluency of speech, and an animated enunciation
of certain great truths, continue to secure their attendance,
no doubt arises as to the blessing under which he is
labouring, or the sufficiency of the Gospel which he
preaches. But during all this time his hearers may only
have been attracted to the talent which dazzled them,
not converted to the truth as it is in Jesus. Their impressions may have been lively, but not deep nor abiding;
their views of the Gospel may have been strong, but
neither full nor consistent; and after several years of
brilliant display, and general admiration, he may find
that his congregation is drawn away to some newer and

more attractive rival : or falling into inconsistencies of
doctrine or practice which affect the very integrity of
their faith. Knowing that such may be the case, and
often has been so, let the extempore preacher remember
that the gift in which he glories, was not given to supersede the necessity of study, of meditation, of laborious
cultivation of his mental powers, but to assist in their
developement, and to contribute to their usefulness.
Like the gift of tongues in Apostolic times it is the most
specious, but it is also the most illusive quality in
the preacher : and though when properly employed
and discreetly used, it may be a powerful instrument
of good, he must never lose sight of its real nature nor
cease to consider it merely as an instrument which
depends on other qualites for the good which it is to
produce.

' But while there are some advantages to be named on
this side, let not any one to whom God does not seem to
have granted the qualities essential to it, be tempted to
despondency on that account. Some of those individuals
whom the grace of God has made eminently and widely
useful, have never seen fit to adopt the practice. Their
heart has spoken through the medium of their pen ; and
the feeling with which they delivered in the pulpit, what
had been prepared in the closet, has rescued their ministrations from the charge of coldness and languor.

' Let but a sermon be prepared under the influence of
prayer; let it be but aimed at the souls of men, and be
delivered from a heart overflowing with love to those who
are addressed, and the difference will be small, whether
it lies on paper before the preacher, or is only lodged in
the recesses of his mind. Its final success depends upon
the grace of God ; and that grace will generally accom- '
pany the most faithful labours and the most earnest

Q 5

prayers, whatever may have been the mode in which they have been exerted.

' Nor should we forget to bear in mind, that those evils which seem to belong to written sermons, may be more easily detected and avoided, while those which belong to the extempore mode, seem inherent in the system itself. The present practice of the Scottish church is strongly in favour of the adoption of written discourses ; and if extempore addresses are best calculated to pro-duce *effect*, it is probable that *edification* will be more generally promoted by those which are written.

' At all events, the dangers connected with extempore preaching, are so many and so obvious, that it should never be attempted by those who are perhaps the most disposed to adopt it, by the young, the warm, and the inexperienced. It should be deferred till the judgment has gained maturity. till the mind has been enriched with a large variety of knowledge, and till some security has been gained by these acquirements against the dangers of sameness and precipitancy.'

(7) **Page 44.** ' I am persuaded,' observes the late Rev. H. Venn, ' that we are very negligent in respect of our *texts.* Some of the most weighty and striking are never brought before the people : yet these are the texts which speak for themselves. You no sooner repeat them, than you appear in your high and holy character, as a messenger of the Lord of Hosts. Within these few weeks I have found it so. In London I preached on— " Thus saith the Lord : cursed be the man that trusteth in man, and maketh flesh his arm, and whose heart departeth from the Lord. For he shall be like the heath in the desert, and shall not see when good cometh, but shall inhabit the parched places in the wilderness, in a

salt land and not inhabited. Blessed is the man that trusteth in the Lord, and whose hope the Lord is. For he shall be as a tree planted by the waters, and that spreadeth out her roots by the river, and shall not see when heat cometh, but her leaf shall be green; and shall not be careful in the year of drought, neither shall cease from yielding fruit." Jeremiah xvii. 5—8. I contrasted the character described in the first verse, with the child of God in the latter. The very reading of my text fixed the attention, and raised as I could see the expectation of the hearers; and much affected they seemed to be. Last Sunday I saw the same impression from—" And the Lord descended in the cloud, and stood with him there, and proclaimed the name of the Lord. And the Lord passed by before him, and proclaimed, The Lord, the Lord God, merciful and gracious, long-suffering, and abundant in goodness and truth." Exodus xxxiv. 5—6, on which I am to preach again, God willing next Lord's day. I feel the good of selecting these passages to my own soul. I have to lament and bewail my ignorance and great defects for so many years, one thousandth part of which I do not yet perceive. I wish you may attend to this point, and be led to make the chief and vital parts, as they may be called, of Scripture, your subjects of discourses." Life and Correspondence of the Rev. H. Venn, p. 453.

(⁸) Page 47. It has always appeared to the Editor. to be very important to the edification of a congregation, that the preacher should be in the habit of directing their attention from time to time to the subjects of the several fasts and festivals of our church. What valuable opportunities will be thus presented to him to direct their attention to an enlarged survey of all the great doctrines of Christianity.

(9) Pape 53. It was the opinion of Vossius, that praying to saints owed its origin partly to the injudicious use of figurative language in funeral orations; to the apostrophes and prosopopœias of the panegyrists. These abuses have driven some good men to lay aside all funeral services whatever.

(10) Page 56. In the Christian Observer for March 1821, occurs a very valuable paper on this important subject, which the Editor is glad to be permitted to extract. "There are clergymen, (observes the writer,) who though they admit the gospel to be a dispensation of mercy to fallen man, perpetually clothe it, I had almost said, in the terrors which accompanied the delivery of the Law at Mount Sinai, and in a hard and unfeeling manner, as if not subject themselves to the like infirmities with their hearers, constantly overwhelm their people with a black and appalling catalogue of their transgressions, and habitually pourtray in the most tremendous colours, the punishment of the wicked in the eternal world; and then, as if mercy formed no part of the scheme of redemption, with scarcely a mention of the way of salvation by Christ, they leave their audience the chilling alternative, of embracing a religion which they have never beheld, but amidst the frowns of justice and the thunders of vengeance, or of persisting in their evil course with the certainty of incurring the awful destruction which the preacher has described. Now what I complain of is, that during the denunciation of these affecting truths, little apparent concern or compassion is manifested for those to whom they are delivered;

so that the good effect which they might otherwise have produced is destroyed, either by a seeming insensibility in the preacher, to the future state of his hearers, or by an impetuosity and warmth of temper, savouring too much of that " wrath of man which worketh not the righteousness of God." Accustomed to hear the threat- ening of Scripture, constantly brought forward, and seeing their minister apparently unconcerned in denouncing them, an audience grows hardened under rebuke; while unused on the other hand, to view religion as the remedy for every moral disease, as the balm of consolation to the wounded spirit, as the only source of real happiness, they recoil from it as calculated only to disturb their peace, to fill their minds with vain apprehensions, and to deprive them of what they esteem the substantial felicities of life.

Let not my meaning, however, be misunderstood by supposing that I am offended at the plain declaration of the truths of Revelation, though of ever so alarming an import; or that I would desire to see Christianity softened down to suit the sickly delicacy of a fastidious ear. The minister of Christ must indeed try all methods, if by any means he may save some of the souls com- mitted to his charge. Now there are in almost every congregation, persons whose attention to religious sub- jects can be excited only by an appeal to their fears: per- sons on whose hearts the merciful tidings of the love of God, and the atonement of Christ make comparatively little impression. The faithful shepherd is therefore obliged to enforce the terrors of the Lord. He is com- pelled to remind his hearers, that " the wicked shall be turned into hell, and all the people that forget God;— that there is no peace to the wicked:—that he who believeth shall be saved, and he who believeth not shall be condemned." These truths constitute a most important part of the disclosures of Revelation, and should be frequently and solemnly enforced; but they should not usurp the place of other truths equally important. I can discover no reason why one part alone of those motives by which men are persuaded to accept of salvation, should be constantly exhibited to the exclusion of all others: and still less why the part selected should be the one most revolting to the human mind. It is granted, indeed, that the natural mind is enmity against God; and that the whole scheme of the Gospel is uncongenial to the vicious taste; but this is an additional inducement to throw no unnecessary stumbling-block in the way of the most hardened sinner, and to avoid giving to the gospel an air of unmerited austerity and repulsiveness, which it does not wear in the wisely-blended pages of sacred writ, and in the preaching of our Lord and his Apostles, who " knowing the terrors of the Lord *persuaded* men." It is, however, the *manner* even more than the *matter*, that constitutes " angry preaching;" and I am not to be understood as arguing that the threatenings of God against sin are not to be earnestly and often dwelt upon; but only that they should be enforced in a way that indicates real Christian sympathy and tenderness of heart upon the part of the preacher, and with a soberness of language and a solemnity of appearance, which show an evident reluctance to wound, except in order to heal. Allow me in confirmation of my remarks, to adduce the testimonies of two or three writers, whose office or character entitles their opinions to attention. The late Mr. Newton in a " letter to a Young Minister," remarks ' there is another strain of preaching, which, though it wears the garb of zeal, is seldom a proof of any power, but the power of self. I

mean angry and scolding preaching. The Gospel is a
benevolent scheme, and whoever speaks in the power of
it will assuredly speak in love. In the most faithful
rebukes of sin, in the most solemn declarations of God's
displeasure against it, a preacher may give evidence of a
disposition of good-will and compassion to sinners, and
assuredly will if he speaks under the influence of the
power of truth. If we can indulge invective and bitterness in the pulpit, we know not what spirit we are of:
we are but gratifying our own evil tempers, under the
pretence of a concern for the cause of God and truth.
Persons of this character may applaud their own faithfulness and courage, and think it a great attainment that
they can so easily and constantly set their congregations
at defiance; but they must not expect to be useful, so
long as it remains a truth that the wrath of man worketh
not the righteousness of God.'

In the "Remains of the Rev. R. Cecil," the sentiments of that eminent servant of Christ are clearly
expressed on this point. "The zeal of some men is
of a haughty, unbending, ferocious character. They
have the letter of truth, but they mount the pulpit like
prize-fighters: it is with them a perpetual scold. This
spirit is a reproach to the Gospel : it is not the spirit of
Jesus Christ. He seems to have laboured to win men.
But there is an opposite extreme. The love of some
men is all milk and mildness? There is so much
delicacy and so much fastidiousness? They touch with
such tenderness! and if the patient shrinks they will
touch no more! The times are too flagrant for such a
disposition. The Gospel is sometimes preached in this
way till all the people agree with the preacher. He
gives no offence, and he does no good !

"But St. Paul united and blended love and zeal.

He must win souls ; but he will labour to do this by all
possible lawful contrivances.   " I am made all things to
all men that I might by all means save some." Zeal
alone may degenerate into ferociousness and brutality :
and love, alone, into fastidiousness and delicacy; but the
Apostle combined both qualities, and more perfectly
than other men realized the union of the '*fortiter in re,*'
with the ' *suaviter in modo.*'

In another part of the work Mr. Cecil observes, ' It
is a foolish project to avoid giving offence ; but it is our
duty to avoid giving *unnecessary* offence. It is necessary
offence if it is given by the truth; but it is unnecessary if
our own spirit occasion it.' 'Our system of preaching must
meet the circumstances of mankind : they must find it possible to live in the bustle of the world, and yet serve God.
After being worried and harrassed with its concerns, let
them hear cheering truths concerning Christ's love, and
care, and pity, which will operate like an enchantment
in dispelling the cares of life, and calming the anxious
perturbations of conscience. Bring forward privileges,
and enforce duties in their proper places and proportions.
Let there be no *extremes :* yet I am arrived at this conviction :—men who lean toward the extreme of evangelical privilege in their ministry, do much more to the
conversion of their hearers than they do who lean toward
the extreme of requirement. And my own experience
confirms my observation. I feel myself repelled, if any
thing chills, loads, or urges me. This is my nature, and
I see it to be very much the nature of other men. But
let me hear, " Return again to me, saith the Lord," and
I am melted and subdued.'

Such are the sentiments of two divines to which I shall
subjoin the testimony of a layman—the poet Cowper.
' No man,' says he ' was ever scolded out of his  sins.

The heart, corrupt as it is, and because it is so, grows angry, if it be not treated with some management and good manners, and scolds again. A surly mastiff will bear, perhaps to be stroked, though he will growl under that operation, but if you touch him roughly he will bite. There is no grace that the spirit of self can counterfeit with more success than a religious zeal. A man thinks he is fighting for Christ, and he is fighting for his own notions. He thinks that he is skilfully searching the hearts of others, when he is only gratifying the malignity of his own, and charitably supposes his hearers destitute of all grace, that he may shine the more in his own eyes by comparison. When he has performed this noble task, he wonders that they are not converted : 'he has given it them soundly ; and if they do not tremble, and confess that God is in him of a truth, he gives them up as reprobate, incorrigible, and lost for ever.' But a man that loves me, if he sees me in an error, will pity me, and endeavour calmly to convince me of it and persuade me to forsake it. If he has great and good news to tell me, he will not do it angrily and in much heat and discomposure of spirit. It is not easy therefore to conceive on what grounds a minister can justify a conduct which only proves that he does not understand his errand. The absurdity of it would certainly strike him if he were not himself deluded.'

These extracts I submit to the most serious consideration of all whom they may concern ; and 1 trust that with some they may have their due weight and influence in producing a conciliatory strain of preaching, accompanied by a conciliatory manner : a mildness and forbearance entirely consistent with the strictest fidelity. A just picture of what a clergyman ought to be in addressing his congregation is incidentally drawn

by the poet just quoted in the person of one 'for years
deserving honour, but for wisdom more.'

> ' With a smile,
> Gentle, and affable, and full of grace,
> As fearful of offending whom he wish'd
> Much to persuade, he plied his ear with truths
> Not harshly thunder'd forth, or rudely press'd,
> But like his purpose, gracious, kind, and sweet.'
>
> Task, book vi.

I add no other comment than an earnest exhortation
to every minister of the Gospel of peace: " Go, and do
thou likewise."

( ¹¹ ) Page 73.   One of the most important considerations in making a sermon, is to disembarrass it as
much as possible.  The sermons of the last century were
like their large unwieldly chairs.  Men have now a far
more true idea of a chair.  They consider it as a piece
of furniture to sit upon, and they cut away from it every
thing that embarrasses and encumbers it.  It requires as
much reflection and wisdom to know what is not to be
put into a sermon, as what is.

' A young minister should likewise look round him,
that he may see what has succeeded and what has not.
Truth is to be his companion, but he is to clothe her so
as to gain her access.   Truth must never bow to fashion
or prejudice; but her garb may be varied.   No man
was ever eminently successful in his ministry who did
not make Truth his friend.   Such a man might not see
her, indeed, in all her beauty and proportions; but certainly he saw and loved her.   A young minister should
remember that she does not wear the dress of a party.
Wherever she is, she is one and the same, however
variously men may array her.   He who is ignorant of
her prominent and distinguished features, is like a mu-

sician who plays half score; it grates on every well-
formed ear, as fatal error finds no corresponding vibration
in the renewed heart. Truth forms an immediate acquaintance with such a heart by a certain fitness and
suitableness to its state and feelings. '

' Knowledge, then, and Truth, are to be the constant
aim of a young minister. But where shall he find them?
Let him learn from a fool, if a fool can teach him anything.' Let him be everywhere, and always a learner.
He should imitate Gainsborough. Gainsborough trans-
fused Nature into his landscapes, beyond almost any of
his contemporaries; because Gainsborough was everywhere the painter. Every remarkable feature of a tree;
every fine stroke of Nature was copied into his pocket-
book on the spot, and in his next picture appeared with
a life and vivacity and nature which no strength of
memory or imagination could have supplied.'—CECIL.

( [12] ) Page 99. The following observations on this
subject by, perhaps, the most eloquent preacher of modern
days, are well worthy of consideration. " May I be permitted, (says he) to remark, though it seem a digression,
that in the mode of conducting our public ministrations,
we are perhaps too formal and mechanical, that in the
distribution of the matter of our sermons, we indulge too
little variety, and exposing our plan in all our parts,
abate the edge of curiosity, by enabling the hearer to
anticipate what we intend to advance. Why should
that force, which surprise gives to every emotion, derived from just and affecting sentiments, be banished
from the pulpit, when it is found of such moment in
every kind of public address. I cannot but imagine the
first preachers of the gospel appeared before their audience with a more free and unfettered air than is con-

sistent with the narrow trammels to which in these
latter days, discourses from the pulpit are confined.
The divine emotions with which they were fraught, would
have rendered them impatient of such restrictions; nor
would they suffer the impetuous stream of argument,
expostulation, and pathos, to be weakened by diverting
it into the artificial reservoirs prepared in the heads and
particulars of a modern sermon.

'Method, we are aware, is an essential ingredient in
every discourse designed for the instruction of mankind,
but it ought never to force itself on the attention as an
object apart; never appear to be an end, instead of an
instrument; or beget a suspicion of the sentiments being
introduced for the sake of the method, not the method
for the sentiments. Let the experiment be tried on some
of the best specimens of ancient eloquence; let an
oration of Cicero or Demosthenes be stretched upon a
Procrustes' bed of this sort, and, if I am not greatly
mistaken, the flame and enthusiasm which have excited
admiration in all ages, will instantly evaporate; yet no
one perceives a want of method in these immortal compositions, nor can anything be conceived more remote
from incoherent rhapsody.'—*Discouragements and Supports of the Christian Minister, by the late Rev. Robert
Hall, M.A.*

(13) Page 114. 'Two extremes have been fallen into,
from not duly attending to the difference between *moral
evidence* and *demonstration*. On the one hand probable
proof has been called demonstration. When a writer has
produced in favour of some important point, a variety
of reasons all of the probable kind, yet of great cogency,
and has shewn, that all the objections against it are
either fallacious, or but of little weight, he often asserts

that he has demonstrated his position. He may, indeed, have so far proved it, as to have excluded all reasonable doubt : yet he has, nevertheless, not demonstrated it. For, the highest degree of probability does not amount to a demonstration ; and nothing can be a demonstration where there is not an intuitive, and necessary connexion between every successive step of the proof. This practice has, probably, arisen from an inclination to magnify every thing important : and from a disposition to the use of figures of speech. As demonstration is the highest species of proof, when we have so fully proved any point, as to have excluded all reasonable doubt, we say, by the figure hyperbole, that we have "demonstrated it." This, however, is improper, because things which differ in their nature, ought to be distinguished by different names : and when different names have been invented for them, it is wrong to confound the things by using the name of the one for the other. It has, besides, a tendency to defeat its own end : for, with all, who have been accustomed to a more accurate use of words, it is calculated rather to weaken than to strengthen the force of the proof; inasmuch as it excites them to inquire, not whether the question has been proved by sufficient evidence, but whether there is an intuitive and necessary connexion between each successive step of that proof; and, as it is evident that there is no such connexion doubts are raised in their minds.

' On the other hand, a position for which sufficient probable evidence is brought, is often denied to be proved. This happens most frequently when an opponent demands our assent to some point, which seems unfavourable to our present interests. But, the word proof ought not to be confined to demonstration, any more than the name demonstration to be given to every

species of proof. Lawyers have their proofs as well as
mathematicians. And should a mathematician censure a
lawyer who had asserted that to be proved, for which
sufficient evidence, according to the established rules of
law, had been adduced, because it had not been demonstrated, he would be considered as absurd. Divines,
too, have their proofs: and though they do not amount
to demonstration, yet, if they be sufficient to exclude all
reasonable doubt, they ought to be admitted to be
proofs. In truth, wherever there is produced, in favour
of any demonstration the highest kind of evidence of
which it admits, and in a sufficient degree ' to outweigh
all that can be urged against it, it may properly be
said to be proved.'—Gambier's Introduction to the Study
of Moral Evidence.

There are few subjects more frequently and I-may add,
more unhappily neglected by theological students than
that of ' Moral Evidence,' and yet what subject is there
more deeply interesting to those who are appointed to be
the guides of the perplexed, and the referees in cases of
conscience? Among the very few writers on this
neglected subject, the Editor refers with feelings of
peculiar interest to the Rev. J. E. Gambier, M. A. to
whose kind and able instructions whilst preparing for the
University he feels deeply indebted.

( 14 ) Page 162. 'The concern of a parish minister,'
(observes Archbishop Secker,) ' is to make the lowest
of his congregation apprehend the doctrine of salvation
by repentance, faith, and obedience ; and to labour, that
when they know the way of life, they may walk in it.
If he doth not these things for them, he doth nothing :
and it requires much consideration to find out the proper
methods of doing them, and much pains and patience to

try one after another. Smooth discourses, composed
partly in flowing sentences which they cannot follow
to the end, containing little that awakens their drowsy
attention, little that enforces on them plainly and home,
what they must do to be saved, leave them as ignorant
and uninformed as ever, and only lull them into a fatal
security. Therefore bring yourselves down to their
level.' Eighty years have now elapsed since this advice
fell from the lips of this pious Archbishop, and well had
it been for our peasantry and our mechanics, if not for
the higher grades of society, if it had been more universally followed by our English clergy. That a great
improvement in this respect has taken place since that
period, and especially during the last twenty or thirty
years should be acknowledged with thankfulness to that
gracious Being who has made our national Church, even
in these troublous times, " for a name and a praise in
the earth."

 (15) Page 185. As the subject of this chapter is of
vast importance, the reader will not object to be detained
by an attentive perusal of the following weighty observations from " Cecil's Remains." ' Christ is God's great
ordinance. Nothing ever has been done, or will be done
to purpose, but so far as he is held forth with simplicity.
All the lines must centre in him. I feel this in my own
experience, and therefore I govern my ministry by it:
but then this is to be done according to the analogy of
faith — not ignorantly, absurdly, and falsely. I doubt
not, indeed, but that excess on this side is less pernicious
than excess on the other; because God will bless his
own especial ordinance, though partially understood, and
partially exhibited. There are many weighty reasons .
for rendering Christ prominent in our ministry :—

' 1. Christ cheers the prospect. Every thing connected with him has light and gladness thrown round it. I look out of my window :—the scene is scowling—dark—frigid —forbidding : I shudder, my heart is chilled. But let the sun break forth from the cloud—I can feel—I can act—I can spring.

' 2. God descending and dwelling with man, is a truth so infinitely grand, that it must absorb all other. ' You are his attendants! Well! but the king! There he is —the king ! '

' 3. Out of Christ God is not intelligible, much less amiable. * * * A sick woman said to me, ' Sir! I have no notion of God. I can form no notion of him. You talk to me about him, but I cannot get a single idea that seems to contain' any thing.' ' But you know how to conceive of Jesus Christ as a man! God come down to you in him, full of kindness and condescension.' ' Ah, Sir! that gives me something to lay hold on. There I can rest. I understand God in his Son.' But if God is not intelligible out of Christ, much less is he aimable, though I ought to feel him so. He is an object of horror and aversion to me, corrupted as I am! 1 fear—I tremble—I resist—I hate—I rebel.

' 4. A preacher may pursue his topic without being led by it to Christ. A man who is accustomed to investigate topics is in danger. He takes up his topic and pursues it. He takes up another and pursues it. At length Jesus Christ becomes his topic, and then he pursues that. If he cannot so feel and think as to bend all subjects naturally and gracefully to Christ, he must seek his remedy in selecting such as are more evangelical.

' 5. God puts peculiar honour on the preaching of Christ crucified. A philosopher may philosophize his hearers,

but the preaching of Christ must convert them. John
the Baptist will make his hearers tremble : but if " the
least in the kingdom of heaven is greater than he," let
him exhibit that peculiar feature of his superiority—
Jesus Christ. Men may preach Christ ignorantly—
blunderingly—absurdly : yet God will give it efficacy,
because He is determined to magnify his own ordinance.

6. God seems, in the doctrine of the cross to design
the destruction of man's pride. Even the murderer and
the adulterer sometimes become subjects of the grace of
the Gospel, because the murderer and adulterer are more
easily convinced and humbled : but the man of virtue is
seldom reached, because the man of virtue disdains to
descend. " Remember me," said a dying malefactor!
" God, I thank thee," condemned a proud Pharisee!

Every minister should therefore inquire, ' What is for
me the wisest way of preaching Christ to men ? ' Some
seem to think that in the choice of a wise way there lurks
always a trimming disposition. There are men, doubtless, who will sacrifice to self, even Christ Jesus the
Lord ; but they, of all men, are the farthest from the
thing. There is a secret in doing it, which none but an
honest man can discover. The knave is not half wise
enough. We are not to judge of one another in these
things. Sufficient it is to us, to know what we have to
do. There are different ways of doing the same thing,
and that with success and acceptance. We see this in
the Apostles themselves. They not only preached
Christ in different ways ; but what is more, they could
not do this like one another. They declare this fact
themselves, and acknowledge the grace of God in their
respective gifts. " Our beloved brother Paul writes,"
says St. Peter, " according to the wisdom given unto
him." But there are Peters in our days who would

say—' Paul is too learned. Away with these things, which are hard to be understood. He should be more simple. I dislike all this reasoning.' And there are Pauls, who would say, ' Peter is rash and unguarded. He should put a curb on his impetuosity.' And there are Johns, who would say, ' They should both discharge their office in my soft and winning manner. No good will come of this fire and noise.' Nothing of this sort! Each has his proper gift of God; one after this manner, and another after that; and each seems only desirous to occupy faithfully 'till his Master come, leaving his brethren to stand or fall to their own Master.

Too much dependence is often placed in a system of rational contrivance. An ingenious man thinks he can so manage to preach Christ, that his hearers will say— ' Here is nothing of Methodism! This has nothing to do with that system !' I will venture to say, if this is the sentiment communicated by his ministry, that he has not delivered his message. The people do not know what he means, or he has kept back part of God's truth. He has fallen on a carnal contrivance, to avoid a cross, and he does no good to souls. The whole message must be delivered, and it is better it should be delivered even coarsely than not at all. We may lay it down as a principle, that if the gospel be a medicine, and a specific too, as it is, it must be got down such as it is. Any attempt to sophisticate and adulterate, will deprive it of its efficacy, and will often recoil on the man who makes the attempt, to his shame and confusion. The Jesuits tried to render Christianity palatable to the Chinese, by adulterating it, but the Jesuits were driven with abhorrence from the empire. If we have to deal with men of learning, let us show learning so far as to demonstrate that it bears its testimony to the truth. But accommodation in manner must often spring from humility. We must condescend to the capacity of men, and make the truth intelligible to them.

If this be our manner of preaching Christ, we must make up our minds, not to regard the little caviller who will judge us by the standard of his favourite author or preacher.

We must be cautious too, since men of God have been and ever will be, the butt and scorn of the world, of thinking that we can escape its sneers and censures. It is a foolish project—to avoid giving offence : but it is our duty to avoid giving unnecessary offence. It is necessary offence if it is given by the truth : but it is unnecessary if our own spirit occasion it.

I have often thought that St. Paul was raised up peculiarly to be an example to others, in labouring to discover the wisest way of exhibiting the gospel : not only that he was to be a great pattern in other points, but designedly raised up for this very thing. How does he labour to make the truth reasonably plain? How does he strain every nerve, and ransack every corner of the heart, to make it reasonably palatable !

We need not be instructed in his particular meaning when he says, " I became all things to all men, if by any means I might save some." His history is a comment on the declaration.

The knowledge of Jesus Christ is a wonderful mystery. Some men think they preach Christ gloriously, because they name him every two minutes in their sermons. But that is not preaching Christ. To understand, and enter into, and open his various offices and characters—the glories of his person and work—his relation to us and ours to Him, and to God the Father, and God the Spirit through-Him—this is the knowledge of Christ. The

Divines of the present day are stunted dwarfs in this knowledge, compared with the great men of the last age.'

It is important, at the same time, to remember, that in preaching Christ we are not at liberty to keep back the " terrors of the Lord." The following observations from an old writer are well deserving of consideration. " Some men say that to proclaim the " terrors of the Lord " has no other tendency than to make unwilling hypocritical professors. This makes me remember how I have heard some preachers of these times blame their brethren for not preaching Christ to their people, when they preached the danger of rejecting Christ, disobeying him and resisting his spirit. Do these men think that it is no preaching Christ (when we have for many years told them the fulness of his satisfaction, the freeness and general extent of his covenant or promise, and the riches of his grace, and the incomprehensibleness of his glory, and the truth of all) to tell them afterwards the danger of refusing, neglecting, and disobeying him? and of living after the flesh, and preferring the world before him? and serving Mammon, and falling off in persecution and avoiding the cross, and yielding in temptation, and quenching the spirit, and declining from their first love, and not improving their talents, and not forgiving and loving their brethren, yea and enemies, &c. ? Is none of this the Gospel? nor preaching Christ? Yea, is not repentance itself (except despairing repentance) proper to the gospel seeing the law excludeth it and all manner of hope. Blame me not, reader, if I be zealous against these men that not only know no better what preaching Christ is, but in their ignorance reproach their brethren for not preaching Christ, and withal condemn Christ himself and all his apostles? Do they think that Christ

himself knew not what it was to preach Christ? or that
he has set us a 'pattern too low for our imitation? I
desire them soberly to read Matthew v. 6, 7;
x. 25. Rom. viii. 4.—from the first verse to the
fourteenth Rom. ii. Heb. ii. and iv. and v. and x.
and then tell me whether we preach as Christ and his
Apostles did.

I say we do set forth God's love and the fulness of
Christ, and the sufficiency of his death and satisfaction
for all, and the freeness and extent of his offer and
promises of mercy and his readiness to welcome return-
ing sinners: this we do first, mixing with this the dis-
covery of their natural misery by sin, which must be
first known, and next we shew them the danger of neglecting Christ and his offer. 2. When we find men
settled under the preaching of free grace in a loose contempt or sleepy neglect of it, preferring the world and
their carnal pleasures and ease, and the indulgence of
their evil tempers before all the glory of heaven, and
the riches of Christ and grace, is it not time for us to
say, " How shall ye escape if ye neglect so great salvation ?" And " of how much sorer punishment shall he
be thought worthy, that treadeth under foot the blood
of the covenant," &c. Doth any of the Apostles speak
more of hell fire, and the worm that never dieth and the
fire that never is quenched than Christ himself doth?
Alas ! what work should we make if we should smooth
and stroke all men with antinomian language ? It were
the way to please all the careless, sensual, ignorant
multitude, but it is wide of Christ's way to save their
souls. I am ready to think that these men would have
Christ preached, as the papists would have him prayed
to, who say, Jesus, Jesus, Jesus, a number of times
together, and call this praying to him : so to have the

name of Jesus Christ often in the preacher's mouth some people think is rightly to preach Christ.

($^{16}$) Page 232. 'A minister must cultivate a tender spirit: if he does this so as to carry a savour and unction into his work, he will have far more weight than other men. This is the result of a devotional habit. To affect feeling is nauseous and soon detected; but to feel is the readiest way to the hearts of others.

The leading defect in Christian ministers is want of a devotional habit. The church of Rome made much of this habit. The contests accompanying and following the Reformation, with something of an indiscriminate enmity against some of the good of that church as well as the evil, combined to repress this spirit in the Protestant writings; whereas the mind of Christ, seems in fact to be the grand end of Christianity in its operation upon man.

There is a manifest want of spiritual influence on the ministry of the present day. I feel it in my own case and I see it in that of others. I am afraid that there is too much of a low, managing, contriving, manœuvering temper of mind among us. We are laying ourselves out more than is expedient, to meet one man's taste, and another man's prejudices. The ministry is a grand and holy affair; and it should find in us a simple habit of spirit, and a holy, but humble indifference to all consequences.'— *Cecil's Remains.*

THE END.